**Europe in Question**

# Europe in Question

Referendums on European Integration

Sara Binzer Hobolt

*This book has been printed digitally and produced in a standard specification in order to ensure its continuing availability*

# OXFORD
UNIVERSITY PRESS

Great Clarendon Street, Oxford OX2 6DP
Oxford University Press is a department of the University of Oxford.
It furthers the University's objective of excellence in research, scholarship,
and education by publishing worldwide in
Oxford  New York
Auckland  Cape Town  Dar es Salaam  Hong Kong  Karachi
Kuala Lumpur  Madrid  Melbourne  Mexico City  Nairobi
New Delhi  Shanghai  Taipei  Toronto
With offices in
Argentina  Austria  Brazil  Chile  Czech Republic  France  Greece
Guatemala  Hungary  Italy  Japan  South Korea  Poland  Portugal
Singapore  Switzerland  Thailand  Turkey  Ukraine  Vietnam

Oxford is a registered trade mark of Oxford University Press
in the UK and in certain other countries

Published in the United States
by Oxford University Press Inc., New York

© Sara Binzer Hobolt 2009

The moral rights of the author have been asserted

Database right Oxford University Press (maker)

Reprinted 2009

All rights reserved. No part of this publication may be reproduced,
stored in a retrieval system, or transmitted, in any form or by any means,
without the prior permission in writing of Oxford University Press,
or as expressly permitted by law, or under terms agreed with the appropriate
reprographics rights organization. Enquiries concerning reproduction
outside the scope of the above should be sent to the Rights Department,
Oxford University Press, at the address above

You must not circulate this book in any other binding or cover
And you must impose this same condition on any acquirer

ISBN 978-0-19-954994-8

*To Dominik*

# Contents

*List of Figures* viii
*List of Tables* x
*Preface* xiii

## Part I. The Theoretical Framework

1. Introduction: Referendums in a European Context 3
2. A Theory of Referendum Behaviour 23

## Part II. A Comparative Study of Referendum Behaviour

3. A Comparative Analysis of Voting Behaviour 65
4. Campaign Effects in Referendums 84
5. Framing Effects in Referendums: Experimental Evidence 110

## Part III. Case Studies

6. Voter Competence: What do Voters Need to Know? 135
7. From No to Yes: The Danish and Irish Referendums on the Maastricht and Nice Treaties 161
8. Campaign Dynamics in the Referendums on the European Constitution 204

## Part IV. Conclusions and Implications

9. Lessons and Future Challenges 233

*Appendix 1: List of Data Sources* 251
*Appendix 2: Descriptive Statistics* 254
*Bibliography* 255
*Index* 271

# List of Figures

| | | |
|---|---|---|
| 2.1. | Development in public support for European integration | 26 |
| 2.2. | Public perceptions of the EU, by member state | 28 |
| 2.3. | Spatial representation of voter choice in EU referendums | 44 |
| 2.4. | Uncertainty about the ballot proposal | 47 |
| 3.1. | Effects of partisanship and government satisfaction | 78 |
| 3.2. | Mediating effect of political awareness | 79 |
| 4.1. | Elements of campaign intensity | 91 |
| 4.2. | Campaign intensity in EU referendums | 95 |
| 4.3. | Campaign intensity and turnout | 96 |
| 4.4. | Campaign intensity and country-level issue voting | 97 |
| 4.5. | Campaign exposure and turnout | 102 |
| 4.6. | Issue voting and campaign intensity | 106 |
| 5.1. | Effect of government evaluation and cues on Euro vote | 127 |
| 5.2. | Effect of political awareness on Lisbon Treaty vote | 128 |
| 6.1. | Voter competence in EU referendums | 142 |
| 6.2. | European party positions on Left-Right and European dimensions | 146 |
| 6.3. | Positions of European mainstream parties | 147 |
| 6.4. | Party and voter positions in Norway on two dimensions | 149 |
| 6.5. | Issue voting across types and levels of information | 155 |
| 7.1. | Danish attitudes towards EU membership | 165 |
| 7.2. | Vote intentions during the 1992 Maastricht referendum campaign | 168 |
| 7.3. | Vote intentions during the 1993 Maastricht referendum campaign | 176 |
| 7.4. | Comparing groups of Danish voters: attitudes and awareness | 179 |
| 7.5. | A spatial illustration of two referendum scenarios | 180 |
| 7.6. | Irish attitudes towards EU membership | 185 |

## List of Figures

| | | |
|---|---|---|
| 7.7. | Vote intention during the 2002 Nice campaign | 192 |
| 7.8. | Comparing groups of Irish voters: attitudes and awareness | 194 |
| 8.1. | Intensity of campaign coverage | 208 |
| 8.2. | Vote intention in France and the Netherlands | 212 |
| 8.3. | Marginal effects on vote choice in France and the Netherlands | 225 |

# List of Tables

| | | |
|---|---|---:|
| 1.1. | Referendums on European integration, 1972–2008 | 9 |
| 3.1. | Modelling vote choice in Danish EU referendums | 72 |
| 3.2. | Modelling vote choice in Irish and Norwegian EU referendums | 73 |
| 3.3. | Modelling vote choice in the ECT referendums | 74 |
| 3.4. | Multilevel model of vote choice in EU referendums | 77 |
| 3.5. | Probability of voting yes given a change in the explanatory variables | 77 |
| 4.1. | Predicting turnout in EU referendums | 101 |
| 4.2. | Predicting ballot-specific knowledge | 104 |
| 4.3. | Issue voting and campaign intensity | 105 |
| 5.1. | Euro referendum split-sample experimental treatments | 119 |
| 5.2. | Lisbon Treaty referendum split-sample experimental treatments | 120 |
| 5.3. | Framing effects in the Euro referendum experiment | 121 |
| 5.4. | Framing effects in the Lisbon Treaty referendum experiment | 122 |
| 5.5. | Multinomial logit of vote choice in the Euro referendum | 124 |
| 5.6. | Multinomial logit of vote choice in the Lisbon Treaty referendum | 125 |
| 6.1. | Public knowledge of national and European politics | 137 |
| 6.2. | Distances between voters and parties | 150 |
| 6.3. | Voting correctly? | 152 |
| 6.4. | Information types and vote choice in the 1994 Norwegian accession referendum | 154 |
| 6.5. | Impact of EU attitude change on the probability of voting yes, across information categories | 156 |
| 7.1. | Attitudes towards European integration in Denmark | 166 |
| 7.2. | Reasons for vote choice in the 1992 Maastricht referendum | 173 |
| 7.3. | Who switched in the Maastricht referendums? | 178 |
| 7.4. | Yes-vote by party preference in the two Maastricht referendums | 181 |
| 7.5. | Reasons for vote choice in the Nice referendums | 189 |

# List of Tables

| | |
|---|---|
| 7.6. Who switched in the 2002 Nice referendum? | 193 |
| 8.1. Issues in the campaign | 210 |
| 8.2. Vote choices by party affiliation in France | 212 |
| 8.3. Vote choices by party affiliation in the Netherlands | 213 |
| 8.4. Reasons for vote choice | 215 |
| 8.5. Factor analysis of attitude indicators in France | 217 |
| 8.6. Factor analysis of attitude indicators in the Netherlands | 219 |
| 8.7. Predicting vote choice in France | 221 |
| 8.8. Predicting vote choice in the Netherlands | 223 |
| 2.1A. Descriptive statistics | 254 |

# Preface

The Danish electorate's unexpected no-vote to the Maastricht Treaty in 1992 first inspired this book. This event presented an intriguing puzzle: Why would voters reject a proposal that was so widely supported by political parties, interest groups and the media? It also raised the more general question of whether voters were actually capable of making competent decisions on complex issues in direct democracy. I set out to examine whether the choices of voters in European Union referendums were related to their preferences on European integration or whether they were based altogether on different reasons. When I embarked on this research project eight years ago, the Irish voters had just followed the Danish example and rejected the Nice Treaty. However, the circumstances surrounding this no-vote in Ireland appeared nothing like the Danish referendum campaign. Whereas the issues of the Maastricht Treaty and European integration were highly salient in the Danish debate, the Irish ballot was preceded by a lacklustre campaign and limited interest in the Nice Treaty. These very different referendum experiences raised the question of whether it would be possible to create a single theoretical framework for understanding how voters choose in referendums. In this book, I have attempted to do just that: Create a simple, but comprehensive, model of voting behaviour in European integration referendums that also takes account of differences in the issue saliency across campaigns and individuals. By doing so, I hope that this book goes some way to explaining the puzzles of past referendums and anticipating the referendum experiences of the future.

This book would not have been possible without the insights, guidance, and support of colleagues and friends. My most sincere gratitude goes to Geoff Evans, Mark Franklin, Michael Marsh, and Pieter van Houten, each of whom have supported my endeavours as a scholar and inspired me to become a better political scientist.

## Preface

Numerous people have given me advice, suggestions, and encouragement throughout the process and commented on various parts of this book. In particular, I would like to thank: Jake Bowers, Claes de Vreese, Jamie Druckman, Geoffrey Edwards, Karin Gilland Lutz, Simon Hug, Ron Inglehart, Avril Keating, Orit Kedar, Michelle Jackson, Robert Klemmensen, Ken Kollman, Michael Levin, Skip Lupia, Brian McElwee, Hans Jørgen Nielsen, Keiko Ono, Rune Slothuus, Jae-Jae Spoon, Palle Svensson, James Tilley, Cees van der Eijk, John Winn, and Chris Wlezien. I am also grateful to the politicians who kindly took the time to share their knowledge and experiences with me, and to Lucie Cerna and Armen Hakhverdian for their excellent research assistance. A special note of thanks goes to Oisín Tansey who read the entire manuscript twice and provided numerous suggestions for improvements.

Chapters 4 and 6 draw on material from two of my previous publications, namely 'Campaign information and voting behaviour in EU referendums' in Claes H. de Vreese (ed.) *The Dynamics of Referendum Campaigns. An International Perspective*, Palgrave MacMillan, 2007, and 'Taking cues on Europe? Voter competence and party endorsements in referendums on European integration', *European Journal of Political Research* 46(2), 2007. I thank Palgrave MacMillan and *European Journal of Political Research* for allowing me to use it here. Moreover, Chapter 8 owes much to the ideas and data provided by Sylvain Brouard.

This study has benefited from the generous financial support provided by various funding bodies and other institutions: the American National Election Studies (ANES), the British Academy (award no. SG-43644), Cambridge European Trust, the Norman Chester Fund, the Danish Research Agency, St. John's College at the University of Cambridge, the University Association for Contemporary European Studies, and the Michael Zilkha Trust at Lincoln College. I am most indebted for their support.

This intellectual journey would have been far less fruitful and enjoyable without the hospitality and inspiring research environments of many academic institutions. The Centre of International Studies and St. John's College at the University of Cambridge provided an excellent base for my doctoral research; and the Departments of Political Science at Trinity College Dublin and at the University of Copenhagen welcomed me as a visiting researcher. I am most grateful to Nancy Burns and Donald Kinder for giving me the opportunity to spend a year as an ANES Fellow at the Center for Political Studies, University of Michigan. My research fellowship at Nuffield College, Oxford, also provided excellent support for research. Finally, I could not ask for a better work environment than the

# Preface

Department of Politics and International Relations and Lincoln College at the University of Oxford. I am particularly grateful to my colleagues at the Centre for Research Methods in the Social Sciences (ReMiSS) for stimulating discussions, invaluable advice, and friendship.

I would also like to express my gratitude to those who worked with me at Oxford University Press: Dominic Byatt, Lizzy Suffling, and Aimee Wright. Moreover, I am greatly indebted to the three anonymous reviewers of this book for their insightful and encouraging remarks.

My deepest gratitude goes to my parents, Naja Binzer and Carsten Hobolt, for their love and encouragement throughout the years. They taught me always to ask questions and have given me the strength to look for some of the answers. Above all, I would like to thank Dominik Mattmann for his love, patience, and unfailing support and with gratitude I dedicate this book to him.

# Part I
# The Theoretical Framework

# 1
# Introduction: Referendums in a European Context

*Democracy is not a state in which people act like sheep.*
—Mahatma Gandhi

Direct democracy has become an increasingly common feature of European politics. During the past four decades, European countries have conducted forty-three referendums on aspects of European integration. In stark contrast to the otherwise elite-driven nature of the integration project, national referendums have provided a direct means of involving citizens in the integration process.

But can citizens make sense of direct democracy? The no-votes to the Lisbon Treaty in Ireland and the Constitutional Treaty in France and the Netherlands led many commentators to suggest that voters are not capable of making choices that are consistent with their interests and preferences. These referendums also raised the question of why a majority of voters would vote no to a treaty when national and European elites were largely united in their support. Was this a rejection of further European integration, a statement of dissatisfaction with the national government and parties, or a random protest vote? One possible explanation is that these referendums were decided by citizens' evaluation of the advantages and disadvantages of European integration. An alternative scenario is that the referendums were polls on the performance of the national government. These rival scenarios have very different implications for our understanding of referendums and far-reaching consequences for democratic decision-making in the European Union (EU).[1]

This book addresses this puzzle: When and why do voters reject a ballot proposal on European integration? To answer this question, the book provides a general theoretical framework for understanding voting behaviour in European integration referendums. The main argument is that vote choices are influenced by citizens' general attitudes about Europe, as well as their feelings about national party politics. But crucially, the information provided to voters during a campaign influences whether feelings about the EU, partisan loyalties, or dissatisfaction with the government play a greater role in the ballot box. Hence, to understand why citizens sometimes accept proposals and reject them at other times, it is vital to analyse the context of the campaign. Moreover, we should not expect all citizens to respond in the same way to the political environment. The book demonstrates that individuals with higher levels of political interest are more resistant to follow elite recommendations and more likely to vote on the basis of their underlying attitudes and preferences.

To understand the relationship between voters and elites in EU referendums, this book examines information both in terms of supply and demand. On the supply side, this study examines the intensity and nature of the information provided in the referendum campaign. On the demand side, it examines how differences in individuals' attention to political information influence patterns of opinion formation and voting behaviour. Political information can thus be seen as a crucial mediating factor that can help us understand variation in voting behaviour between individuals, across countries and over time.

The theoretical framework also highlights another important aspect of vote choices in referendums, namely that the perceived cost of a no-vote is as important as the professed benefits of accepting the proposal. When voters decide in these referendums, they are not only choosing between the proposed treaty and status quo, but they also assess the potential consequences of rejecting the proposal. The real challenge for the advocates of a proposal is therefore to convince voters that the dangers of voting no are greater than the cost of accepting the treaty.

To examine why people vote the way they do, the role of political elites, and the impact of the campaign dynamics, the book presents a comparative analysis of EU referendums in Denmark, France, Ireland, Luxembourg, the Netherlands, Norway, and Spain in the period from 1972 to 2008. This is presented in a mix of comparative analysis (Part II) and case study chapters (Part III), relying on a variety of different data sources and methods, including statistical analysis of survey data, content analysis of media coverage, experimental studies, and elite interviews.

This introductory chapter discusses the notion of direct democracy in theory and practice, followed by a classification and historical overview

## 1.1. Direct democracy in theory and practice

'Direct democracy' is an umbrella term for a variety of decision processes by which ordinary citizens vote directly on policy matters. Often, direct democracy is contrasted with representative democracy in which citizens delegate decision-making to elected representatives (Butler and Ranney 1978, 1994; Setälä 1999; Qvortrup 2005). This distinction is, however, rather artificial since we know of no political regimes that use direct democracy as their main legislative system. Moreover, the notion of 'direct democracy' implies that voters have a direct impact on legislation. In reality, political behaviour in referendums is mediated by elites and institutions (Mendelsohn and Parkin 2001). This book therefore examines referendums as decision-making processes that operate *within* representative systems and seeks to understand the interplay between voters and the institutions and actors of representative democracy, notably political parties. The term 'referendums',[2] in this context, is used to designate all the procedures whereby voters directly cast ballots on an issue. This includes the most common type of referendum in the European context that permits voters to accept or reject a proposal put to them by their representatives, as well as the less common 'initiatives'[3] that allow citizens to place proposals on the ballot for voter decision.

The institutional device of referendums is flourishing in most developed democracies. In the decade from 1993 to 2003, 497 national referendums were held worldwide, more than double that of the previous decades. The vast majority of these, 301, took place in Europe[4] and the most voted on question has been that of European integration (Kaufmann and Waters 2004: 3). Most of the new constitutions of the post-communist EU member states contain provisions for referendums and initiatives. Moreover, countries that have previously never held referendums, such as Britain and the Netherlands, have resorted to this device in recent decades. Yet, the use of referendums remains controversial, despite their increasing popularity.

The relative merits of direct and representative democracy have interested scholars for centuries. Proponents of direct democracy celebrate citizen engagement and the responsiveness of the political system to citizens' wishes. But more often, commentators are sceptical of the virtues of direct legislation. A well-known critique of direct democracy was put forward in the Federalist Papers by James Madison, who argued that direct democracy will lead to the tyranny of the majority, since 'a common passion or interest will, in almost every case, be felt by a majority of the whole; a communication and concert results from the form of Government itself; and there is nothing to check the inducements to sacrifice the weaker party, or an obnoxious individual' (Madison 1787: No. 10). Another prominent criticism levelled against direct democracy is that citizens generally lack not only knowledge, but also informed opinion, about the issues submitted to a vote (Butler and Ranney 1978; Bowler and Donovan 1998; Lupia and Matsusaka 2004). Many scholars of voting behaviour have pointed out that voters lack the interest, sophistication, and information required to make reasoned decisions in elections. Campbell et al. (1980: 543) famously characterized the American electorate as 'almost wholly without detailed information about decision making in government... it is almost completely unable to judge the rationality of government actions; knowing little of particular policies or what has led to them, the mass electorate is not able to appraise either its goals or the appropriateness of the means chosen to serve these goals'. It is therefore hardly surprising that there have been concerns raised about whether voters are competent enough to make reasoned decisions on issues that are placed directly on the ballot. As Matsusaka (2003: 4) comments: 'an obvious concern with direct democracy is that it places decision-making power in the hands of the uninformed'. The normative critiques of referendums thus stress that under direct democracy voters are less competent, outcomes are less likely to make sense, and policies are more abusive to minorities. These arguments seem compelling; yet because the literature on direct democracy, at least until recently,[5] is mostly descriptive or normative, we have a limited understanding of whether these concerns about referendums are in fact warranted (Lupia and Matsusaka 2004).

The purpose of this book is not to engage in the normative debate about the relative merits of direct versus representative democracy, but rather to provide a theoretical framework and empirical analyses that contribute to our understanding of how elites and voters interact in referendums. By doing so, however, this book also speaks to the normative issues addressed in the literature. One of the key concerns in the debate on direct democracy is whether citizens can make decisions that are consistent with their interests and desires, and how far voters are subject to elite manipulation. This question of whether voters are able to make competent decisions in referendums is addressed both theoretically and empirically (see, in particular, Chapters 3, 6, and 9). Another key issue in the literature is under what conditions referendums are likely to produce better outcomes—both in terms of responsiveness to public preferences and voter competence. The book also addresses this issue by exploring whether and how the campaign context and elite cues are conducive to competent voting behaviour (see Chapters 4 and 5).

This book therefore addresses some of the key debates in democratic theory from the perspective of European integration referendums. These referendums have been chosen not only because they provide apposite cases for the study of referendum behaviour in a comparative perspective, but also because direct democracy has played—and will continue to play—a significant role in the process of European integration. Understanding the mechanisms of political behaviour in EU referendums is important if we want to comprehend the current and future path of European integration.

The following section gives an overview and provides a framework for classifying referendums on European integration.

## 1.2. European integration and referendums

Direct democracy played no role in the early stages of the European integration process, but has become an increasingly important way to make decisions on important European issues. During the past four decades, forty-three referendums on aspects of European integration have been conducted in member states and candidate countries.[6] The outcome of this public consultation has occasionally both surprised and dismayed national and European political elites. The Danish rejection of the Maastricht Treaty in 1992 dealt a serious blow to the integration project, even though the decision was overturned in a subsequent referendum (see Chapter 7). The effect of the Danish rejection was exacerbated by the near-failure of the treaty ratification in the French referendum only three months later. These Maastricht referendums marked for many the end of the 'permissive consensus' that had characterized the first decades of the integration process (Lindberg and Scheingold 1970). Despite this forewarning, Irish elites were still taken by surprise when the otherwise

Europhile Irish decided to reject the innocuous Nice Treaty in 2001. In 2005, the negative outcomes of the referendums on the Constitutional Treaty in France and the Netherlands sounded the death knell for the process of establishing a European Constitution and caused a political crisis in Europe. After a 'period of reflection', European leaders revamped the Constitutional Treaty, removing the grand constitutional gestures and any provisions that could potentially trigger a referendum, and created the Treaty of Lisbon. Ten countries had announced a referendum on the Constitutional Treaty, but only one country held a ballot on the reformed Lisbon Treaty, namely Ireland. This resulted in a repeat of the 2001 Nice referendum with a no-vote in 2008 and once again left the efforts to reform the decision-making processes and institutions of the EU in difficulty.

Direct democracy has forced national and European elites to consider how to garner public support for the integration project. What is particularly noteworthy about the no-votes in Denmark, France, Ireland, and the Netherlands is that these ballot proposals were backed by a broad consensus amongst national elites. Hence, referendums have introduced a popular element into the process of European integration that is at least partly out of the control of the elected and appointed representatives in Brussels and the national capitals, yet has important implications for both national and European politics. This section provides an overview of European integration referendums held to date.

### 1.2.1. Classifying referendums on European integration

Direct democracy played no role in the early stages of the European integration process. From its conception in the post-war period, the European integration project was conceived as an elite-driven project with limited popular involvement. The dual executive of the Union was made up by a Commission of nationally appointed bureaucrats and a Council consisting of members of national governments. The European Parliament had only negligible powers and its members were not directly elected until 1979. The first European integration referendum held in France in 1972 introduced a hitherto unseen aspect of public involvement in the integration process. Since then, forty-two further referendums on aspects of European integration have taken place in member states and candidate countries. In order to give an overview of the use of direct democracy in the EU, it is useful to classify the referendums according to certain criteria (see also Table 1.1).

# Introduction

**Table 1.1.** Referendums on European integration, 1972–2008

| Year | Country | Object | Type | Turnout (%) | Yes (%) |
|---|---|---|---|---|---|
| 1972 | France | Enlargement of EC (I) | NR and NB | 60 | 68.3 |
| 1972 | Ireland** | EC membership (M) | R and B | 71 | 83.1 |
| 1972 | Norway** | EC membership (M) | NR and NB | 79 | 46.5 |
| 1972 | Denmark** | EC membership (M) | R and B | 90 | 63.3 |
| 1972 | Switzerland | EC-EFTA Treaty (T) | R and B | 52 | 72.5 |
| 1975 | United Kingdom | EC membership (M) | NR and NB | 64 | 67.2 |
| 1986 | Denmark** | Single European Act (T) | R and B | 75 | 56.2 |
| 1987 | Ireland** | Single European Act (T) | R and B | 44 | 69.9 |
| 1989 | Italy | Mandate for MEPs (I) | NR and NB | 85 | 88.1 |
| 1992 | Denmark** | Maastricht Treaty (T) | R and B | 83 | 49.3 |
| 1992 | Ireland** | Maastricht Treaty (T) | R and B | 57 | 68.7 |
| 1992 | France | Maastricht Treaty (T) | NR and B | 70 | 51.1 |
| 1992 | Switzerland | EEA accession (M) | R and B | 78 | 49.7 |
| 1993 | Denmark** | Maastricht Treaty (T) | NR and NB | 87 | 56.8 |
| 1994 | Austria | EU membership (M) | R and B | 82 | 66.6 |
| 1994 | Finland | EU membership (M) | NR and NB | 70 | 56.9 |
| 1994 | Sweden | EU membership (M) | NR and NB | 83 | 52.3 |
| 1994 | Norway** | EU membership (M) | NR and NB | 89 | 47.8 |
| 1997 | Switzerland | EU candidature (M) | NR and B | 35 | 25.9 |
| 1998 | Ireland** | Amsterdam Treaty (T) | R and B | 56 | 61.7 |
| 1998 | Denmark** | Amsterdam Treaty (T) | R and B | 76 | 55.1 |
| 2000 | Switzerland | Bilateral agreements (T) | NR and B | 48 | 67.2 |
| 2000 | Denmark** | Single currency (I) | NR and B | 88 | 46.9 |
| 2001 | Switzerland | EU candidature (M) | NR and B | 55 | 23.2 |
| 2001 | Ireland** | Nice Treaty (T) | R and B | 35 | 46.1 |
| 2002 | Ireland** | Nice Treaty (T) | R and B | 49 | 62.9 |
| 2003 | Malta | EU membership (M) | NR and NB | 91 | 53.6 |
| 2003 | Slovenia | EU membership (M) | R and B | 60 | 89.6 |
| 2003 | Hungary | EU membership (M) | R and B | 46 | 83.7 |
| 2003 | Lithuania | EU membership (M) | R and B | 63 | 91.1 |
| 2003 | Slovakia | EU membership (M) | R and B | 52 | 92.5 |
| 2003 | Poland | EU membership (M) | R and B | 59 | 77.5 |
| 2003 | Czech Republic | EU membership (M) | R and B | 55 | 77.3 |
| 2003 | Estonia | EU membership (M) | R and B | 64 | 66.8 |
| 2003 | Sweden | Single currency (I) | NR and NB | 83 | 42.0 |
| 2003 | Latvia | EU membership (M) | R and B | 73 | 67.0 |
| 2003 | Romania | EU membership (M) | R and B | 56 | 89.7 |
| 2005 | Spain** | Constitutional Treaty (T) | NR and NB | 42 | 76.7 |
| 2005 | France** | Constitutional Treaty (T) | NR and NB | 69 | 45.3 |
| 2005 | The Netherlands** | Constitutional Treaty (T) | NR and NB | 63 | 38.2 |
| 2005 | Switzerland | Schengen agreement (I) | NR and B | 56 | 54.6 |
| 2005 | Luxembourg** | Constitutional Treaty (T) | NR and NB | 89 | 56.5 |
| 2008 | Ireland** | Lisbon Treaty (T) | R and B | 53 | 46.6 |

*Notes:* **Referendums included in the analyses in this book. M = membership referendum, T = treaty ratification referendum, I = single issue referendum, NR = non-required, R = required, NB = non-binding, B = binding.

Most existing literature classifies referendums according to various institutional characteristics (see for example, Butler and Ranney 1978, 1994; Suksi 1993; Hug 2002). While some of these classifications are formal legalistic distinctions of little practical relevance in this study, others may be informative. The most common institutional classifications differentiate between referendums that are required (R) and non-required (NR), and ones that are binding (B) and non-binding (NB) (Suksi 1993; Hug 2002). The first institutional criterion concerns whether there are particular constitutional provisions demanding a popular vote on particular legal acts. If this is the case, a referendum may be required. Yet, in reality, it is often difficult to establish whether a referendum is mandatory or not. An example is the Danish Constitution's Article 20, which states that a binding referendum is mandatory if national sovereignty is transferred to international authorities, unless approved by five-sixths of the members of the Danish Parliament. In practice, what constitutes 'transfer of national sovereignty' often becomes a political rather than purely legal matter. In 1986, for example, the Danish government decided to hold a referendum after the ratification of the Single European Act could not be passed in Parliament, but in 2001 and 2007 the Danish Ministry of Justice decided that referendums on the ratification of the Nice Treaty and the Lisbon Treaty were not required since these treaties did not involve a considerable transfer of sovereignty.

The second important institutional criterion concerns whether or not the referendum outcome is legally binding. A vote is binding only if it must be accepted and adopted by parliament and government or if the vote in itself is the decisive act. Some constitutions have clear provisions for advisory referendums, where the government is not obligated to heed to the wishes of the voters. However, in practice the distinction is often inconsequential, since even 'consultative' referendums usually have the same effects as their binding counterparts (Uleri 1996: 7). Certainly there is no example in the history of European integration referendums of a government ignoring the wishes of the voters without a second referendum.[7]

These specific institutional provisions may influence the strategies available to elites; yet such rules tend to play a limited role in the campaigns leading up to the referendums and voters are generally unaware of the institutional rules governing a specific vote. Hence, a more useful way of classifying EU referendums is by focusing on the types of issues that are on the ballot. The specific nature of the ballot issue has important implications both for the strategies adopted by elites and the opinion

## Introduction

formation process of voters. Broadly speaking, we can distinguish between three types of issues decided in EU referendums: membership, treaty ratification and single policy issues.

*Membership referendums* (M) are the most common type of European integration referendums. Twenty-one referendums of this kind have taken place. Most countries that have joined the EU since the 'founding six' have subjected the decision to popular will. In membership referendums, voters are asked to decide on whether or not to join the EU. Some national constitutions contain provisions that render it mandatory to hold a referendum in order to accede to an international organization, but even without such provisions governments may decide to consult the citizenry before acceding to the Union. In either case, national governments have considerable agenda-setting control in these referendums, since they have significant influence over the negotiation of the membership agreement as well as the timing of the referendum. Voters, however, have no direct experience with the EU in accession referendums and will thus have to rely considerably on information and cues provided by elites.

After the French referendum in 1972 paved the way for the first enlargement of the European Community (EC), three such membership referendums took place in the candidate countries, namely Ireland, Norway, and Denmark. In the Norwegian referendum, the accession proposal was narrowly defeated. In contrast, membership was accepted by a large majority of the electorates in Ireland and Denmark. Britain also joined the EC in 1973 but without a referendum. When the British Labour Party gained power in 1974, it was split on the issue of Europe and decided to call a referendum on continued membership in which two-thirds of British voters said yes to stay in the EC. The subsequent enlargements of the Union in 1981 (Greece) and 1986 (Spain and Portugal) were not preceded by referendums, partly because these countries had only recently emerged from authoritarian dictatorships. The next membership referendums took place in 1994 in Austria, Sweden, Finland, and Norway. The order of these referendums was not wholly accidental, but engineered to create a 'domino effect' letting the most pro-European country, Austria, go first and the most Eurosceptic country, Norway, last. The strategy was, however, not entirely successful since the Norwegian voters rejected membership for a second time (as discussed in Chapter 6). The citizens of Austria, Finland, and Sweden, on the other hand, accepted membership and the countries acceded to the Union in 1995. In 2003, nine membership referendums paved the way for the fifth enlargement, the largest in EU history. Of the ten candidate countries, only Cyprus decided not to hold an accession referendum. With the exception of Malta, where only 54 per cent voted in favour of accession, these membership referendums were very easily passed. After this series of accession referendums, Romania held a referendum on a constitutional amendment preparing it for membership of the Union, and the ballot was supported by almost 90 per cent of the voters. Romania and Bulgaria both joined the Union in 2007.

In addition to these EU accession referendums, Switzerland has held several referendums on EU-related issues. Switzerland is in many ways a unique case, since it has the most developed institutional provisions for referendums in Europe and more than any other country resembles a 'referendum democracy'. Although Switzerland remains outside the Union, Swiss voters have regularly voted on their relations with Europe. In 1972, the Swiss agreed to a free trade agreement between the European Free Trade Association (EFTA) and the EC, but in 1992 they narrowly rejected membership of the European Economic Area (EEA). In 2000, they agreed to adopt bilateral agreements with the EU and in 2005 to join the Schengen agreement, but in two referendums held in 1997 and 2001, Swiss voters overwhelmingly voted against starting accession negotiations with the EU.

The second most common type of EU referendums involves *treaty ratification* (T). All member states need to ratify a treaty revision. Most countries do so by a simple majority in their national legislatures. Some countries, such as Denmark and Ireland, have constitutional provisions that make referendums mandatory before signing up to new supranational treaties. In other cases, such as the referendums on the Constitutional Treaty in Spain, France, the Netherlands, and Luxembourg, governments may simply decide to consult the public. In most cases, however, national governments will only hold referendums to ratify new EU treaties if they are constitutionally required to do so.[8] Generally, national governments have more limited agenda-setting powers in treaty ratification referendums than in membership referendums. The interest accommodation in treaty negotiations is a collective process involving all member states, and consequently the outcome cannot be fully controlled by individual governments. Moreover, treaty ratifications are usually restricted to a predetermined time period and this limits governments' ability to determine the timing of the referendum. The decision-making process of voters also differs in this type of referendums, since they have first-hand experience with the EU institutions and the integration process when deciding. Conversely, the consequences of a no-vote are often more uncertain in these referendums. Since EU treaties are required to be ratified by every single member state, a rejection in one country could

# Introduction

mean the failure of the treaty. It may also have specific repercussions for the country that rejects the treaty, and could potentially lead to the exit from the Union. In two of the instances where the electorates failed to ratify a treaty—Denmark in 1992 and Ireland in 2001—a second referendum on a similar issue was held which overturned the first decision.[9] In contrast, the Constitutional Treaty was abandoned after the French and the Dutch no-votes. Not only did this involve two founding member states, but further no-votes were anticipated in countries such as Britain if the ratification process had continued. In the most recent example of an 'involuntary defection' caused by the Irish rejection of the Lisbon Treaty, the wider implications are still in doubt. These types of referendums thus present the voters with considerable uncertainty regarding the consequences of their choice.

The *single-issue referendum* (I) is the least common type of EU referendum. Whereas all referendums are essentially issue-specific, the membership and treaty ratification referendums touch upon a number of interconnected economic and political issues related to the integration process. In contrast, single-issue referendums address a single policy issue (although these issues are also related to the European integration process in general). National elites tend to have extensive control over the specific ballot proposal as well as the timing of the referendum. Examples of single-issue referendums include the first French referendum on enlargement in 1972 and the Italian referendum giving a 'constituent mandate' for the Italian members of the European Parliament to pursue further European integration in 1989 (Uleri 1996: 107). Other examples of single-issue referendums include the two Scandinavian referendums on joining the Euro in 2000 and 2003, which both failed at the hands of the electorate. Using this classification system based on institutional and issue criteria, Table 1.1 provides an overview of all the European integration referendums held to date.

Table 1.1 illustrates considerable variations in outcomes across these referendums: The percentage of the electorate voting in favour of the proposal has ranged from 23 to 92 per cent with turnout rates from 35 to 91 per cent. The factors that influence these variations in outcomes and turnout will be discussed in the ensuing chapters of this book.

## 1.2.2. Implications of EU referendums

The distinction between membership, ratification, and single-issue referendums provides a framework for classifying the growing number of referendums on European integration, and highlights some important differences concerning the agenda-setting power of elites and the complexity of the choice facing voters. However, despite the differences, there are also important similarities that allow for and warrant a comparative study of these referendums. Although the specific ballot proposition may vary, the main choices facing elites and voters in these referendums concern European integration, and, in practice, all of the campaigns leading up to these referendums have dealt with political, economic, and cultural issues of the integration process. Moreover, each of these referendums has important implications for the integration process, both directly and indirectly. The direct implications are evident, since these referendums—both the binding and advisory types—have decided many important issues, sometimes at odds with the consensus among the majority of national elites. The carefully negotiated Constitutional Treaty was abandoned due to the no-votes in France and the Netherlands. Moreover, it is owing to referendums that Norway and Switzerland remain outside the EU and that Denmark and Sweden have stayed outside the Euro-zone. EU referendums have also had tangible consequences in the domestic political arena, in some countries leading to the division of established parties, to the formation of new parties and political alliances and, in other cases, to the resignation of governments.

The *indirect* consequences of national EU referendums are more difficult to observe and measure, yet no less important. It seems plausible that the anticipation of a national referendum on a treaty or policy issue could impact the positions that governments adopt in intergovernmental negotiations, particularly if they face a Eurosceptic electorate at home. They may also be able to use the forthcoming national referendum to their advantage in the bargaining situation. Formal models have shown that governments can use the 'ratification threat' of referendums strategically to improve the terms of an integration agreement (Schneider and Cederman 1994; Hug and König 2002). Moreover, the public sentiments in national referendums have had other indirect effects on the positions adopted by European elites. The outcomes of the Maastricht referendums were in many ways instrumental in fostering the debate about the 'democratic deficit' in the EU. The increased awareness among political elites that public support for European integration could no longer simply be taken for granted was evident in the Laeken Declaration adopted by the EU's heads of state and government in December 2001:

## Introduction

Within the Union, the European institutions must be brought closer to its citizens. Citizens undoubtedly support the Union's broad aims, but they do not always see a connection between those goals and the Union's everyday action (...) This is even perceived by some as a threat to their identity. More importantly, however, they feel that deals are all too often cut out of their sight and they want better democratic scrutiny.[10]

In an attempt to make the Union more relevant to its citizens, the Laeken summit set out a plan for the constitutional Convention on the Future of Europe. The remit of this assembly, composed of representatives of national governments and national parliaments, included the task of making 'the European Union more democratic and closer to its citizens'. Whether the Convention and the subsequent Constitutional Treaty achieved this goal is of course debatable in the light of the failure to ratify the Treaty. There is little doubt that both the referendums that preceded the negotiations on the Constitution and the ones that were anticipated influenced the final outcome. In the drafting of the Reform Treaty, renamed the Lisbon Treaty, EU leaders deliberately removed many of the 'constitutional' aspects of the Treaty in an effort to avoid the necessity of further referendums and thus the potential of another ratification failure. As former Italian prime minister and vice president of the Convention Giuliano Amato noted: 'They [EU leaders] decided that the document should be unreadable. If it is unreadable, it is not constitutional, that was the sort of perception (...) Any Prime Minister can go to the Commons and say "look, you see, it's absolutely unreadable, it's the typical Brussels treaty, nothing new, no need for a referendum"' (Kirk 2007). This strategy was successful to the extent that only Ireland decided to hold a referendum on the Treaty; yet this did not prevent another no-vote.

It is thus evident that EU referendums, both directly and indirectly, have important implications for both the decision-making process in the Union and for the democratic legitimization of this process. This raises several questions: Are national referendums on European integration an appropriate method of decision-making and citizen involvement in the EU? Are voters competent to vote directly on matters of such complexity as aspects of European integration? Should we endorse the use of an institutional device which allows citizens to undercut their elected representatives? The answers to these questions ultimately depend on our understanding of how citizens make choices in EU referendums. Yet, the growing body of literature on EU referendums still leaves many of these questions unanswered. We have limited understanding of the relative importance of different factors influencing voting behaviour in EU referendums. Existing studies do not inform us under which conditions citizens are more or less likely to follow the recommendations of national elites. Part of the reason for our limited understanding of political behaviour in EU referendums is that comparative studies are still few and far between. Single-country or single-referendum studies cannot uncover some of the important relationships that may be crucial in determining voting behaviour. In particular, these studies cannot investigate systematically how the national and the campaign context interact with the decision-making processes of individuals. Moreover, the importance of general political awareness is poorly understood in the context of EU referendums, because existing studies tend to treat voters as a uniform mass that responds in the same way to elite cues, but differs in preferences and attitudes.

By providing a general theoretical framework and a detailed empirical analysis of political behaviour in EU referendums in a comparative perspective, this book aims to contribute to our understanding of the decision-making process in these referendums and thereby also inform some of the important normative debates about the use and implications of referendums in the EU.

### 1.2.3. *Overview of the argument*

To understand the nature of referendums on European integration, this book takes its starting point in exploring voting behaviour: How do voters decide in these referendums? Are they swayed by elite endorsement? Do they use their vote to express their feelings about the government? Or, do they choose on the basis of their underlying feelings about European integration and their risk assessments of the consequences of either accepting the proposal or rejecting it? While much of the existing literature has argued in favour of one of these scenarios, this book seeks to explain when and why voters decide in a certain way. It argues that the key factor that can help us explain why some voters and some electorates will be more likely to use EU referendums as a ballot on the incumbent and other voters will be more likely to carefully assess the pros and cons of the ballot question is *information*. The book focuses on both the forces that determine the supply of information and the factors influencing the demand for, or procession of, information. On the supply side, this concerns the quantity and quality of information supplied to citizens. When the issue of Euro-

# Introduction

pean integration is highly salient in the public sphere, we would expect citizens to be more motivated to participate in the democratic process and base their vote choices on an evaluation of the issues at stake. The nature of the campaign will influence how people decide. If they only receive one-sided messages in favour of the proposals, they are likely to follow this lead. However, in an intense campaign with conflicting messages, voters will also assess whether these elite endorsements are compatible with their feelings about European integration. The campaign will provide them with the tools to perform a risk assessment: Are the risks associated with further European integration greater than the risks associated with a no-vote and potential loss of the benefits associated with full membership of the EU? Hence, context matters. But even when exposed to the same campaign context, not all voters will respond in the same way. On the demand side, the book examines how voters' levels of political awareness, or interest, influences the way in which they make choices. Someone who is very interested in and knowledgeable about politics is more likely to be able to vote on the basis of a cost–benefit analysis of the issues at stake and critically evaluate elite cues than someone who pays very little attention to politics. Hence, we expect voters to rely on slightly different decision criteria, and to respond differently to the information provided by elites, depending on their level of interest in politics.

This argument is explained in much greater detail in Chapter 2 and tested empirically in Parts II and III of this book.

## 1.3. Research strategy

To develop and evaluate these propositions, this book investigates relationships and interactions at two levels. At the *individual level*, it examines variations in individual patterns of voting behaviour. At the *contextual level*, the impact of the campaign environment of each referendum is investigated. Importantly, these two levels of analysis are not seen as separate or independent of each other. Rather, the aim is to examine micro-level units (individual voters and politicians) as nested within diverse and influential macro-level contexts (the campaign context and national public sphere). In other words, this book investigates how individual-level political behaviour varies within and across the specific context of the referendum and the national political setting.

This book adopts a four-stage multi-method approach to the questions examined by combining theory, statistical testing, experimental methods, and case study methods. The first component of this research design involves the specification of a model of voting behaviour that accounts for the relationship among the variables and from which testable hypotheses are derived (Chapter 2). The second component consists of the statistical evaluation of these hypotheses using large-N cross-national survey data (Chapters 3 and 4). Statistical methods enable us to find patterns of behaviour that are similar across a large number of units and to identify significant variables and suggest possible causal effects. Yet, statistical methods are often weaker at identifying causal mechanisms and key processes. To more fully explore the micro-foundations of the causal mechanisms, the book relies on experimental methods (Chapter 5). This enables us to clearly distinguish cause from effect and to examine the influence of elite framing and endorsement on opinion formation and vote choices in a controlled environment. Yet, when using survey experiments we do not fully capture the actual *processes* of campaign dynamics and opinion formation. As Laitin has pointed out, 'if statistics addresses questions of propensities, narratives address questions of process' (Laitin 2002: 2). Hence, the fourth and final component of this methodological design involves case study methods. Chapter 6 examines the Norwegian accession referendum in 1994, focusing on voter competence. In Chapter 7, the dynamics of the campaigns in two pairs of 'controlled comparison' referendums in Denmark and Ireland are explored and Chapter 8 investigates the multifaceted nature of campaigns and attitudes in the context of the French and Dutch votes on the Constitutional Treaty. Case study methods provide a better tool for discovering the causal mechanisms in the relations between elites and voters and to identify variables that have been omitted from the statistical models, which may be of particular importance in individual cases.

This book thus combines qualitative and quantitative methods and relies on various different data sources—notably national survey data, experimental data, content analysis of newspapers, and interviews with politicians—to empirically examine patterns of vote choices. In the large-N analysis, we analyse survey data from nineteen referendums held in Denmark, France, Ireland, Luxembourg, the Netherlands, Norway, and Spain between 1972 and 2008. These cases not only represent about half of all referendums ever held of EU questions (see Table 1.1), but also provide large variation in types of referendums (4 membership, 14 treaty ratification, and 1 single issue), in outcomes (7 no-votes and 12 yes-votes), and in terms of popular support for European integration (Irish and Luxembourgian citizens are among the most Europhile, whereas

# Introduction

Danes and Norwegian are among the most Eurosceptic) and partisan polarization. Moreover, the campaign environments have varied from barely noticeable (e.g. the Irish referendum on the Amsterdam Treaty) to very intense affairs (e.g. the Norwegian referendums on membership).

The aim of examining these cases is two-fold: First, to provide a better understanding of mass—elite dynamics in these referendums on European integration that have had important implications for national as well as European politics. Second, to propose and evaluate a theoretical model of voting behaviour that not only is applicable to referendums, specifically those on European integration, but that also provides general insights into patterns of political behaviour under processes of direct democracy.

## 1.4. Plan of the book

This book is divided into three parts. The first part presents a theoretical model of voting behaviour in referendums. The second part presents the statistical analysis of survey data and experimental data. In the third part, the case studies of individual referendums are presented. Below is a more detailed overview of the remaining chapters of the book.

The second chapter lays out the theoretical framework for the analysis. The core component of the theory is a model of voting behaviour, which outlines how attitudes shape vote choices, influenced by the information that voters receive from political parties and other elites. The framework highlights that differences in political interest among individuals also lead to diverse patterns of voting behaviour, and that the campaign context shapes electoral outcomes. These two aspects of referendum behaviour—individual-level differences and campaign effects—are examined in a comparative analysis of EU referendums in the two subsequent chapters.

Chapter 3 presents a comparative analysis of voting behaviour in nineteen referendums held in Denmark, France, Ireland, Luxembourg, the Netherlands, Norway, and Spain between 1972 and 2008. It relies on statistical analysis of survey data from these referendums to evaluate the theoretical framework presented in Chapter 2. The results reveal the influence of European attitudes, partisan loyalties, and feelings about the government on voters' decisions. They also highlight that voters differ in their voting patterns depending on their level of interest in and knowledge of politics. While Chapter 3 focuses on the influence of individual characteristics, the subsequent chapter examines how the campaign shapes the vote.

Based on analysis of media coverage, opinion polls, and elite polarization, Chapter 4 evaluates how the campaign context shapes vote choices. The key finding is that as the intensity of the referendum campaign increases, voters will rely more heavily on sophisticated criteria, such as attitudes and issue positions, and political elites will find it more difficult to persuade citizens to vote a certain way.

The purpose of the fifth chapter is to examine how different 'frames' influence individual vote choices in referendums. Framing effects occur when people's responses to an issue depend on how it is portrayed. This chapter relies on survey experiments to examine two types of framing effects in (hypothetical) EU referendums. First, it explores the influence of party endorsements on partisan and non-partisan voters. Second, it examines the effect of describing different consequences of voting yes or no on vote choices. This experimental evidence complements the analysis of the survey data by exploring how voters respond to elite recommendations and how the framing of the context influences the choice between two options.

Chapter 6 explores voting behaviour in EU referendums from a normative perspective by considering the issue of voter competence. It addresses the question: What do voters need to know? The main argument put forward in the chapter is that competent voting in EU referendums is based on issue-specific preferences and requires political knowledge, but not necessarily high levels of factual political information, since information short cuts such as party cues can act as substitutes for detailed information. These theoretical questions are evaluated empirically in an analysis of the 1994 Norwegian referendum on EU membership. This case study reveals that most citizens can vote 'competently' by relying on the recommendations of political parties; although it does not follow those voters necessarily adhere to this advice.

In the second case study (Chapter 7), four critical referendums are examined in greater detail: the two Danish referendums on the Maastricht Treaty and the two Irish referendums on the Nice Treaty. In both cases, the initial no-votes were overturned in a second vote. This chapter asks the question: Why did some voters change their minds? These case studies trace the dynamics of elite behaviour and public opinion formation during the course of the campaigns. Through in-depth analyses of newspapers, campaign material, opinion polls, and interviews with key actors in the campaign, this chapter gives a rich description of political behaviour

# Introduction

in the campaigns leading up to the referendum votes. It also provides a detailed analysis of how differences in the political environment—and specifically the information disseminated by political elites—influenced the behaviour of citizens in these referendums on European integration.

The final of the three case studies (Chapter 8) explores perhaps the most significant votes on Europe so far: the referendums on the European Constitutional Treaty in 2005. This chapter examines the two failed referendums in France and the Netherlands. It addresses the questions: Why did the French and the Dutch reject the Constitutional Treaty? Why did the governments fail the task of convincing voters? What was the role of the campaign? Based on systematic research of the campaigns and analyses of the survey data, this chapter provides a comprehensive account of campaign dynamics and voting behaviour in these referendums that ultimately led to the downfall of the European Constitution.

The concluding chapter summarizes the key argument and findings of the book. It discusses the normative and policy implications of this study, focusing particularly on the issue of voter competence and the arguments for and against direct democracy. Finally, it offers some general thoughts and recommendations on the use of direct democratic institutions in the EU.

## Notes

1. The European Union only officially came into existence with the ratification of the Maastricht Treaty in 1993; yet, for the sake of simplicity this term and its acronym (EU) is used in this book as a general description of the organization that was founded in 1957 to bring about economic integration in Europe. This organization has undergone several, often confusing, name changes: The European Community (EC), most important of three European Communities, was originally founded in 1957 by the signing of the Treaty of Rome under the name of European Economic Community (EEC). The 'Economic' was removed from its name by the Maastricht Treaty, which at the same time effectively made the European Community the first of three pillars of the EU, called the Community (or Communities) Pillar. The Treaty of Lisbon states that 'The Union shall replace and succeed the European Community'. This would thus abandon the pillar system in the EU.
2. This book uses 'referendums' as the plural form of referendum, as recommended by the editors of the Oxford English Dictionary: 'In terms of its Latin origin, *referendums* is logically preferable as a modern plural form meaning ballots on one issue (as a Latin gerund *referendum* has no plural); the Latin plural

gerundive *referenda*, meaning "things to be referred", necessarily connotes a plurality of issues'.
3. These initiatives are used frequently in Switzerland, and more infrequently in Italy (the so-called abrogative referendums). In the US, more than half of the States have provisions for initiatives.
4. One hundred and thirty-five of these referendums took place in Switzerland.
5. Recent examples of empirical studies of referendums include Bowler and Donovan (1998) and Mendelsohn and Parkin (2002). In a European context, Hug (2002) is one of the few examples of comparative empirical research on referendums.
6. This figure was correct as of December 2008, and excludes referendums in the Principality of Liechtenstein and the autonomous territories, Greenland (Denmark) and the Åland Islands (Finland), as well as related Swiss votes on free movement of persons in 2005 and cohesion contribution in 2006.
7. Voters have been asked to vote twice on very similar matters, when they rejected the proposal the first time around, in Denmark in 1992 and 1993 and Ireland in 2001 and 2002 (see Chapter 7).
8. An example of this was the Irish referendum on the Single European Act. This referendum was only called after the Irish Supreme Court established that the government was not entitled to ratify a treaty that restricted the freedom of future governments to decide on matters of foreign policy without a constitutional amendment (and thus a referendum). See *Crotty* v. *An Taoiseach* 09 Apr 1987 [1987] IESC 4, [1987] IR 713.
9. Although in the first case, the Danes were guaranteed important opt-outs in the areas of defence, justice, and home affairs; citizenship; and a single currency. In the Irish case, a 'neutrality clause' was added to the ballot proposition. These referendums are described in more detail in Chapter 7.
10. Extract from the Laeken Declaration. The European Council in Laeken on 14–15 December 2001 adopted a Declaration on the Future of Europe and established the method and timetable for the discussion and preparatory phase that preceded the 2004 Intergovernmental Conference.

## 2
# A Theory of Referendum Behaviour

> *The democratic citizen is expected to be well informed about political affairs. He is supposed to know what the issues are, what their history is, what the relevant facts are, what alternatives are proposed that the party stands for, what the likely consequences are. By such standards the voter falls short.*[1]
> —Berelson, Lazarsfeld, and McPhee

The above quote addresses a key dilemma of modern democracy: on the one hand, normative theories of democracy expect citizens to have a basic understanding of party platforms and public policy issues. On the other hand, the empirical evidence shows that citizens are poorly informed about political affairs. We know from numerous studies of elections that citizens are not just ignorant about specific policy issues, but also about the basic structure of government and how it operates. More recent studies, however, have emphasized that in spite of imperfect information, voters are often capable of making competent decisions in elections by relying on a variety of cues, such as partisan identification and group endorsements. At the heart of this debate is the link between political information and voting behaviour, which is also highly relevant in the context of European referendums. If voters are poorly informed in elections, this problem is likely to be even greater in referendums where they are asked to vote on often complex and unfamiliar issues.

The view that European politics is too complex for ordinary people to decide on has been widely expressed during the arguments that have followed the referendums on the European Constitutional Treaty (ECT) and the Lisbon Treaty. In the opinion of the Commission President, José Manuel Barroso, referendums represent a 'populist trend' which threatens to 'undermine the Europe we are trying to build by simplifying important and complex subjects'. Equally, Margot Wallström, European

Commissioner, has commented that complexity of the European Constitution leads voters to 'use a referendum to answer a question that was not put to them'.[2] Indeed, one of the most prominent explanations for these no-votes is that French and Dutch voters used the Constitutional referendums as an opportunity to express their dissatisfaction with the government of the day, rather than as a vote on the substantive issue of the Constitution. Following the Irish rejection of the Lisbon Treaty, politicians were also eager to stress that the Irish No had very little to do with the treaty itself. As Ireland's EU Commissioner, Charlie McCreevy put it: 'this vote is not a vote against the European Union. It is about a myriad of other issues'.[3]

These arguments over the no-votes in EU referendums raise the more general question of how voters decide in referendums on European integration. How do they make up their mind in referendums where they are asked to vote directly on complex and unfamiliar issues? Are their votes decided by their views on Europe, the recommendations of their preferred party or protest over domestic politics? These questions also concern the issue over how the information provided to citizens in the campaign influence patterns of voting behaviour. This chapter outlines a theoretical framework for understanding voting behaviour in EU referendums, emphasizing the mediating impact of political information.

In spite of the importance of information in shaping political behaviour, no comparative studies on EU referendums have systematically examined the impact of political information. The main debate in the literature concerns whether citizens vote according to their own attitudes towards the issue of European integration or whether they vote on the basis of the endorsements and performance of national political parties. The central argument of this book is that political information plays a crucial role in mediating the relative importance of these factors. Political information concerns not only the type of information and elite cues that are available in the political environment (*supply of information*), but also the handling of this information by individual voters (*processing of information*). Both processes can crucially determine the salience of European integration and the centrality of EU attitudes and moreover influence individuals' reception of elite cues and consequently their vote choice. The main proposition is that patterns of voting behaviour vary according to the intensity of the campaign environment as well as the political awareness of the individual. More specifically, intense campaigns will lead to more issue voting, and reduce the importance of domestic politics. Equally, voters who pay more attention to politics are likely to be less susceptible to the recommendations of national politicians and instead rely more on their own opinions about European integration.

This chapter begins by providing a brief overview of the developments in public attitudes towards European integration, before proceeding to review the existing explanations of voting behaviour in EU referendums. The theoretical framework of voting in referendums developed in this chapter draws on theories of opinion formation and communication as well as spatial models of voting behaviour. A brief discussion of these theories and the body of literature precedes the presentation of the theoretical model. The core component of this theoretical framework is a proximity model of voting behaviour in referendums that incorporates the mediating effect of political knowledge.

## 2.1. Public attitudes and behaviour in the EU

Recent decades have seen fluctuations in public support for European integration. This contrasts with the predictions of Ronald Inglehart (1970a, 1970b, 1971, 1977) in the 1970s, who forecasted that support for integration would be on the rise because of increasing education levels and because the younger generations born after the Second World War would be favourably disposed towards post-materialist values and international cooperation. Yet the 1990s saw a significant fall in public enthusiasm for the European project across the member states. The lack of public support for the EU that became evident in the Maastricht referendums gave rise to a number of studies addressing the issue of the 'democratic deficit' of the Union and the correlates of support for European integration. Despite the fact that national EU referendums provided the impetus for this renewed interest in the public's European attitudes, few comparative studies have examined citizens' behaviour in EU referendums. Understanding why citizens express positive (or negative) attitudes towards the EU is important, but it is equally important to know how these attitudes affect actual behaviour, and hence the focus of this book is to understand the factors influencing political behaviour rather than attitude formation. In this section, we present a brief overview of the variation in attitudes towards European integration before proceeding to examine the behaviour of citizens in referendums on European integration.

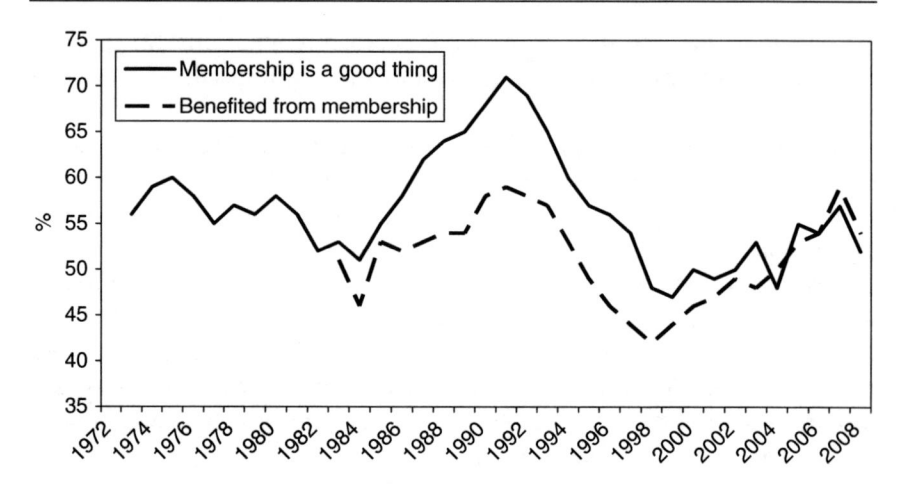

**Figure 2.1.** Development in public support for European integration
*Source*: Eurobarometer surveys, 1973–2008

### 2.1.1. *Public support for European integration*

Since the early 1970s, public attitudes towards the integration project have been tracked in the biannual Eurobarometer surveys. These surveys measure 'diffuse' as well as 'concrete' support for the integration project[4] (Reif 1984; Reif and Inglehart 1991; Niedermayer and Sinnott 1995). Figure 2.1 shows the general trend in support for European integration in the member states during the past three decades.

Figure 2.1 shows that public support for the EU has picked up since the late 1990s. In particular, there has been a marked increase in the number of people who think that their country has benefitted from membership. It is worth noting, however, that while these levels of support for European integration among citizens may seem relatively high, there is still a considerable gap between public and elite support for European integration. More than 90 per cent of national elites think that that EU membership is a good thing, compared with just over a half of the citizens (Hooghe 2003: 3). A study by Hooghe (2003) has demonstrated that this divide is more pronounced in areas of 'high politics', where elites are significantly more in favour of integration, than in 'low' public policy areas of social policy and redistribution.

The aggregate trend of citizen support shown in Figure 2.1 conceals considerable variation in support between member states. Historically, citizens of the six founding member states have been the most pro-European together with citizens of Ireland, Greece, and Portugal, whereas the British and the Nordic publics have been amongst the most Eurosceptic. Figure 2.2 shows more recent trends in the public perception of the EU across all twenty-seven member states.

According to Figure 2.2, Irish citizens have the most positive image of the EU, followed by the most recent entrants, the Romanians and Bulgarians. The most negative assessments of the EU are found among the publics in Northern Europe (Austria, the UK, Sweden, and Denmark) as well as among the citizens in some of the post-Communist countries that joined in 2004: Latvia and Hungary. The black bars highlight the countries with referendums examined in this book—Ireland, Spain, Luxembourg, France, the Netherlands, and Denmark (as well as Norway)—and clearly indicate the variation in public perception of the EU across these countries. This figure also suggests that attitudes alone cannot account for negative outcomes in EU referendums, given that ballots were rejected not only in Denmark and the Netherlands, but also among more the more pro-European electorates in France and Ireland.

There are several attempts in the literature to explain these cross-national and cross-temporal variations in public support for European integration and determine individual-level correlates of support, such as 'postmaterialist values' (Inglehart 1971, 1977), economic cost-benefit-analysis (Gabel 1998*a*; Kaltenthaler and Anderson 2001), and culture and identity patterns (McLaren 2002, 2004, 2006; Hooghe and Marks 2004). While there are many explanations of what drives citizens to support or oppose European integration, less attention has been given to the question of how these attitudes affect political behaviour. Studies have shown that attitudes towards European integration generally play a limited role in determining people's vote choices in European elections where behavioural patterns are mainly driven by domestic political considerations and 'national political cues' (Irwin 1995; Marsh and Franklin 1996: 11; van der Eijk and Franklin 1996, 2004; Marsh 1998; van der Brug and van der Eijk 2007; see also Hobolt, Spoon and Tilley 2009). European issues have also been of limited importance in national elections, with some notable exceptions (Evans 1998, 1999, 2002; Mair 2000; de Vries 2007). But while attitudes towards European integration may have played a rather limited role in national and European elections, they would be expected to influence behaviour in referendums where voters are asked specifically to decide on Europe. However, this central role of European attitudes has been disputed by many studies on voting behaviour in

**Europe in Question**

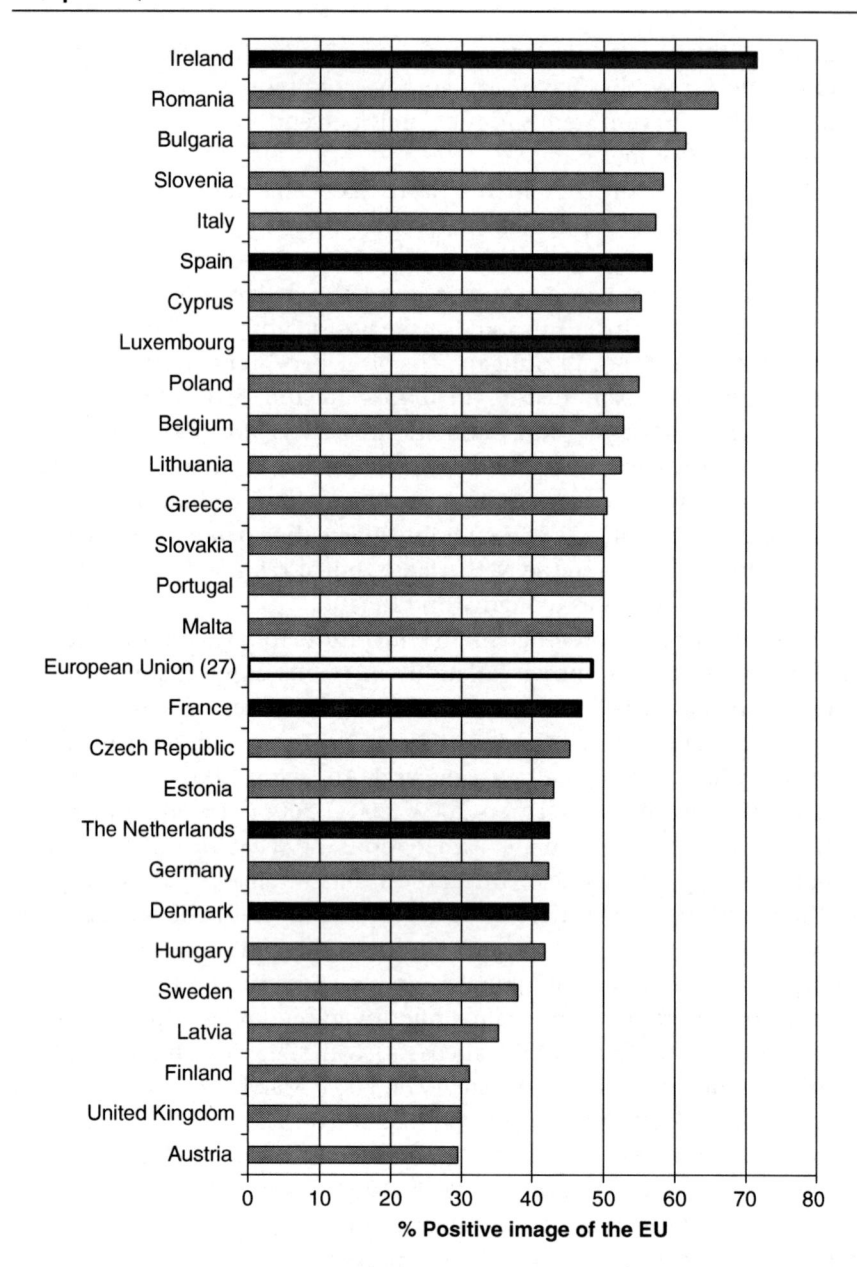

**Figure 2.2.** Public perceptions of the EU, by member state

*Source*: Eurobarometer surveys, 2005–2008 (average). Answer 'very/fairly positive' to the question: 'In general, does the EU conjure up for you a very positive, fairly positive, neutral, fairly negative or very negative image?'

referendums. The following section presents an overview of the literature on political behaviour in referendums on European integration, focusing particularly on the question of whether and when European attitudes matter in EU referendums.

## 2.1.2. Voting behaviour in EU referendums

Scholarly interest in EU referendums has grown during the past decade, as the frequency and importance of these referendums have risen. Nonetheless, comparative empirical studies of political behaviour in these referendums are still few and far between and attempts of general theorizing are rare. Most studies of EU referendums have focused on a single case or referendums in a single country.[5] These studies provide many important insights into EU referendums but one of the major drawbacks of single-country studies is that they rarely allow for generalization beyond their specific context.

This lack of theory building and comparative empirical work has meant that many important questions about political behaviour in referendums still remain unanswered. As Hug (2002: 4) has pointed out, 'in the absence of any detailed comparative studies of voting behaviour in such referendums we cannot disentangle country-idiosyncrasies from more general patterns'. Yet, there have been some important contributions to the literature that have attempted to present more general hypotheses about patterns of voting behaviour in EU referendums and to test these propositions empirically; notably in the wake of the Maastricht referendums where a number of competing explanations of patterns of voting behaviour emerged in the literature (Franklin, Marsh, and McLaren 1994; Franklin, Marsh, and Wlezien 1994; Franklin, van der Eijk, and Marsh 1995). These studies spurred an ongoing debate between two competing schools: the 'attitude' (or 'issue voting') school and the 'second-order election' school. The first school focuses on individuals' values and preferences and argues that voting behaviour in EU referendums reflects people's underlying broad attitudes towards Europe (Siune, Svensson and Tonsgaard 1992, 1994*a*, 1994*b*; Siune and Svensson 1993; Svensson 1994, 2002; Aardal et al. 1998). Broadly speaking, this approach suggests that individuals' attitudes towards European integration, described in the previous section, are the key factors that determine referendum outcomes and reversions in outcomes. Behaviour in EU referendums is thus not dissimilar from issue voting in elections where voters opt for the choice (or candidate) that has the closest proximity to their own ideal point on an issue dimension (Downs 1957).

A competing explanation of voting behaviour in EU referendums is inspired by the 'second-order' theory of elections (Reif and Schmitt 1980). The important characteristic of 'second-order' elections (local and regional elections also fall into this category) is that they are regarded of lesser importance than national elections ('first-order'), and consequently voter turnout is lower, protest-voting and voter-switching are more common, and national issues tend to dominate the election campaigns. Following this logic, voters are expected to use referendums on European integration as a means of signalling their satisfaction or dissatisfaction with the government and parties. Several studies have applied this second-order model to EU referendums and have linked referendum outcomes with attitudes towards national governments (Franklin, Marsh and McLaren 1994; Franklin, Marsh and Wlezien 1994; Franklin, van der Eijk and Marsh 1995; Franklin 2002). According to these studies, voters who are dissatisfied with the performance of the government may use EU referendums to punish the government by voting against the proposals; whereas voters who are satisfied may follow the recommendations of the parties in power. As Franklin, Marsh and McLaren note: 'voters may take advantage of the opportunity provided by a referendum to express a protest against government policy generally' (Franklin, Marsh and McLaren 1994: 462). The second-order model, however, does not necessarily imply that voters will vote no, but rather that attitudes towards European integration play a limited role, whereas the cues of national elites and the credibility of these cues play crucial roles in determining the outcome.

In the literature, these two approaches are often presented as 'quite distinct from each other' (Garry, Marsh, and Sinnott 2005: 205), and there is a continuing battle as to which approach provides the most accurate description of patterns of voting behaviour. Moreover, the implications of these competing explanations are also seen as different and far-reaching. As Palle Svensson (2002: 733) notes, it is a question of whether voters 'really address the issues and involve themselves actively in the policy-making process on a vital issue or... merely vote for or against the current government'. While the implications of these alternative approaches are undoubtedly significant, it seems misguided to present the two approaches as mutually exclusive. Rather the challenge must be to examine why and under what circumstances individual voters are more likely to rely on attitudes or when second-order factors take prominence.

Some authors have examined how different factors may play a role in mediating the importance of these factors in referendums. In Simon Hug's important book *Voices of Europe* (2002), he focuses on the impact of legal-constitutional factors (see also Schneider and Weitsman 1996; Hug and Sciarini 2000). Hug argues that government supporters are more likely to follow government recommendations (and vote yes) in non-required and binding referendums than in required and nonbinding ones. Franklin (2002) has suggested that *salience* may influence the degree to which government popularity matters: 'on matters of low salience to voters, a referendum called by a government and opposed by opposition parties should generally be seen as a test of the standing of that government rather than as test of support for the policy nominally at issue' (Franklin 2002: 756, see also Hobolt 2005). This argument is not further developed in the article, but it provides an apposite starting point for a more rigorous examination of how salience levels and the political environment of the campaign affect attitudes and reception of elite cues and, in turn, how this influences behaviour in referendums.

In summary, the last decade has produced some valuable comparative studies of clusters of EU referendums. An important contribution of these studies has been to highlight the role of both people's attitudes towards European integration and various elite cues in determining the outcome of a referendum. Yet, no study has satisfactorily explained to what extent and under what circumstances these factors are likely to matter to the individual voter or the aggregate outcome. The remainder of this chapter presents a theoretical model that seeks to answer these questions. The main proposition of this model is that political information acts as a crucial intervening variable that mediates the relative weight of attitudes and elite cues in determining voting behaviour. The *supply of information* determines the extent to which individuals have the opportunity to form attitudes towards the issue of European integration in the first place and the information environment also dictates the type of cues and endorsements that elites make available to voters. The *processing of information* affects how attentive and receptive individuals are to informational cues and elite endorsements. This theoretical framework builds on theories of information effects in voting and opinion formation and this body of literature will be reviewed in the following section before proceeding to the discussion and specification of the model.

## 2.2. Theories of information and voting behaviour

> In general, it is irrational to be politically well-informed because the low returns from data simply do not justify their cost in time and other scarce resources. Therefore many voters do not bother to discover their true views before voting, and most citizens are not well enough informed to influence directly the formulation of those policies that affect them.[6]
>
> Anthony Downs

Downs famously proposed that it is rational for most citizens to remain ignorant about political affairs due to the low marginal benefits of acquiring political information, and thus he concluded that 'true political equality is impossible' (Downs 1957: 259). The lack of political knowledge among citizens is well-documented, especially in the American context. Despite the democratic ideal of an electorate that chooses among candidates and parties on the basis of an informed understanding of policy issues and party platforms, numerous studies have pointed to evidence suggesting that many people know of the existence of few, if any, of the major issues of policy. The influential study of voting behaviour in the US, *The American Voter* (Campbell et al. 1960), found that voters have limited ability to think in the abstract about candidates and issues and that they lack factual information (see also Butler and Stokes 1969, 1974). Converse (1964) expanded this study of political sophistication and found that citizens' attitudes towards political issues are characterized by incoherence and instability: 'as one moves from elite sources of belief systems downwards, one encounters a drop in levels of information, the disappearance of a belief system as such and of constraint between ideas that are in fact related' (1964: 115). Voter ignorance is not a uniquely American phenomenon. Only shortly after the European Constitution was signed by European leaders in a high-profile ceremony in 2004 in Rome, 33 per cent of the European public declared that they had never heard of the document and another half responded that they knew very little about the content of the Constitution. More than a third of people were also unable to express any preferences about the document.[7]

These findings of voter ignorance have even led some scholars to suggest that, 'the low level of political knowledge and the absence of ideological reasoning have lent credence to the charge that popular control of the government is illusory' (Iyengar 1987: 816). In recent years, however, a number of studies have moved away from this very pessimistic view of voter competence and rallied behind Key's (1966) dictum that 'voters are not fools'. Most of these studies have changed their focus from information levels to individual and collective information processing (Bartels 1996). The basic argument is that voters can make reasoned choices based on very limited information by using cues and information shortcuts. To understand how information matters to vote choice, we must therefore first consider the main theories of voting and then proceed to a discussion of how heuristics (information short cuts) can help voters with the informational demands inherent in these voting models.

## 2.2.1. Models of voting behaviour

How do voters decide between candidates and parties in an election? This question has vexed political scientists for decades. Broadly speaking we may refer to two general approaches to this question: the sociological approach and the rational choice approach (Merrill and Grofman 1999; Clarke et al. 2004). While the theoretical framework developed in this chapter builds on the rational choice approach to political behaviour, some of the insights of the sociological approach are also incorporated into the model.

In classic works of American politics, scholars developed the so-called 'Michigan model' of voting where *party identification* was the central concept (see Campbell et al. 1960). Party identification refers to relatively stable and enduring affective attachments to parties that predispose the individual to vote for the party with which they 'identify'. This concept was imported to the British electoral studies in the 1960s by Butler and Stokes (1969) and has remained pervasive in the European context, although it has been challenged in recent decades (see for example Crewe et al. 1977; Clarke et al. 2004; see also Wattenberg 1998). Butler and Stokes (1969) argued that voters in a divided class society possess powerful and pervasive class identifications that are transmitted to the electoral arena via durable identifications with political parties thought to represent the economic interests of those classes. According to this sociological approach, most identifiers acquire their party identification during their early formative years. Empirically, party identification has proven a strong predictor of patterns of voting behaviour and as a result, it is usually accorded a pivotal causal role in the determination of voting preferences. But party identification is an important concept in electoral studies not only because it is a powerful predictor of vote choice in elections, but also because it acts as a filter for the interpretation of political messages and cues, as will be discussed later. In the context of referendums, this latter indirect effect is more important than the former direct effect, since voters are asked to vote on issues and not parties.

An alternative approach to voting in elections is the rational choice approach, which posits that vote choice depends on a calculation of personal cost and benefit (utility) of voting for a certain party and candidate.[8] The basic idea of this spatial theory of voting, originally popularized by Downs, is that voters vote for the party holding policy positions most similar to their own positions (Downs 1957; Davis, Hinich, and Ordeshook 1970; Enelow and Hinich 1984). From a rational choice perspective, choices are derived from maximization of voters' individual utility functions representing the evaluation of various party positions. However, spatial models could equally be derived in the framework of cognitive models used in political psychology theory, i.e. voters' choices of parties are determined by voters' emotional responses to symbols.

Since voters maximize their utility by voting for the party (or candidate) that is located closest to their own position (or 'ideal point') on the dominant policy dimension (e.g. left-right), the proximity model requires voters to have a certain amount of information about the position of parties or candidates as well as their own positions in order to vote 'rationally'. As Downs pointed out, 'a man's evaluation of each party depends ultimately upon (1) the information he has about its policies and (2) the relation between those of its policies he knows about and his conception of the good society' (Downs 1957: 46). The basic paradox of the knowledge requirements implied by the spatial models is that, as Downs observed, 'voters are not always aware of what the government is or could be doing, and often they do not know the relationship between government actions and their own utility incomes' (Downs 1957: 80). Not only do people have very low levels of information about policy positions, this lack of knowledge about political affairs can also be seen as a rational consequence of the low value of that information to most individuals set against the relatively high cost of acquiring such information. According to the rational choice perspective, an individual's investment in obtaining information should be determined by the cost of the information, the value this information has to her in terms of making the correct decisions (optimizing utility), and the relevance of the decision being made (Downs 1957; Lupia and McCubbins 1998). The low return of acquiring information means that it is irrational for most voters to acquire political information. As discussed above, numerous empirical studies have shown that voters do indeed possess very low levels of political information.

This lack of voter information has important implications not only for our empirical understanding of how people vote, but also normative repercussions for our conception of democracy. If the marginal benefit of acquiring information is so low that most people do not bother, can they still vote 'rationally' or competently, as stipulated by the spatial theories of voting as well as many normative theories of democracy? According to much of the recent work on voting, the answer is yes, since poorly informed voters can make rational decisions by using heuristics and informational shortcuts. Indeed, Downs argued that party identification could be used as an informational shortcut as the basis of vote choices. As Samuel Popkin has noted in his discussion of the contributions of Downs:

Party identification viewed from the perspective of low-information rationality is an informational short-cut or default value, a substitute for more complete information about parties and candidates (...) Party identification is a standing decision; even so, it is affected by the information they obtain in their daily lives and connect with government policies, and by the information they absorb simply because it is interesting or entertaining (Popkin 1991: 14).

Hence, from the perspective of information processing and cue-taking, the core concept of the sociological approach, party identification, can be incorporated into the spatial models of voting, where it provides a useful information short cut about the proximity and direction of parties, as well as a general filter mechanism for elite cues.

### 2.2.2. The use of cues and heuristics

The basic idea of much of the recent research on the relationship between information and voting is that limited information need not prevent people from making reasoned (or 'rational') vote choices, since voters can rely on cues and heuristics—such as party identification, campaign events, polls, and opinion leaders—to overcome their information shortfalls (Brady and Sniderman 1985; McKelvey and Ordeshook 1985; Sniderman, Brody, and Tetlock 1991; Lupia 1994, 2006; Lupia and McCubbins 1998). In order to understand the underlying idea of 'cue-taking', it is necessary to distinguish between information and knowledge (Downs 1957; Lupia and McCubbins 1998). On the one hand, *knowledge* refers to the ability of individuals to predict the consequences of actions, for example, the implications of voting for a specific party with respect to one's personal utility. On the other hand, *information* is the data that allows people to acquire knowledge. Hence, 'although you cannot have knowledge without having information, you can have information without having knowledge' (Lupia and McCubbins 1998: 25). This distinction between information and knowledge is central to the renaissance of the 'reasoning voter' in the literature. The main proposition is that high levels of information are not necessarily required for a voter to have sufficient knowledge to make a *reasoned choice*; that is, to choose the same way as they would have done if perfect information were available. Instead of acquiring 'encyclopaedic' information about politics, voters can use information shortcuts or cues as substitutes. In a spatial framework, this would imply that voters can use information shortcuts to opt for the party or candidate that has the closest proximity to their own position. McKelvey and Ordeshook have summarized the argument as follows:

Citizens possess highly imperfect information about candidates and public issues, and in deciding how to vote they rely on a variety of indirect and possibly irrelevant cues, such as partisan identification, group endorsement, and the opinions of friends, as well as the personality, appearance, and "style" of candidates (McKelvey and Ordeshook 1986: 910).

Information shortcuts may therefore take various forms. In their study, McKelvey and Ordeshook (1986) emphasize how citizens use opinion polls to learn about the policy position of candidates on issues. Other scholars have emphasized the usefulness of alternate heuristics, such as party identification (Downs 1957), campaign events and information (Popkin 1991; Lupia 1992; Lodge, Steenbergen and Brau 1995), opinion leaders (Sniderman, Brody and Tetlock 1991), elite endorsements (Zaller 1992; Lupia 1994), and the media (Iyengar and Kinder 1987). Whether these cues work as effective substitutes for complex information depends crucially on the availability and quality of the information itself, as well as the processing of this information by the individual voter. In *The Democratic Dilemma*, Lupia and McCubbins (1998) develop a framework for understanding how people use cues, when these cues are substitutes for detailed information, and when they are deceptive. They argue that most people acquire knowledge by learning from others (i.e. listening to cues), but for such persuasion to be enlightening rather than deceptive or simply ineffective, it requires the citizen to perceive the information provider as knowledgeable and trustworthy. People are more easily persuaded by information providers believed to have common interests to their own (e.g. perceived shared ideology). Yet, persuasion is not always enlightening. One of the greatest threats to democracy is that the information provided by political elites and others leads to deception, that is, a reduction in people's ability to make accurate predictions about their actions. According to Lupia and McCubbins, a persuasive and knowledgeable 'speaker' can bring about either enlightenment or deception. The only condition that separates these two processes is when either actual common interest or external forces induce the speaker to reveal what he knows, and hence be truthful. Absent of common interests, 'external forces' such as costly effort, threats of claims being verified, and penalty for lying are necessary to avoid deception. Lupia and McCubbins' (1998) formal model of persuasion provides a framework for understanding when and how informational cues may be used as substitutes for more detailed information. At the heart of their theory is the question of how citizens process cues provided by elites.

The issue of the processing of elite cues is highly relevant in the context of EU referendums where political elites, such as parties and interest groups, play an important role in disseminating endorsements and other cues that influence voting decisions. Such cues may provide important tools for voters to make reasoned choices on the basis of limited information but, as Lupia and Johnston have pointed out, 'short cuts are no panacea. If used incorrectly, reliance on short cuts can lead to grave errors' (2001: 196). To understand opinion formation and voting behaviour in EU referendums, we must therefore examine the types of elite cues available as well as the processing of these cues by individuals.

### 2.2.3. Variation in political awareness and reception of elite cues

The studies discussed above have emphasized that voters in many cases can make reasoned choices without possessing encyclopaedic knowledge by using information cues and shortcuts. Yet, while poorly informed voters may be capable of approximating the behaviour of 'fully informed' voters by using shortcuts, the way in which they arrive at this decision is not necessarily identical. In other words, the information processing, and hence relative weight of different factors determining vote choices, may vary depending on the individual's attention to political information. As Sniderman, Brody, and Tetlock (1991: 165–6) pointed out, 'it is not reasonable to assume that the voter who is exceedingly well informed about politics and the one who is largely ignorant of it would enumerate potentially relevant considerations with the same exhaustiveness; or foresee consequences of alternative choices with the same distinctness'.

Numerous studies of opinion formation have shown that people vary greatly in their attentiveness to political communication and that this variance influences the process of opinion formation (see for example, Converse 1975, 2000; Zaller 1992; Alvarez and Brehm 2002). Downs (1957) has provided a plausible model of why citizens vary in their attentiveness to politics. As discussed previously, it is generally too costly for citizens to be well informed about political issues. Costs of acquiring information include transferable costs that can be borne by other individuals (gathering, analysing and evaluating information) and non-transferable costs that must be borne by the individuals themselves (learning information and relating it to attitudes and behaviour). But some citizens are better able to reduce these information costs than others, which implies that there will be significant differences in the political awareness of voters (Downs 1957).[9] Consequently, there is considerable heterogeneity in *political awareness*, defined as the extent to which an individual pays attention to, and understands, politics (Zaller 1992: 21). But while the variation in individuals' level of political awareness is well-documented, we know less about how this may affect patterns of voting behaviour. As Converse has noted, 'the degree of heterogeneity [of political information] is widely underestimated, and the implications of that dramatic heterogeneity seem even less well understood' (2000: 332). One important contribution to this question is John Zaller's (1992) well-known theory of opinion formation, which explicitly examines how variations in political awareness may affect opinion formation, and in particular, the reception of elite cues.

Variation in an individual's attentiveness to politics is at the heart of Zaller's (1992) Receive-Accept-Sample (RAS) model of opinion formation. Zaller argues that the formation (and change) of public opinion is driven by political messages delivered by the elites. Hence, this model is a top-down model of elite-driven public opinion; yet, the important stipulation of the model is that people do not generally accept elite cues mechanically without qualifications. On the contrary, there are several 'filter mechanisms' that determine whether people (voters) choose to follow the elites. As Lupia and McCubbins (1998: 10) point out, 'people respond to the advice of some experts or interest groups and not others'. They suggest that knowledge and trust are the fundamental factors that make elite cues persuasive. But before people can 'decide' whether or not to be persuaded by elites, they need to pay attention to these cues in the first place. In Zaller's model this attentiveness to politics is specified as the *Reception Axiom*: the greater a person's level of cognitive engagement with an issue, the more likely she is to be exposed to and to comprehend political messages concerning the issue (Zaller 1992: 58). In other words, the higher the level of political awareness, the more likely a person is to *receive* elite messages. However, the reception of elite cues does not necessarily imply that an individual will internalize and act in accordance with these messages. The second axiom in Zaller's model is the *Resistance Axiom*: people tend to resist arguments that are inconsistent with their political predispositions, but they do so only to the extent that they possess the contextual information necessary to perceive the relationship between the message and the predisposition (1992: 58).

The impact of people's value predispositions always depends on whether citizens possess the contextual information needed to translate their values into support for particular policies or candidates, and the possession of such information can... never be taken for granted (Zaller 1992: 25).

Hence, political predispositions, that is, stable individual-level traits and attitudes, regulate the acceptance or non-acceptance of the political communications a person receives. Moreover, the level of political awareness influences the extent to which an individual can make the link between the elite cues and these underlying political attitudes. Following this logic of Zaller's RAS model, citizens with high levels of political awareness are more exposed to, and more capable of, understanding and receiving political messages from the elites (reception axiom). Yet, they are also better equipped to assess whether these cues are consistent with their underlying political attitudes, and are thus more likely to reject the cues if they are incompatible (resistance axiom). Hence, Zaller's RAS model focuses on how variation in an individual's attentiveness to politics may affect how she responds to elite cues and, in turn, whether or not she decides to act on these cues. Moreover, the context in which these cues are delivered and processed is also important. According to Lupia and McCubbins (1998), the institutional environment can affect whether or not elite persuasion is enlightening by altering the incentives for elites to provide truthful information and by influencing the perception of this information among citizens.

In summary, these theories of political information and voting behaviour have highlighted important issues concerning the role of information in democratic processes: first, the nature of elite cues and the context within which they are delivered influence political behaviour and second, the way in which people process these information cues guides behaviour. The remainder of the chapter draws on these theories of opinion formation and voting to build a theoretical framework of how people make vote choices in referendums on European integration.

## 2.3. A model of referendum behaviour

The previous sections have emphasized that the ability of voters to make reasoned decisions in elections depends crucially on the supply of informational cues and the processing of these cues. Hence, to understand patterns of voting behaviour in referendums, it is important to determine how cues are supplied and processed and how this impacts the vote choice of individuals. As Lupia and Johnston (2001: 196) have pointed out, 'the key to understanding referendum voters' competence is to determine *how* they use short cuts available to them'. Yet, while a great deal of attention has been paid to the role of information and voter competence in elections, especially in American elections (see, for example, Ferejohn and Kuklinski 1990; Alvarez 1997; Lupia and McCubbins 1998), few studies have examined this question in the context of European integration referendums. Yet, some studies have examined the role of information in other referendums. In an influential article on direct democracy, Lupia (1994) examines how voters with limited information used elite endorsement to make 'reasoned decisions' in Californian insurance referendums. Another important contribution to this literature is Bowler and Donovan's (1998) book on how voters make choices in referendums given the information available to them. They examine this issue empirically in the context of American state-level referendums and find that vote choices are affected by the information demands associated with ballots. When ballots are lengthy and complex, voters are more likely to abstain and more likely to vote no. Yet, they also find that voters use cues, such as elite endorsements, to place proposals within a partisan frame. They also find that higher levels of campaign spending tend to increase voters' awareness of a ballot proposal. A number of studies have examined the role of information in Swiss referendums. For example, Christin, Hug, and Sciarini (2002) demonstrate that individual-levels of political awareness conditions voting behaviour in Swiss referendums. Following Zaller's RAS model, Bützer and Marquis (2002) and Sciarini, Bornstein, and Lanz (2007) have shown the effect of political predispositions on vote choice is mediated by political awareness, and that this effect in turn varies according to the campaign context (intensity and elite division) in Swiss ballots. Kriesi (2005) also presents a sophisticated analysis of how Swiss voters use cues to make sense of direct democracy.

This book builds on this literature on the role of information in elections and referendums to develop and test a model of vote choice in European referendums. By examining how the type and quantity of information in the political environment and variation in political awareness affect the way in which people make up their minds in EU referendums, we can arrive at a better understanding of voting behaviour in these settings. On the one hand, variation in knowledge of policy issue positions may be context-dependent and elite-induced; that is, it can be dependent on the type of information supplied by elites. On the other hand, it may be endogenous to the voter, that is, dependent on the general political awareness of the individual citizen (Enelow and Hinich 1984; Alvarez 1997). Whereas most studies focus exclusively on only one of these 'information' effects, this book will consider both.

This section develops a theoretical model of the impact of political information on voting behaviour in referendums. To begin with, the section discusses the intuition behind the model. Thereafter, the full model of the voter's expected utility of a ballot proposal in a referendum is presented and the various elements of the model are discussed in turn, and finally, this chapter derives implications for the strategies available to elites from this model.

### 2.3.1. Intuition

Imagine a left-wing French voter who has only a limited interest in European politics, but is broadly supportive of European integration as a project of peace and solidarity and believes that the EU enhances French influence in the world. She is asked to cast a vote on the ratification of the Constitutional Treaty. Several considerations might influence her decision. First of all, she considers whether the Treaty is broadly in line with her preferences on Europe (*proximity hypothesis*). Given that she knows very little about the Constitution, she is unsure whether it will benefit France and promote the kind of Europe that she wants (*political awareness hypothesis*). Given these fears, she considers voting no to be on the safe side or abstaining (*uncertainty hypothesis*). However, she also considers whether a rejection of the Constitution would damage France's reputation in Europe and maybe even diminish the leadership role of France within the Community. Given her indecisiveness, she seeks guidance from the political party that she normally votes for, the Socialist Party (*endorsement hypothesis*). It appears, however, that the Socialists are divided on the issue and this leaves her wavering. Moreover, the French President Jacques Chirac, whom she deeply distrusts, is enthusiastically advocating a vote in favour the Constitution, and this makes her suspicious about the proposal. As the campaign takes off, our voter becomes more interested in the issues at stake and starts to pay attention to the lively debate for and against the Constitution (*campaign intensity hypothesis*). She senses that the European Constitution will lead to less solidarity and social welfare in Europe, whereas a no-vote may allow for a renegotiation of the Treaty to include more social provisions. As a consequence, she decides to vote no. This voter thus chooses not to follow the recommendation of her party to vote yes, but instead to vote on the basis of her views on the issues that are on agenda in the campaign. Her decision is also influenced by her perception that a no-vote may lead to a more optimal solution (*reversion point*). Without the information provided in the campaign, she would have been more likely to abstain or to vote on the basis of her feelings about national politics.

### 2.3.2. A spatial model of voting in referendums

This basic intuition about opinion formation and vote choices in EU referendums can be depicted more formally. Building on the spatial models of voting behaviour and the literature on information effects, this book proposes a simple model of voting in referendums. To give an overview of the model, this section first briefly introduces the full model (Equation 2.1), and thereafter the remainder of the chapter discusses each of the components of the model in greater detail.

The full model presents the expected utility of voting in favour of a specific ballot proposal as follows:

$$E[U_{ix}] = w_{ix}(-(p_x - I_i)^2 - \sigma_{ix}^2) + (1 - w_{ix})c_{ix} \qquad (2.1)$$

Equation 2.1 is based on a model of the expected utility $E[U]$ of a ballot proposal $x$ for an individual voter $i$, consisting of several components. At the core of the model is the *proximity component* $(-(P_{ix} - I_i)^2)$: the perceived utility of voting for proposal $x$ depends on the (squared) distance between the perceived position of the proposal ($P_{ix}$) and the voter's own ideal point ($I_i$). Moreover, Equation 2.2 includes $c_{ix}$ which is a term that represents all the considerations involved in the voter's overall evaluation not related to the ballot proposal itself. In the context of EU referendums, this term captures, for example, considerations about domestic political matters ('second-order' factors). Importantly, political information also conditions the relative weight of proximity considerations versus other considerations in the utility calculus. This is denoted by $w_{ix}$, which defines the relative weight of each component. It is assumed that this weight is proportional to the salience of the ballot issue and/or the voter's knowledge about the issue at stake and that it is constrained so that $0 \leq w_{ix} \leq 1$. This means that the closer $w_{ix}$ is to 1, the more the issue preferences will matter to the overall utility of the proposal relative to other non-issue specific considerations. But the overall expected utility is reduced by the variances in the voter's perception of the location of the ballot proposal, that is the *uncertainty* component of the model, denoted by $\sigma_{ix}^2$. Hence, according to this model, information conditions the impact of the utility of the proposal in two ways: first, by influencing the knowledge and certainty of the location of the alternative options and second, by affecting the extent to which these proximity considerations matter to the overall evaluation of the proposal. In the following sections, each of the components of the model are discussed in more detail and specific hypotheses are presented. First, we recast the classic spatial proximity model in the context of referendums. Second, we introduce the element of uncertainty, and finally, we discuss the information weights of issue salience and awareness.

### 2.3.3. Proximity voting in referendums

The spatial models of voting discussed above were originally developed in the context of a two-party system where voters have to choose between two distinct candidates and where they are assumed to vote for the candidate who has issue positions closest to their own ideal point (Downs 1957; Alvarez 1997). Although this theory is rarely explicitly applied to direct democracy, it can render some important insights into voting in referendums. Just as in a two-party system election, referendums on European integration allow citizens to make a binary choice between two alternatives. We can thus use the spatial proximity model to illustrate the choice that voters face in referendums, assuming that voters will choose the option that is closest to their own ideal point on a single-issue dimension, related to European integration.[10] In other words, this simple model assumes that issue preferences (here attitudes towards European integration) are the only factor that determines the perceived utility of a ballot proposal.

In a referendum on European integration voters are asked to choose between two alternatives; the proposal described on the ballot, $x$, and the policy entailed by a no-vote, the reversion point $r$ (which will be discussed in more detail below). Put simply, all the rational voter needs to do is to figure out whether the policy described on the ballot is better or worse than the alternative. We assume that voters have single-peaked

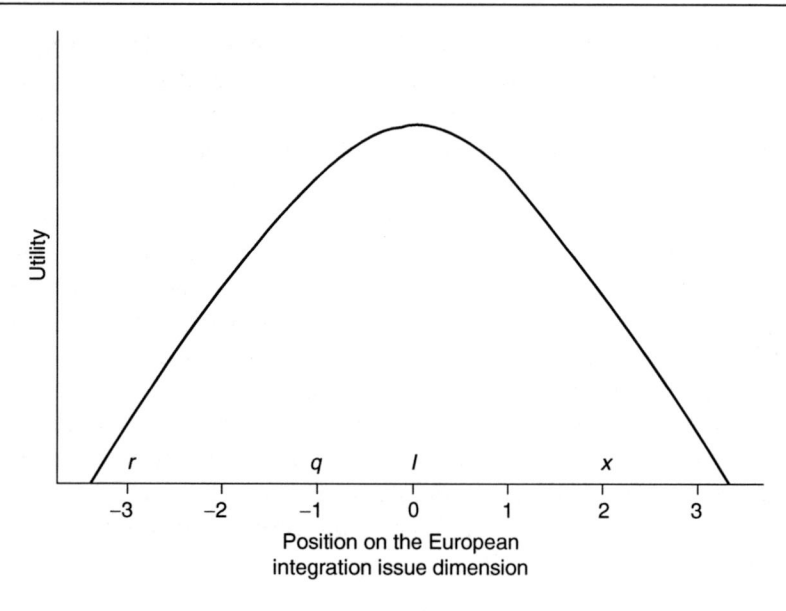

**Figure 2.3.** Spatial representation of voter choice in EU referendums

symmetric preferences over a policy outcome and have a most preferred or ideal point (*I*) on a single policy dimension of more or less European integration. Following the logic of the proximity theory what matters is which of the alternative policy outcomes, *x* or *r*, is closer to *I*. This can be illustrated in a simple spatial representation (Figure 2.3).

In this example, the ballot issue, *x*, may be the ratification of a treaty or the adoption of a specific policy (such as the common currency), and the continuum represents a range of policy options from less European integration (e.g. exit from the EU) to more European integration (e.g. the creation of the United States of Europe). The voter's utilities are a quadratic function of the expected distance between both the ballot proposal and reversion point and the voter's ideal point. In other words, voters are expected to optimize their utility by choosing the option closest to their own preferences, and in this case, a rational and informed voter with the ideal point at 0 would vote for the proposal as this is closer to her ideal point than the reversion point *r* (albeit further away than status quo *q*). The perceived utility of the ballot proposal (*x*) can also be expressed as follows:

$$U_{ix} = -(P_{ix} - I_i)^2 \qquad (2.2)$$

where each voter's evaluation of the ballot proposition's $x$ utility depends in part upon the squared distance between the ballot position as perceived by the voter, $P_{ix}$, and the voter $i$'s own preferred position $I_i$ on a single issue dimension. However, voters are also likely to include non-issue- or non-policy-specific considerations in their evaluation of a candidate or a ballot proposal (see Bartels 1986; Alvarez 1997). Hence, to account for the impact of such considerations, the equation can be restated as:

$$U_{ix} = c_{ix} - (P_{ix} - I_i)^2 \qquad (2.3)$$

where $c_{ix}$ is a term representing all the considerations involved in the voter's overall evaluation of $x$ other than those pertaining to the specific issue dimension included in the model, such as 'second-order' factors relating to national politics.

The proximity model in Equation 2.3 represents the utility of the ballot proposal to the voter. But in order to choose in a referendum, the voter must decide between two alternatives: the ballot proposal and the policy entailed if the proposal is defeated. Figure 2.3 includes two alternatives to the ballot proposal: the status quo $q$ and the reversion point $r$. It is often assumed that voters simply choose between the ballot and the status quo. Yet, it is important to consider the reversion point, because the policy entailed by a no-vote in referendums does not necessarily equal the status quo. Voters cannot be certain that a vote against the proposal will simply lead to a continuation of the pre-existing status quo, since a no-vote in a treaty ratification or single issue referendum may have consequences for the Union in its entirety and may have specific consequences for the country that fails to ratify, such as exit from the Union. Equally, voters cannot be guaranteed if they choose in a membership referendum to remain outside the Union that relations with the EU and market expectations will remain the same as before. A possible scenario is that the country that rejects membership will be punished economically by less favourable trade relations and uncertainty in the market. Hence, in the context of EU referendums, it is less useful to think in terms of the continuation of a pre-existing status quo and more meaningful to refer to the voter's choice as a binary choice between the ballot proposal and the reversion point, that is, 'the outcome to occur if the proposal offered by the agenda setter is defeated' (Banks 1990: 446).

In the formal literature, several studies have emphasized the importance of the reversion point to outcomes in referendums (see Romer and Rosenthal 1979; Banks 1990, 1993). Romer and Rosenthal (1979) have developed a monopoly agenda setter model of referendums in which voters have only the choice between an institutionally defined reversion point and the proposal offered by the proposal setter. They found that the outcome depends crucially on the reversion point. The agenda setter model is highly relevant in the context of EU referendums where voters are equally presented with a binary choice between an exogenously determined proposal and a reversion point. Banks (1990, 1993) has extended this model by incorporating asymmetric information into the model. He has argued that the setters (e.g. the government) have an informational advantage because they know the reversion points, whereas voters lack information and will try to infer from a given proposal exactly what the true reversion level is and then respond accordingly. Hence, voters are dependent on the information provided by the agenda setter and the interaction between the agenda setter and the voters can thus be modelled as a 'signalling game with one of the principal issues being the willingness and ability of the setter to signal the location of the status quo through her choice of proposals, when faced with an uncertain response by voters' (Banks 1993: 432). While two of the assumptions of Banks' model may not hold in EU referendums—namely, that the agenda setter has perfect information about the location of the reversion point and can freely choose the proposal—there are important insights that can be drawn from this incorporation of two-sided uncertainty in the monopoly agenda setter model. The first important point to note is that voters have limited information about the location of the reversion point. This will be discussed in further detail below. The second important insight is that the degree to which they are certain about the location of the reversion points depends on the information and cues provided by political elites.

In summary, the proximity component of the model stipulates that a voter will vote in favour of the proposal if the utility of the ballot proposal is greater than the expected utility of the reversion point[11] (given that $c_{ix}$ is kept constant): $U_{ix} \geq U_{ir}$. On this basis, we can specify the first *proximity hypothesis*:

**Hypothesis 2.1:** Voters are more likely to vote in favour of the ballot proposal if it is perceived as closer to their ideal point than the reversion point, all other things being equal.

Notice that the above proximity calculation emphasizes the *expected* and *perceived* utility rather than the actual utility. This is because voters may be uncertain about the exact location of the ballot position and the reversion point. The implication of this uncertainty for our model will be discussed next.

## 2.3.4. Uncertainty and voting in referendums

The above section presented a simple proximity model of voting in referendums assuming that voters know the location of the two alternatives as well as their own ideal point. Yet, voters may be unsure about the exact position of the ballot proposal and of the reversion point. The issue of imperfect information—or voter uncertainty—has been addressed in the literature on issue voting. Several scholars have incorporated considerations about information and uncertainty into the familiar spatial model of voting by representing candidate positions not by points on a policy dimension, but as probability distributions over a policy dimension (see Shepsle 1972; Enelow and Hinich 1981; Bartels 1986; Alvarez 1997). This modification of the spatial model allows for the possibility that voters may be uncertain about the candidates' or parties' actual positions when they have limited or ambiguous information. This way of thinking about knowledge and uncertainty is also useful in the context of referendums. Hence, following the path of Enelow and Hinich (1981), Bartels (1986) and Alvarez (1997), we can extend the simple proximity model of voting to include uncertainty about positions and apply this to the context of EU referendums. In order to reflect the variation that is due to differences in knowledge about the ballot position, we can define $P_{ix}$ of Equation 2.3 as a random variable composed of a central point, and a distribution of points around the mean, a variance. The smaller the distribution is around the mean, the more certain the voter is about the position of the ballot proposal. This is illustrated in Figure 2.4.

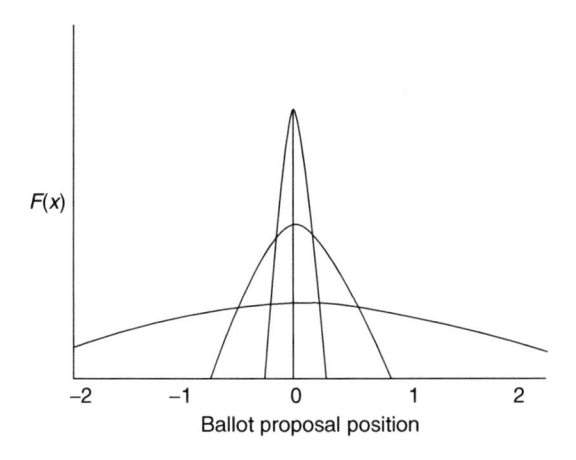

**Figure 2.4.** Uncertainty about the ballot proposal

In Figure 2.4 the potential locations of the ballot proposal on the continuum of the dimension are given on the x-axis, whereas the y-axis gives the possible distributions of the ballot proposal position. The three curves depict the level of voter knowledge about the location of the position. In this figure, the mean of the ballot positions is the same (zero), yet the variances are very different showing the differences in the voter's certainty. Under conditions of low uncertainty, the variance in the voter's perception is quite small and clusters around the central tendency (zero), whereas under circumstances with limited information the variance can be so large that the voter finds it difficult to discern where in the issue space the ballot proposal is located.

Taking into account voter uncertainty means that $P_{ix}$ is expressed as the sum of the estimated position of the ballot $p_x$, and the variance in the voter's perception of this position $\sigma_{ix}^2$. As we think of $P_{ix}$ as a probability distribution rather than single points, we need to recast the model as expected utilities. Hence, the expected utility of voting for proposal $x$ in a referendum is:

$$E[U_{ix}] = E[c_{ix} - (P_{ix} - I_i)^2] \qquad (2.4)$$

After a few minor steps,[12] this equation can be recast as:

$$E[U_{ix}] = c_{ix} - (p_x - I_i)^2 - \sigma_{ix}^2 \qquad (2.5)$$

where $\sigma_{ix}^2$ is the voter's variance in perceptions of the position of the ballot proposal, that is, voter uncertainty. It is clear from Equation 2.5 that the expected utility of voting for proposal $x$ depends not only on the (squared) distance between the expected positions of the candidate and the voter's own ideal point, but also on the degree of voter uncertainty, $\sigma_{ix}^2$. The implication of this model is that voters' utility of voting for the proposal is reduced when they know little about the position. This is because of the assumption of global risk aversion in the quadratic utility function of the model, implying that the voter's utility is a quadratic function of the expected distance that the proposal falls from the voter and a linear function of the variance of the (perceived) location of the proposal. Put simply, voters are expected to be risk averse since uncertainty about the ballot proposal adversely influences their evaluation of that proposal. In the context of referendums, it does not seem unreasonable to assume that individuals will be risk averse. Empirical evidence from psychological studies has suggested that rather than being risk-neutral utility optimizers, people tend to have a particular aversion to losses that makes them risk averse in their evaluations of questions such as candidate choices, and

Alvarez (1997: 33) has found strong empirical support for this in the context of American elections (see also Kahneman and Tversky 1979, 1984; Enelow and Hinich 1984; Bowler and Donovan 1998).[13] On the basis of this extended proximity model, we would expect that voters in referendums are less likely to vote in favour of proposals when they had little knowledge of its location. However, while this may be the case, we need to remember that voters decide on whether or not to vote in favour of proposal $x$ by comparing the expected utility of voting in favour of the proposal with the expected utility of the reversion point $r$. Hence, a voter will vote in favour of the proposal if the expected utility of the ballot proposal is greater than the expected utility of the reversion point: $E[U_{ix}] \geq E[U_{ir}]$.

In sum, vote choice depends on two factors: the relative proximity of the proposal and the reversion point to the voter's ideal point, and the relative knowledge (or uncertainty) that the voter has about the position of the ballot proposal and the reversion point. Greater proximity leads to greater utility, whereas greater uncertainty reduces expected utility. In addition to the proximity hypothesis, we can therefore specify the *uncertainty hypothesis*:

**Hypothesis 2.2:** The more uncertain voters are about the position of a ballot proposal relative to their uncertainty about the position of the reversion point, the less likely they are to vote in favour of the ballot proposal, all other things being equal.

Or, put differently, if voters are more uncertain about the reversion point (what will happen if they reject the proposal) than they are about the ballot proposal (what will happen if they accept the proposal), then they are more likely to vote in favour of the proposal, *ceteris paribus*. This is because greater uncertainty reduces the attractiveness (or utility) of either alternative.

Since uncertainty about the ballot proposal diminishes its utility to voters, we also expect it to affect turnout rates in referendums. More information about the ballot proposal will reduce uncertainty, and thereby increase the utility and the benefits (and reduce the cost) associated with participating in the referendum. This leads us to the *turnout hypothesis*:

**Hypothesis 2.3:** The more certain voters are about the position of a ballot proposal, the less likely they are to abstain, all other things being equal.

Hence, one of the effects of information is that it influences the overall utility of proposal and reversion points for voters by affecting uncertainty. But, as we have seen, both proximity and certainty matter in the voting decision. Another effect of information is that it may influence the relative weight of the issue proximity considerations. This will be discussed next.

### 2.3.5. *Issue salience and proximity voting*

The importance of issue preferences depends partly on the ability of voters to use these issue preferences in their evaluation of the issue at stake. According to the model presented above, we assume that a rational voter will consider the relative distances between her own ideal point and both the ballot proposal and the reversion point, when deciding in a referendum. However, if the voter has very limited knowledge about the ballot position, it is difficult for the voter to employ these considerations in her decision-making. In other words, the relative weight of the proximity component ($-(P_x - I_i)^2$) of the voting model is also variable. Consequently, the voter may rely more on non-issue specific considerations (captured as $c_{ix}$ in the model), which are more readily available, such as partisan loyalties and satisfaction with government performance.

We can distinguish between two different effects that mediate the relative importance of the proximity component: the *salience of the issue* and the extent to which the individual voter is capable of processing political information, what we may refer to as *political awareness*. It is reasonable to assume that the more salient the issue, the more likely voters are to employ issue preferences in their decision. Moreover, voters may vary in their attentiveness to politics and their capability of processing political information, which will affect their ability to employ 'proximity' considerations in decision-making. While the salience and political awareness hypotheses are conceptually distinct, they have a similar effect in the context of our model of voting behaviour, namely to influence the relative weight of issue considerations (proximity calculus) vis-à-vis other considerations ($c_{ix}$) in the overall vote decision. Hence, both factors can be presented as a relative weight on the proximity and non-issue specific components of the voter's expected utility.

The *salience* of an issue is likely to be highly significant for determining the extent to which information will be supplied and processed, and this in turn will influence the knowledge that voters have about the relative proximity between their own position and the proposae. The higher the salience, the more capable voters are at employing issue preferences

## A Theory of Referendum Behaviour

in their utility calculus. As Alvarez (1997: 38) has pointed out, 'if the candidate gives great emphasis to an issue, the voter may know the candidate's position with relatively greater certainty, and accordingly the issue would factor more heavily in her decision making'. Salience has long been viewed as central to an understanding of electoral behaviour (see, for example, Berelson et al. 1954; Campbell et al. 1960; Franklin and Wlezien 1997). A salient issue is defined as an issue that people care about and have meaningful opinions on. Research on the attitude-behaviour relation indicates that attitudes will be consistent with behaviour to the extent that those attitudes are readily retrievable or accessible in behavioural situations (Krosnick 1988*a*, 1988*b*; Lavine et al. 1996: 297). As people are more easily able to retrieve attitudes that are highly important to them than those that are less important, attitude accessibility is partly responsible for the electoral impact of salience. The theoretical literature on the attitude-behaviour relation suggests that highly salient attitudes influence voting behaviour preferences, as they facilitate perceptions of between-party and candidate differences and are more accessible in memory. In the context of referendums, it is equally reasonable to assume that the salience of the issue on the ballot influences the degree to which issue preferences matter. The referendum context, of course, differs from the election in an important way since voters are not evaluating parties or candidates on the basis of issues, but actually evaluating the issue itself. This, however, does not imply that there can be no variation in the intensity or salience associated with the issue. The salience of the issue of European integration varies considerably across countries and over time. This variation in the salience attached to the issue is likely to affect the intensity and certainty of voters' preferences on the issue. Hence, when analysing the vote choice of individuals in referendums, we need to consider that the evaluation of the best alternative (the one that maximizes utility) is mediated by issue salience.

This can be formulated algebraically by weighting the issue distance and non-issue-specific component of the voter's expected utility calculus, denoted in Equation 2.1 by $w_{ix}$. When $w_{ix} = 0$ the issue position is irrelevant to the vote decision and the voter will instead rely on non-issue-specific considerations. Conversely, when the weight is close to 1, the proximity of the voter's issue preferences to the ballot proposal will be a strong determinant of vote choice (or at least of the expected utility of the ballot), whereas other considerations, captured by $c_{ix}$, will play a marginal role. If the salience of the issue is high and the voter has great certainty about her own preferences and the location of the proposal, then the weight will be close to 1, whereas if the salience is very low, then the weight will be closer to zero, and voters will tend to rely more on considerations that are not directly related to the location of the proposal on the issue dimensions, such as satisfaction with the parties in government. On the basis of the model, we can formulate the following *salience hypothesis*:

**Hypothesis 2.4:** The more salient the issue, the more likely voters are to employ issue preferences in their voting calculus, all other things held constant.

While the salience of European integration is likely to influence the extent to which voters have stable issue preferences that they can employ in referendums, voters will not just rely on their general EU attitudes, but also require informational cues that are specific to the task at hand. The cues are likely to be provided in the context of the referendum campaign. Hence, the *intensity of the campaign*, defined broadly as 'the level of information disbursement' in a given referendum (Westlye 1991: 17), is going to determine how much information is available to the voter and this, in turn, may influence the criteria people employ when deciding on a ballot proposition. More information is likely to reduce uncertainty and thus increase utility, according to our spatial model. However, since vote choice is dependent on the *relative* proximity and utility of the ballot proposal and the reversal point (according to the *uncertainty hypothesis*), low intensity campaigns may lead to lower turnout, but they are not necessarily going to increase the probability of a rejection of the vote. While low intensity campaigns may reduce the utility of the ballot proposal there is also likely to be uncertainty associated with the reversion point. In both cases, the overall utility is likely to be decided mostly by non-issue-specific considerations $c_{ix}$, given the low salience context, and this could favour either side of the argument. High intensity campaigns are going to provide more information about the location of both the ballot proposal and the reversion point on the issue dimension, and hence we would expect that people are more capable of employing their issue preferences in the decision-making. Campaign intensity should thus produce effects similar to high issue salience. Whereas issue salience enhances voters' knowledge of their own issue preferences, intensive campaigns are likely to also provide additional knowledge about the position of the particular proposal and the alternative (the reversion point). Hence, we can formulate the following *campaign intensity hypothesis*:

**Hypothesis 2.5:** The more intense the referendum campaign, the more likely voters are to employ issue preferences in their voting calculus, all other things held constant.

This hypothesis concerning the impact of the campaign context is examined empirically in Chapter 4. Both the campaign intensity hypothesis and the issue salience hypothesis concern how the political environment (or context) can affect patterns of voting behaviour at the individual level. But variation may also exist at the individual level, e.g. voters may vary in how interested they are in different issues or how much attention they pay to the information provided during the campaign. However, empirical studies show that knowledge of political issues tends to be more voter specific than issue-specific. In other words, people who know a lot about political issues will tend to be well-informed about all the issues that are salient in the public sphere (political sophisticates or experts), whereas people who pay little attention to politics tend to know very little about political affairs across the board. This variation in attentiveness to political awareness at the individual level is also likely to affect the extent to which voters employ proximity considerations when deciding in referendums. This will be discussed in more detail in the following section.

### 2.3.6. Political awareness and proximity voting

While a great deal of attention has been paid to the implications of voter ignorance in the literature, the effects of *variation* in voter ignorance have been given less attention. In the words of Sniderman et al. (1990: 117): 'that the average citizen tends not to know a lot about politics, lamentable though it is, has obscured the rather more crucial fact that some of them know markedly more than others'. The literature on cue-taking has provided an optimistic picture of how 'ignorant' voters can use cues to make 'reasoned' decisions. Yet, even if we find this to be the case in the context of referendums as well, this does not necessarily imply that there are no systematic differences between well-informed and less well-informed citizens in their processing of these cues and the basis of their vote choices. The model of voting behaviour in referendums presented in Equation 2.1 allows us to consider the possibility that different people make up their minds in different ways, and thus examine the impact of heterogeneity in demand for political information. This model predicts that as knowledge about the relative proximity of your own issue position and the location of the ballot proposal increases, the issue proximity calculus becomes more relevant in the decision-making process. In other words, the more aware people are of politics in general, the more likely they are to employ such consideration in their utility calculus. This leads to the *political awareness* hypothesis:

**Hypothesis 2.6a:** The more knowledgeable a voter is about the issue, the greater her ability to employ issue preferences in her voting calculus and the less likely she is to rely on non-issue-specific considerations, all other things held constant.

Since the hypothesized effect of political awareness is the same as issue salience, the political awareness hypothesis is also represented by the weight $w_{ix}$ included in the general spatial voting model specified in Equation 2.1. In the context of European integration referendums, this would imply that, as attitudes towards European integration become more certain and knowledge about the integration process increases, these attitudes should become a more important determinant of voting behaviour. This model is also compatible with Zaller's model of opinion formation (Zaller 1992). According to the resistance axiom of Zaller's model, people tend to resist arguments that are inconsistent with their issue preferences, but they do so only to the extent that they possess the contextual information necessary to perceive the relationship between the message and the predisposition (1992: 58). We would thus expect that people with higher levels of political awareness would be less likely to vote according to party cues that are incompatible with their own issue preferences. We can thus formulate another hypothesis, the *endorsement hypothesis*:

**Hypothesis 2.6b:** The higher the individual's level of political awareness the more likely she is to resist party endorsements that are incompatible with her issue preferences, all other things being equal.

This model has implications beyond predicting that the effect of issue attitudes is conditional on knowledge of issue positions. If the voter is very uncertain about her own issue position and the location of the ballot proposal, she will need to rely upon issues that are not directly related to the issue dimension. Such considerations are encompassed in the $c_{ix}$ term in the one-dimensional spatial model developed above. But what does this mean in practice? In the literature on issue voting, such 'non-issue-specific' considerations include factors like the personal characteristics of the candidate (Kinder 1986; Rahn et al. 1990) and partisanship (Downs 1957; Campbell et al. 1960). In other words, they include informational shortcuts and heuristics. Cue-taking is not a process that necessarily stands in opposition to issue voting. Rather, it can be one of the mechanisms by which issues come to have meaning in the minds of voters.

As discussed above, elite cues may sometimes give relevant information about the policy positions that enables people to vote as they would have done if they had perfect information about the relative proximity of their own position to that of candidates or parties. But at other times, this may not be the case and reliance on cues, such as partisanship and personalities, can potentially create a different outcome than a more 'informed' reliance on knowledge of issue positions. In the context of referendums, the situation is both similar and somewhat reversed, since voters are asked to evaluate the issue itself rather than evaluate candidates/parties on the basis of issue positions. In this context, voters do not use issue positions as cues about which candidate to choose, but rather use candidate (elite) endorsements as cues about whether to vote for or against the issue proposal. With perfect knowledge about the relationship between their own preferences and the location of the proposal and reversion point, we would assume voters to base their choices mainly on this proximity calculus. However, in situations with uncertain preferences and little knowledge about the location of the proposal and status quo, voters will have to rely on other cues, such as endorsements by parties and interest groups and views on the performance of the *setter* (normally the government). Such cues may facilitate issue voting in referendums by signalling to voters where they are located in relation to the two alternatives on the ballot, that is, by informing the voter which choice is better for them. But relying on elite cues does not necessarily lead to choices that are in accordance with issue preferences. First, voters may rely on cues that are largely unrelated to the ballot question, such as the government's domestic performance. Second, while heuristics can help voters overcome information shortfalls, the effective use of endorsements also requires information (Kuklinski and Quirk 2000). Finally, under certain circumstances, elite cues may in fact mislead citizens. Not only may citizens lack the necessary information about the endorser to use the cues effectively, they may also be misinformed. As Lau and Redlawsk (2001) have observed, endorsements can work against voters when the question at hand is not structured in the typical manner, and this may be the case in most EU referendums. In elections, partisanship has strong and consistent historical connections to policy outcomes, but in referendums the lack of a strong and reliable party-performance connection will make cues less dependable.

As specified in Hypothesis 2.6a, we would expect that the lower the knowledge about their own issue position and the ballot location, the more voters will rely on these non-issue-specific factors. These non-issue considerations may provide informational cues that are closely correlated with detailed information on issue positions. A voter who has little or no knowledge about the ballot proposal may vote in the same way as she would have done with perfect information simply by following the recommendation of her preferred political party. In other cases, however, the use of these non-issue-specific cues may lead to decisions that vary greatly from those voters would have taken had they relied on knowledge of relative issue proximity. As an example, imagine French voter who is generally left-leaning, but sceptical about further European integration. She has little opportunity or inclination to acquire detailed information about a ballot proposal that implies further European integration (e.g. a treaty ratification), so she chooses to follow the recommendation of the Socialist Party that she votes for in national elections. However, although the Socialist Party is located close to the voter on the left-right dimension of domestic politics, its position on Europe is far more pro-integration than the voter's position, and hence the party recommends a yes vote. In this situation, the voter would have voted differently had she acquired more knowledge about the actual ballot proposal and the party's position on the issue of European integration, rather than purely relying on partisan cues.

The model presented here makes an important contribution to the debate in the EU referendum literature discussed in section 2.1 of this chapter. If we recall the competing explanations of voting behaviour, the attitude school emphasizes the role of attitudes and issue preferences, whereas the 'second-order-election' school stresses the importance of elite cues, such as partisanship and government satisfaction. This model provides a framework for understanding under what circumstances either of these explanations provides the most explanatory power. First, this model suggests that the relative uncertainty about the ballot proposal vis-à-vis the reversion point will affect the voter's utility calculations. Moreover, it specifies the conditions under which attitudes towards European integration (issue preferences) and second-order election factors (non-issue-specific considerations) are going to be important. Both issue salience and political awareness act as mediating factors that regulate the relative importance of issue proximity considerations. When issue salience and voter knowledge is low, we can expect non-issue-specific (or 'second-order') factors to play a greater role. These factors, captured by $c_{ix}$ in the model, need not necessarily reduce the expected utility of the ballot proposal (although the utility of the ballot is reduced by uncertainty about its location). In other words, relying on non-issue-specific considerations could potentially make the voter *more* likely to vote in favour of the proposal (for example, if there is a strong 'mainstream effect' of consensual political endorsements) or make her *less* likely to vote in favour (for example, if she is expressing her dissatisfaction with the government). The crucial point is that when issue salience and political awareness are low, issue proximity (and thus attitudes towards European integration) matters less to the voter and consequently, other factors that are not directly related to the ballot proposal become more important in the decision-making process. Hence, this model suggests that, while issue preferences may play a crucial role in determining outcomes in EU referendums, this role depends not only on the general information about the ballot proposal, but also on how the reversion point is perceived by voters, the salience of the issue, and the political awareness of the individual.

In conclusion, this chapter has presented a generic model of voting behaviour in referendums which stipulates that voters' decision-making criteria and their susceptibility to elite endorsements depend not only on the supply of information, but also on the variations in individual demand for information. By introducing political awareness as an intervening variable in the model, we can arrive at a more sophisticated and accurate understanding of the patterns of opinion formation and voting behaviour in referendums than by using a uniform model. In addition to providing a framework for understanding voting behaviour in referendums, this model offers insights into the possible strategies employed by political elites in referendums, which will be discussed in the following section.

## 2.4. Information supply and elite strategies

At the core of the model is the notion of supply and processing of political information. Examining information supply allows us to go beyond the exclusive focus on voters and look at how elites decide to promote an issue and, in turn, how this affects the opinion formation of citizens (see Hobolt 2006). An analysis of the supply of information should thus also focus on strategies employed by elites, the nature of informational cues provided by the elites as well as their effect on voting behaviour. Following the reasoning of the model, the information supplied by political elites can influence referendum outcomes in three interrelated ways: first, information supply influences the perceived position of the ballot proposal and the reversion point. Second, the quantity and diagnostic value of the information disseminated influences the uncertainty concerning those positions that, in turn, affects their relative utility. Third, elite positions and campaigning affect the salience of the ballot issue, which influences the relative importance of issue preferences to vote choices. In other words, elite cues can influence both voters' perception of the ballot proposal and the (un)certainty of their position as well as the importance of these issue proximity considerations in the overall utility calculation. As an example, a successful yes-campaign would not only need to persuade a majority of voters that the ballot proposal is close to their bliss point, but should also provide sufficient persuasive information to make these voters feel that they can confidently rely on this evaluation when they place their final vote. We would expect political elites to act strategically in a manner that optimizes the chances of a majority in favour of their preferred outcome. We would therefore expect elites in favour of (against) the proposal to frame the reversion point in a manner so it appears as far away from (or close to) the median voter's ideal point. Following this we can formulate the *issue framing hypothesis:*

**Hypothesis 2.7:** Political elites in favour of the ballot proposal will present the proposal as located close to the median voter position and the reversion point as extreme, while political elites opposing the ballot proposal will present the reversion point as close to median voter position and the ballot proposal as an extreme position.

The uncertainty concerning these positions may also be influenced by strategic elite behaviour. According to our model of opinion formation, greater uncertainty will reduce the overall utility of the proposal to the voter and less knowledge will impair the ability of voters to use issue preferences in their evaluation. In the context of referendums, voters are often asked to vote on very unfamiliar topics where they have limited knowledge of issue positions, both of their own and that of the ballot proposal/reversion point. Since most voters will only vote in one or very few EU referendums, this may impair their ability to judge the credibility (trustworthiness) of information providers. Moreover, familiar informational cues such as partisanship may give less reliable information about issue proximity on the European integration dimension, as discussed above. Elites may also deliberately try to suppress and obscure information on European integration if they believe that the ballot proposal is located far from the location of the median voter. We would expect political elites to use these considerations strategically, not only to frame the position about the alternative choices, but also the uncertainty about these positions. Hence, political elites would be expected to provide more factual information and assurances about their preferred outcome (e.g. the ballot proposal) and conversely provide less factual information but more explicit threats about the alternative outcome to induce uncertainty.

**Hypothesis 2.8:** Political elites will supply factual information about the proposal they favour to promote certainty, whereas they will provide more generic arguments and threats about the alternative outcome to bring about voter uncertainty.

This model thus highlights the way in which political elites can use information supply strategically and how this is likely to affect voting behaviour in referendums. These propositions concerning elite behaviour will be examined empirically in the case studies of chapters 7 and 8.

## 2.5. Conclusion

> The acquisition of information must be analyzed, since it is itself the result of decisions.[14]
> —Kenneth Arrow

This chapter has presented a general theoretical model of voting behaviour in European integration referendums, emphasizing the impact of information and knowledge on voting patterns. According to this model, voters will tend to vote in favour of a ballot proposal if they perceive it to be closer to their own ideal point than the alternative (the 'reversion point'). However, the relative utility of the proposal will be reduced if voters have greater uncertainty about the location of the ballot proposal than the location of the reversion point. Moreover, the model posits that the relative importance of issue preferences in the overall evaluation of the ballot proposal depends on the salience of the issue and the political awareness of the individual. Put differently, the more a voter knows about European integration and elite positions, the better able she is to judge whether a specific proposition on the ballot is compatible with her own preferences, and the more likely she is to vote on the basis of these preferences and to resist elite recommendations that are contrary to her views. To understand both the causes and the implications of variations in political knowledge, we can think of political knowledge as a function of the sum of individual information processing capability and the supply of contextual information. In other words, the individual voter's knowledge of ballot proposal positions and issue preferences are determined in part by her own interest in and understanding of politics and in part by the information available in the environment.

In the following chapters, these different components of information processing are elaborated and examined in more detail and the theoretical propositions are tested empirically. Chapter 3 examines empirically the model of voting behaviour presented in this chapter. By analysing voting behaviour in nineteen European referendums, we test the individual-level determinants of referendum behaviour and the impact of political awareness. The influence of contextual factors is examined in Chapter 4, where the effect of variations in information supply—campaign intensity—is examined empirically. Using survey experiments, Chapter 5 examines how elite endorsements and framing effects influence voters. Chapter 6 examines how different types of information enhance and impede voter competence. Finally, chapters 7 and 8 explore the theoretical propositions of the model in a qualitative case study analysis of selected referendum campaigns.

## Notes

1. Berelson, Lazarsfeld, and McPhee (1954: 308).
2. Quotations about the Constitutional Treaty cited in Furedi (2005).
3. Quote from *The Times*, 13 June, 2008.
4. Diffuse support is measured using the 'membership' question ('Do you think that your country's membership in the Common Market is a good thing?'). Concrete support is measured using the 'benefit' indicator ('Would you say that your country has on balance benefited or not from being a member of the EC').
5. Single-country case studies of referendums include Nielsen 1993; Siune, Svensson, and Tonsgaard 1992, 1994a, 1994b; Svensson 1994, 2002, 2003; Saglie 2000; Aylott 2002; Buch and Hansen 2002; Gilland 2002; de Vreese 2004; Widfeldt 2004; Sauger, Brouard, and Grossman 2007; Schuck and de Vreese 2008. Edited volumes on European referendums also exist, such as Butler and Ranney 1978, 1994; de Vreese 2007; Gallagher and Uleri 1996; LeDuc 2003; Kaufmann and Waters 2004; Szczerbiak and Taggart 2004.
6. Downs 1957: 259.
7. These results are taken from the special Eurobarometer number 214, conducted by TNS Opinion Social and EOS Gallup Europe between 27 October and 29 November 2004.
8. This approach also provides a theory of the decision to vote, leading to the 'paradox of voting' where it is irrational for most voters to turn out to vote

given that the cost will tend to outweigh the benefits of voting (Aldrich 1993).
9. Downs mentioned that the total amount of political information that an individual receives depends on three factors: First, the time he can afford to spend assimilating it; second, the kind of contextual knowledge he has; third, the homogeneity of the selection principles behind the information with his own selection principles. Downs noted that education is the primary source of contextual knowledge (Downs 1957).
10. For the sake of simplicity we address the case in which votes have quadratic utility functions over the single issue of European integration (see also Enelow and Hinich 1981).
11. The equation for the expected utility of the reversion point $E(U_{ir})$ is assumed to be the same as for the expected utility of the ballot $E(U_{ix})$, shown in Equation 2.1.
12. We can expand Equation 2.4, so that, $E[U_{ix}] = E[c_{ix} - (P_{ix}^2 - 2P_{ix}I_i + I_i^2)]$. To simplify this model, we move the expectations operator through to the right-hand side of the equation, meaning that,

$$E[c_{ix}] = c_{ix}; E[P_{ix}^2] = p_x^2 + \sigma_{ix}^2; E[2P_{ix}I_i] = 2p_xI_i; E[I_i^2] = I_i^2.$$

This yields, $E[U_{ix}] = c_{ix} - p_x^2 - \sigma_{ix}^2 + 2p_xI_i - I_i^2$, which can then be simplified as specified in Equation 2.5.
13. In an article, Berinsky and Lewis (2007) criticize this assumption of global risk aversion inherent in the studies on voting uncertainty. They argue that this assumption is problematic and that 'there is good reason to doubt that policy risk plays much of a role in voting' (2007: 140). In our model, we find the assumption of risk aversion justifiable and thus use the conventional quadratic utility function.
14. Arrow (1974: 48).

Part II

# A Comparative Study of Referendum Behaviour

# 3

# A Comparative Analysis of Voting Behaviour

*Never overestimate the information of the electorate,*
*but never underestimate its intelligence.*[1]
—Mark Shields

How do voters decide in referendums on European integration? Do decisions in referendums reflect underlying policy attitudes or are the choices that citizens make in referendums capricious, reflecting unrelated concerns or elite manipulation? These are some of the critical questions debated by scholars and commentators concerned with European integration referendums. To address these questions, Chapter 2 developed a general theoretical framework for understanding voting behaviour in referendums. According to this spatial model, voters are expected to base their vote choice on issue proximity considerations; that is, they vote on the basis of their attitudes towards European integration. Yet, this model also suggests that the relative importance of issue proximity considerations is mediated by two factors, namely the salience of the issue and the extent to which the individual voter is capable of processing political information, that is, political awareness.

This chapter tests the individual-level components of this model in a statistical analysis of voting behaviour in referendums on European integration. The objective of this chapter is thus twofold. First, to examine which factors influence voting behaviour in EU referendums, and thereby also evaluate the explanatory power of existing theories of voting behaviour using comparative data. Second, to test the hypotheses derived from the model of voting behaviour presented in Chapter 2 and, in particular, examine the mediating impact of voters' political awareness on patterns of voting behaviour. The hypotheses concerning the mediating effect of issue salience and campaign intensity will be explored in Chapter 4.

Most existing studies of referendum behaviour control for individual-level variation in demographic characteristics, such as age, gender, and income, but they tend to overlook the potential impact of differences in political awareness. In this chapter, the impact of variations in political knowledge on vote choices is evaluated explicitly, by examining not only the direct impact of knowledge, but also the conditioning effect of knowledge on attitudes. This chapter proceeds as follows: first, it summarizes the main propositions concerning the determinants of voting behaviour in EU referendums presented in Chapter 2; and second, it describes the survey data used to evaluate these propositions and discusses the operationalization and measurement of the variables in the model. Finally, statistical models are estimated to test the theoretical propositions, using individual referendum surveys as well as pooled data from a range of EU referendums. These analyses show that both EU attitudes and elite cues have a significant impact on vote choice across these referendums, but that voters with higher levels of political awareness are more likely to rely on their attitudes than those who are less informed about political affairs. This chapter thus shows that voters are not primarily concerned with domestic politics when they vote in European referendums.

## 3.1. Explaining voting behaviour in EU referendums

The scholarly debate on voting behaviour in referendums on European integration has predominantly focused on how much citizens' attitudes towards European integration matter when voters decide in EU referendums (see Chapter 2). The 'attitude' approach to EU referendums has argued that European attitudes drive voting behaviour, while the 'second-order election' approach has contended that citizens use their vote as a means of signalling their satisfaction or dissatisfaction with the government or to follow the recommendations of national parties. The spatial model presented in Chapter 2 provides both an extension and a synthesis of these explanations by introducing the salience of European issues and political awareness as conditioning factors that influence the extent to which attitudes and second-order election factors are relevant.

This model builds on the spatial proximity model of voting, where voters base their choices on considerations regarding the location of the policy alternatives relative to the voter's own preferences. Hence, Hypothesis

2.1 emphasizes that issue attitudes matter: voters are more likely to vote in favour of a ballot proposal if it is located closer to their 'ideal point' of European integration than the alternative. But attitudes towards European integration are not the only factors that influence voting behaviour. Since voters often have limited information about the issue at stake, they rely on recommendations and heuristics provided by political elites and other groups. With perfect knowledge about the relationship between their own preferences and the location of the proposal and reversion point, we would assume voters to base their choices mainly on these proximity considerations. However, in situations with uncertain preferences and little knowledge about the location of the proposal and reversion point, voters will have to rely on other cues, such as endorsements by parties and views on the performance of the government, as suggested by the 'second-order' approach. Hence, we expect that supporters of parties who recommend a yes-vote are more likely to vote yes than supporters of parties recommending a no-vote. Moreover, we expect that voters who are dissatisfied with the performance of the government of the day are more likely to vote no. However, the relative weight of issue proximity considerations versus other second-order factors is influenced by individuals' level of political awareness. People who are more politically aware are more capable of employing such issue considerations in their vote choice (Hypothesis 2.6a) and of resisting party recommendations which are incompatible with their own attitudes (Hypothesis 2.6b). These hypotheses are tested empirically in the following sections of this chapter.

## 3.2. Data and methods

This section evaluates the theoretical model of referendum behaviour using survey data from eighteen referendums (more details on each of these surveys can be found in Appendix 1). These referendums were conducted in France, Denmark, Ireland,[2] Luxembourg, the Netherlands, Norway, and Spain over the past three decades (see Table 1.1). As described in Chapter 1, these cases are representative of the general 'population' of EU referendums. Four of them are membership referendums, thirteen are ratification referendums, and one is a single-issue referendum (on joining the Euro). In seven of these cases, the ballot proposal was rejected. The surveys used in the empirical analyses are national and Eurobarometer surveys[3] conducted after the referendum had taken place, with a nationally representative sample of over 1,000 respondents. Many questions on issues such as vote choice, party preferences, EU attitudes, and demographics are repeated in all of these surveys. Nevertheless, these surveys are not identical, which presents us with considerable challenges in a comparative research design. Two steps have been taken to alleviate the potential problems associated with using survey data from different sources and to ensure that the results are robust. First, the hypotheses are tested analyzing each survey separately. By estimating the models separately, we can make full use of all relevant question items in the surveys to test the theoretical propositions and we can evaluate whether the suggested patterns of correlations can be detected across countries and over time. Second, the model has also been estimated using a pooled dataset of all referendum surveys to evaluate whether the hypothesized relationships hold up in a cross-sectional time-series dataset and to present the general trends in voting behaviour in a more concise manner. By conducting both separate and pooled analyses, it can be shown that the findings are robust across countries and over time. In the following section, the measurement of each of the variables in the model is discussed in detail.

### 3.2.1. *Variables in the Model*[4]

The dependent variable in the models presented here is a yes/no vote in the referendum. Only respondents who actually voted are included in the analysis, since the aim is to explain and predict actual voting behaviour.[5] Due to the binary nature of the dependent variable all of the models have been estimated using logistic regression.

The key independent variable in the model is the individual voter's *attitudes towards the EU*; that is a proxy measurement of the voter's 'ideal point' on the dimension of European integration. In the literature, this is often measured by using a single survey item, such as the Eurobarometer question: 'Generally speaking, do you think your country's membership of the EU is a good thing, a bad thing, neither a good or a bad thing?' (see, e.g. Gabel 1998*a*; Steenbergen and Scott 2004; Garry, Marsh, and Sinnott 2005). However, there are several potential problems with using a single item for measuring attitudes. Single-item measurements tend to have considerable random measurement error and suffer from question wording biases. Moreover, an individual item cannot discriminate among fine degrees of attitude differences and is unlikely to adequately represent the theoretical construct that we are interested in. McIver and Carmines (1981) add that, 'the fundamental problem with single item measures is not merely that they tend to be less valid, less accurate, and less reliable than their multi-item equivalents. It is rather that the social scientist rarely has sufficient information to estimate their measurement properties. Thus, their degree of validity, accuracy, and reliability is often unknowable' (1981: 15).

Hence, rather than using a single survey item, the attitude variable is constructed as a scale using multiple survey items on attitudes towards different aspects of European integration.[6] The method used is the summated rating (or 'Likert') method where answers to different survey items relating to attitudes towards European integration are added to produce a single scale score. Responses to questions such as the respondents' attitudes towards European integration in general, the United States of Europe, and further integration in specific policy areas were recoded on the same scale and added together with each item given equal weight. On average twelve items were used to create the scales in each survey. The scales were then transformed to a 21-point scale[7] of attitudes towards European integration. The summated rating method assumes that people respond to separate specific EU attitude and policy questions on the basis of their underlying attitudes towards European integration and that the items display monotone homogeneity; that is, they reflect a single underlying trait (DeVellis 1991; Jacoby 2000: 764). Theoretically, it is reasonable to assume that individuals have underlying attitudes towards the EU that guide their responses to specific questions on European integration. This assumption of unidimensionality has been tested using a variety of techniques, including multi-dimensional scaling, Mokken scaling, and principal component analysis. The clear picture that emerges from these analyses is that there is a strong underlying attitude dimension that structures respondents' answers to all EU attitude questions in each of these surveys, and this dimension can reasonably be interpreted as attitudes towards more or less transfer of national sovereignty to the European level.[8] Reliability analyses and inter-item analyses also confirm that the attitude scales are highly reliable and internally consistent (Cronbach's alpha is more than 0.80 for all of the attitude scales).[9] Hence, for the purposes of the comparative analyses presented in this chapter it makes both theoretical and empirical sense to measure a single underlying dimension of attitudes towards European integration, especially since this makes it possible to compare across different contexts. Yet, in more in-depth studies of individual referendums it is often possible to tease out different aspects of attitudes towards Europe that were salient to the vote choice, and this may provide a more detailed understanding of the type of concerns that mattered most to the voter. We adopt such an approach in Chapter 8, which explores the multidimensionality in the attitudes towards European integration, and their effect on vote choice in the referendums on the European Constitution.

The *political awareness* variable measures people's knowledge about European integration.[10] This scale has also been constructed using the summated scaling technique. Zaller has evaluated the advantages of different measures of political awareness on the basis of attitude stability, consistency and the attitude-behaviour relation and has found that neutral factual information is on both theoretical and empirical grounds the preferred measure (Zaller 1992: appendix; see also Converse 2000). Hence in this study, the European political awareness scale has been measured using items of neutral political knowledge. However, since many of the surveys only have few items with 'factual knowledge' questions, these items have been supplemented by measures of subjective political knowledge and political interest.[11] The awareness scales (1–13) all have alpha reliabilities in the 0.80–0.90 range, and thus have high internal consistency.

To test for the impact of the *cues of political parties*, the endorsements given by each party have been coded. The recommendation of each party has been coded as a 4-point scale,[12] where 4 is given to a party that is united in favour of the ballot proposal, 1 is given to a party united against the proposal, and 3 and 2 are given to parties that are for or against, but with considerable dissenting voices within the party. By creating a scale, rather than a dichotomous yes/no party variable, this allows us to differentiate between parties that are united in the support of (or opposition to) the referendum and parties that are split on the issue, and consequently send mixed cues to their supporters.[13] Party cues are linked to each respondent by recoding the question of party support, according to the answer to the question: 'If there were an election tomorrow, which party would you vote for?'.[14] We are more interested in the party identification or party sympathy than actual vote choice, but since such questions are not asked in all of the surveys, we have opted for the 'vote intention' question. Moreover, in the surveys where the 'party support' question is asked in several different ways (party sympathy, party identification, last vote, intended vote), the correlation between the different measures is very high (above 0.85), thus indicating that vote intention provides a good measure of general party support.

To test the significance of other *'second-order' factors*, we include an indicator of satisfaction with the government's performance, measured as a single-item Likert scale (4-point scale). Unfortunately, the question does not appear in all surveys, therefore we also include alternative indicators of 'second-order' factors, such as trust in (national) politicians as well as satisfaction with the national economic situation, when these question items are available. The model also includes control variables relating to the respondents' socio-economic status, namely class,[15] as well as demographic controls of age, gender, and region (urban versus rural dummy). The next section presents the results of estimating this model.

## 3.3. A comparative analysis of voting behaviour

In the following steps this section tests the theoretically derived hypotheses presented above. First, we estimate the effect of attitudes, partisanship, second-order factors, and the mediating effect of political awareness on voting in each of the seventeen referendums.[16] Second, the model is tested using the cross-sectional pooled dataset and predicted probabilities of voting yes given a change in each of the independent variables presented.[17]

### 3.3.1. Country-by-country analyses

The tables below show the results of applying the vote choice model to Danish referendums (Table 3.1), Irish and Norwegian referendums (Table 3.2) and finally, the referendums on the Constitutional Treaty and the Lisbon Treaty (Table 3.3). The results in these tables indicate that attitudes towards European integration and party recommendations are important factors determining voting behaviour across all EU referendums. The more that people are in favour of steps towards further integration, the more likely they are to vote in favour of the ballot proposal. Equally, individuals who support parties recommending a yes-vote are more likely to vote in favour of the proposal. These variables are significant in each of the eighteen referendums evaluated. Satisfaction with the government also has a positive impact on the yes-vote, in all but three cases, as the 'second-order election' approach would predict. Apart from EU attitudes and second-order factors, no set of variables are consistently robust in their effect on vote choice across referendums.

Table 3.1. Modelling vote choice in Danish EU referendums

| Independent variables | Denmark: Accession 1972 Logit (S.E.) | Denmark: SEA 1986 Logit (S.E.) | Denmark: Maastricht 1992 Logit (S.E.) | Denmark: Maastricht 1993 Logit (S.E.) | Denmark: Amsterdam 1998 Logit (S.E.) | Denmark: Euro 2000 Logit (S.E.) |
|---|---|---|---|---|---|---|
| EU attitudes | 0.26** (0.09) | 0.25** (0.05) | 0.36** (0.03) | 0.55** (0.16) | 0.22** (0.01) | 0.62** (0.04) |
| Party recommendation | 1.36** (0.13) | 1.19** (0.14) | 0.73** (0.11) | 0.72** (0.15) | 0.57** (0.04) | 0.49** (0.11) |
| Government satisfaction | −0.04 (0.09) | — | 0.92** (0.17) | 0.41* (0.16) | — | 0.07 (0.15) |
| Political awareness | −0.10 (0.10) | −0.15 (0.10) | −0.33* (0.14) | −0.40* (0.29) | −0.17** (0.03) | −0.31 (0.23) |
| Social class | 0.02 (0.09) | 0.12 (0.17) | −0.12 (0.10) | 0.05 (0.10) | 0.12** (0.03) | 0.18 (0.10) |
| City | −0.24 (0.19) | −0.28 (0.29) | 0.17 (0.38) | −0.06 (0.37) | −0.02 (0.08) | −0.21 (0.25) |
| Gender (female) | −0.22 (0.17) | 0.24 (0.29) | 0.02 (0.22) | 0.24 (0.22) | −0.12 (0.07) | −0.17 (0.25) |
| Age | −0.02 (0.06) | 0.04 (0.11) | −0.03 (0.08) | 0.12 (0.08) | 0.28** (0.03) | 0.13 (0.09) |
| Awareness* attitudes | 0.02* (0.01) | 0.04** (0.00) | 0.05** (0.01) | 0.03** (0.01) | 0.06** (0.00) | 0.02** (0.01) |
| Constant | −5.50** (1.01) | −6.01** (0.95) | −6.17** (1.12) | −8.33** (1.78) | −6.93** (0.23) | −8.66** (1.55) |
| % correctly predicted | 84 | 88 | 83 | 86 | 83 | 89 |
| McFadden R Squared | 0.40 | 0.63 | 0.44 | 0.49 | 0.34 | 0.62 |
| N | 1131 | 756 | 692 | 906 | 6366 | 965 |

* Significant at 0.05
** Significant at 0.01

Note: This model predicts the yes-vote using logistic regression.

*Government satisfaction* is measured using the 'trust in politicians question' in the following surveys: Denmark 1993, 2000; Ireland 1972, 1994. *Political awareness* is measured using an education measure in Luxembourg 2005, Denmark 1986, 1998, and Ireland 1992.

**Table 3.2.** Modelling vote choice in Irish and Norwegian EU referendums

| Independent variables | Ireland: Accession 1972 Logit (S.E.) | Ireland: Maastricht 1992 Logit (S.E.) | Ireland: Amsterdam 1998 Logit (S.E.) | Ireland: Nice 2001 Logit (S.E.) | Ireland: Nice 2002 Logit (S.E.) | Norway: Accession 1972 Logit (S.E.) | Norway: Accession 1994 Logit (S.E.) |
|---|---|---|---|---|---|---|---|
| EU attitudes | 0.06 (0.06) | — | — | 0.38** (0.10) | 0.46** (0.04) | 1.17** (0.12) | 0.83** (0.05) |
| Party recommendation | 0.44** (0.11) | 0.76* (0.39) | 0.43** (0.06) | 0.35** (0.08) | 0.38** (0.08) | 0.77** (0.09) | 0.87** (0.07) |
| Government satisfaction | 0.31** (0.10) | 0.22** (0.07) | — | — | 0.65** (0.12) | — | −0.23 (0.14) |
| Political awareness | −0.22* (0.10) | 0.22** (0.06) | — | −0.10 (0.22) | −0.07 (0.06) | 0.06 (0.22) | −0.17* (0.08) |
| Class | 0.42* (0.20) | 0.12 (0.08) | −0.08 (0.08) | −0.05 (0.07) | −0.04 (0.12) | 0.09 (0.07) | 0.17* (0.08) |
| City | −0.34 (0.24) | 0.15 (0.20) | 0.05 (0.05) | 0.24 (0.17) | −0.03 (0.20) | 0.52* (0.23) | 0.45* (0.17) |
| Gender (female) | −0.17 (0.24) | −0.13 (0.19) | −0.41** (0.09) | −0.18 (0.16) | 0.17 (0.19) | 0.37 (0.20) | −0.18 (0.14) |
| Age | 0.08 (0.09) | 0.03 (0.03) | 0.28** (0.06) | 0.08 (0.97) | 0.00 (0.07) | 0.26** (0.10) | 0.02 (0.06) |
| Awareness* attitudes | 0.03* (0.01) | — | — | 0.02 (0.01) | 0.02** (0.00) | 0.00 (0.01) | 0.04** (0.00) |
| Constant | −2.98 (1.04) | −1.48* (0.63) | −0.88 (0.33) | −7.25** (1.51) | −3.23 (0.64) | −17.45** (0.96) | −8.60 (1.02) |
| % correctly predicted | 83 | 84 | 66 | 80 | 80 | 93 | 89 |
| McFadden R Squared | 0.22 | 0.05 | 0.04 | 0.30 | 0.31 | 0.73 | 0.60 |
| N | 634 | 935 | 2167 | 1008 | 762 | 1979 | 2832 |

\* Significant at 0.05
\*\* Significant at 0.01

*Note*: This model predicts the yes-vote using logistic regression.

**Table 3.3.** Modelling vote choice in the ECT referendums

| Independent variables | Spain:<br>ECT 2005<br>Logit(S.E.) | France:<br>ECT 2005<br>Logit(S.E.) | Netherlands:<br>ECT 2005<br>Logit(S.E.) | Luxembourg:<br>ECT 2005<br>Logit(S.E.) | Ireland:<br>Lisbon 2008<br>Logit(S.E.) |
|---|---|---|---|---|---|
| EU attitudes | 0.47** (0.11) | 0.72** (0.04) | 0.62** (0.12) | 0.30** (0.05) | 0.33** (0.03) |
| Party recommendation | 0.67** (0.11) | 0.71** (0.13) | 0.48** (0.08) | 0.52* (0.23) | 0.54** (0.16) |
| Government satisfaction | — | 0.67** (0.14) | 0.25* (0.10) | — | 0.68** (0.12) |
| Political awareness | −0.13* (0.06) | −0.27* (0.13) | −0.01 (0.20) | 0.10 (0.08) | — |
| Class | 0.09 (0.13) | 0.04 (0.08) | 0.05 (0.10) | 0.23* (0.11) | 0.14 (0.08) |
| City | −0.13 (0.26) | −0.26 (0.25) | −0.65* (0.29) | −0.07 (0.19) | 0.12 (0.22) |
| Gender (female) | 0.48 (0.26) | 0.53** (0.19) | 0.36 (0.19) | 0.10 (0.18) | 0.35 (0.22) |
| Age | 0.19* (0.08) | 0.23** (0.06) | 0.35** (0.07) | 0.34** (0.07) | 0.19** (0.07) |
| Awareness* attitudes | 0.04* (0.02) | 0.02* (0.01) | 0.01 (0.01) | 0.00 (0.00) | — |
| Constant | −8.31** (1.62) | −11.61** (1.18) | −14.03** (1.62) | −8.10** (1.22) | −8.75** (0.83) |
| % correctly predicted | 93 | 89 | 86 | 80 | 82 |
| McFadden R Squared | 0.51 | 0.61 | 0.48 | 0.33 | 0.41 |
| N | 1101 | 1391 | 1130 | 938 | 710 |

* Significant at 0.05
** Significant at 0.01

Note: This model predicts the yes-vote using logistic regression.

Social class has a positive and significant effect on yes-vote in only four out of the eighteen referendums. In each case, people who belong to the middle class are more likely to favour the ballot than working class voters. The urban-rural divide only appears to matter in Norway, where people living in the more remote and rural areas are less likely to endorse accession to the EU, compared with voters in the capital. Equally, there is no consistent gender gap across referendums, when controlling for attitudes. On the other hand, age has a significant impact in eight out of eighteen cases: older people are more likely to vote in favour of treaty changes. In contrast to the predictions of Inglehart's (1971, 1978) post-materialist theory, younger voters are consistently more reluctant to endorse an EU treaty change compared with older voters in the most recent referendums on the European Constitutional Treaty (ECT) and the Lisbon Treaty.

Perhaps surprisingly to some observers, political awareness does not seem to have a considerable direct impact on how people vote in most of these referendums, when we estimate the direct effect (without an interaction). A higher level of knowledge of the EU has a positive and significant impact on voting yes in the Irish Maastricht and Nice referendums, as well as the Norwegian membership referendum of 1972, whereas it is negatively associated with the yes-vote in the second Danish Maastricht referendum. This supports the theoretical proposition that the impact of political awareness is primarily indirect (conditioning other factors), rather than direct. In other words, knowing more about European politics does not necessarily make voters more inclined to vote for treaty changes and accession. Instead it makes them more likely to follow their underlying attitudes toward European integration when voting in referendums. In contrast, knowing less means that voters are more likely to vote with reference to second-order issues.

In order to test our hypothesis regarding the impact of political awareness, we include an interaction term between awareness and attitudes in the models. This is a common way of assessing the conditioning effect of a moderator variable on the effect of other independent variables (Jaccard 2001). On the basis of our Hypothesis 2.6a, we would expect the multiplicative interaction term between different levels of political awareness and attitudes to be positive and significant, indicating that attitudes matter more for voters who are more politically aware. Indeed, Tables 3.1–3.3 show that the interaction term is positive in all cases and significant in all but four cases. These results thus support Hypothesis 2.6a: the more knowledgeable voters are about the issue, the greater their ability to employ issue preferences in their voting calculus.

While these results present a clear pattern of determinants of vote choices across referendums, the logistic regression estimates make it difficult to interpret the magnitude of the effects. Hence, in the next section we estimate a pooled regression analysis and present the effects on vote choice graphically.

### 3.3.2. Analysing pooled referendum data

In addition to estimating the model using each of the referendum surveys separately, we have also pooled the referendum surveys in one dataset in order to be able to test general patterns of voting behaviour and present these concisely. Variables have only been pooled when the survey question items were considered comparable.[18] When constructing scales, several scaling techniques have been used to ensure that the different questions tap into the same underlying dimension and that inter-item reliability within and between referendum surveys is high. Finally, the pooled model has been estimated using a multilevel logistic regression model with individuals nested within each referendum to alleviate the statistical issues associated with the nested structure of the data and to model the variation of the determinants of vote choices across different contexts (Snijders and Bosker 1999). Both the intercept of the model and the slope of EU attitudes are random effects in this model, that is, they are allowed to vary across referendum contexts, whereas the remaining explanatory variables are fixed.

The results of estimating this model are shown in Table 3.4. We can see that the variances around both the intercept and the EU attitude slope are highly significant. This indicates significant similarities between individuals within each referendum context and also suggests that the effect of attitudes varies across referendums. In other words, the context of a particular campaign partly determines how voters make up their minds in referendums. This conditioning impact of the referendum context on the effect of attitude on vote choice is explored in more detail in Chapter 4. In this analysis, we focus on the individual-level characteristics that influence vote choice. As indicated by the individual survey analyses, attitudes towards European integration have a great impact on vote choice in EU referendums. But domestic politics also matter: voters take cues from their preferred parties and they are more likely to support the proposal when they are satisfied with government performance. In this pooled analysis, class and age also matter: older middle class people are more likely to vote yes compared to younger working class voters. Gender and geography, on the other hand, do not play a significant role across all referendums. Finally, the results show that political awareness conditions the impact of attitudes on votes: more politically aware citizens rely more on their attitudes towards European integration when deciding.

Table 3.4 indicates which factors are significantly associated with the outcome (yes-vote); yet interpreting the substantive effects of each of the variables is not straightforward in logit models, where the coefficients express log odds. This is further complicated when the model includes interaction terms. One way of interpreting the impact of explanatory variables in this logit model is to use statistical simulation to demonstrate how the referendum vote would change as the value of each independent variable changed *ceteris paribus*. The predicted impact of a change in the variables included in the model is calculated using simulation techniques to estimate the change in the probability of voting yes given half a standard deviation change in each of the explanatory variables.[19] The predicted probabilities are reported in Table 3.5, including the 95 per cent confidence interval for each prediction.

**Table 3.4.** Multilevel model of vote choice in EU referendums

| Independent variables | Logit | S.E. |
|---|---|---|
| EU attitudes | 0.40** | 0.06 |
| Party recommendation | 0.65** | 0.02 |
| Government satisfaction | 0.63** | 0.04 |
| Political awareness | −0.15** | 0.02 |
| Class | 0.09** | 0.02 |
| City | 0.00 | 0.05 |
| Gender (female) | 0.01 | 0.04 |
| Age | 0.19** | 0.02 |
| Awareness* attitudes | 0.04** | 0.00 |
| Constant | −8.96** | 0.86 |
| Variance (constant) | 10.46** | 3.92 |
| Variance (attitudes) | 0.06** | 0.02 |
| Deviance | 16353.41 | — |
| N (groups, individuals) | 15, 22723 | — |

*Significant at 0.05
**Significant at 0.01
Note: This is a multilevel logit model. A random slope of EU attitudes is included, whereas all other independent variables are fixed across referendums.
The government satisfaction variable combines government satisfaction items with items on trust in politicians.

The results reported in Table 3.5 clearly indicate that a positive change in attitudes has the greatest impact on the probability of voting yes. A 1-point change on a 10-point attitude scale (equal to half a standard deviation) makes voters 17 percentage points more likely to vote yes. In comparison, a half point change in partisanship on a 4-point scale and a half point increase in government satisfaction increase the probability of voting yes by 8 and 4 per cent respectively. As we can see, changes in age,

**Table 3.5.** Probability of voting yes given a change in the explanatory variables

| Independent variables | % impact of 1/2 std.dev. change in variable | Change in yes-vote (C.I.) |
|---|---|---|
| EU attitudes | 17 | 57–74% (73–75%) |
| Partisanship | 8 | 57–65% (64–66%) |
| Government satisfaction | 4 | 57–61% (61–62%) |
| Age | 2 | 57–59% (58–60%) |
| Political awareness | 1 | 57–58% (58–59%) |
| Class | 1 | 57–58% (58–59%) |
| City | 0 | No change |
| Gender | 0 | No change |

Source: Pooled dataset.

**Europe in Question**

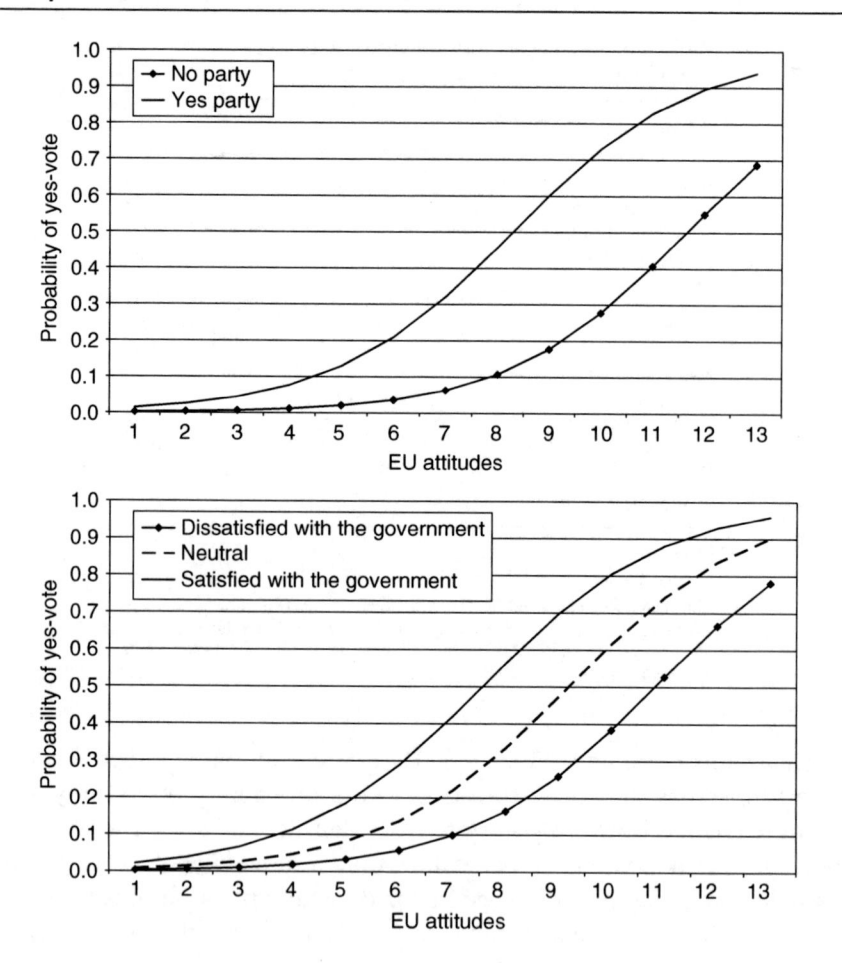

Figure 3.1. Effects of (*a*) partisanship and (*b*) government satisfaction

political awareness, and class have an even smaller impact, while gender and urban location make no difference. These predicted probabilities thus confirm our findings in Hypothesis 2.1, since 'issue proximity voting' is the most important consideration in EU referendums.

An even more intuitive way of illustrating the effect of the main explanatory variables, namely attitudes, partisanship, and government satisfaction is to show the predicted probabilities graphically. Figure 3.1 shows the probability of voting yes for segments of the electorate with different (a) partisanship and (b) government satisfaction, conditioned by their level of support for European integration.

# A Comparative Analysis of Voting Behaviour

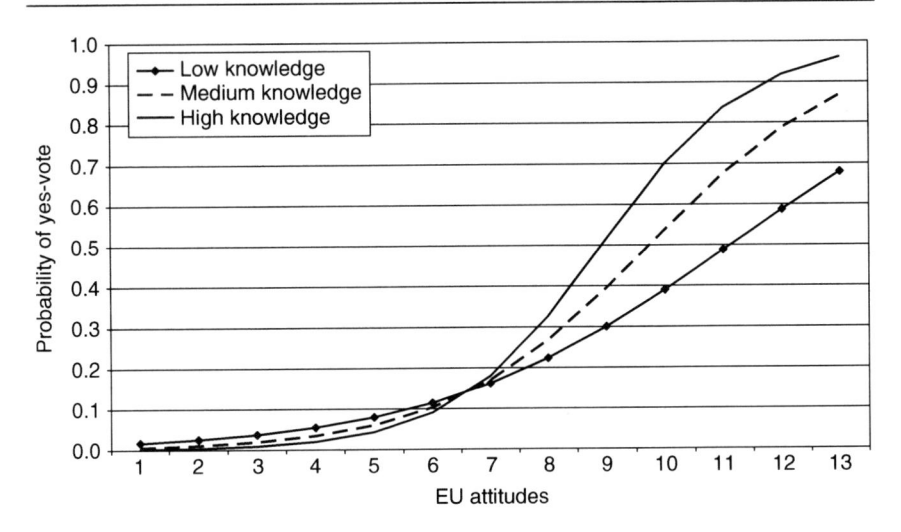

**Figure 3.2.** Mediating effect of political awareness

Figure 3.1 provides a more intuitive illustration of the effects of the explanatory variables than the coefficients shown in the preceding tables and also enables us to detect possible interaction effects. As the figures show, attitudes towards the EU are the major determinant of vote choice, but for voters who are neither strongly Eurosceptic nor strongly Europhile, but somewhere in the middle of the spectrum (with a score of between 8 and 12 on the 21-point scale), partisan cues and government satisfaction can matter a great deal. Imagine an average voter with an EU attitude score of about 10. The voter has an above 70 per cent likelihood of voting yes if she is supportive of a party that recommends a yes-vote, but only 28 per cent likelihood if she supports an anti-ballot party. The same voter would be almost certain to vote yes if she was satisfied with the government's performance, whereas her probability of voting yes would fall below 0.5 if she was dissatisfied with the government's performance.

The distance between the slopes shows the direct impact of the independent variable represented by these slopes (partisanship, and government satisfaction) on the probability of voting yes ($y$-axis), whereas the differences in the steepness of these slopes in a graph indicates that an interaction effect exists between this variable and EU attitudes ($x$-axis). In Figure 3.2 we can see that political awareness not only has a direct effect—higher political awareness increases the probability of voting yes—but also a conditioning effect: the slope is steeper for people with high levels of awareness.

## 3.4. Conclusion

As Zaller has noted, 'most of the time, when scholars attempt to explain public opinion and voting behaviour, they build models that implicitly assume all citizens to be adequately and about equally informed about politics, and hence to differ mainly in their preferences and interests. In other words, they build models that ignore the effects of political awareness' (1992: 18). This chapter has provided a corrective for this practice in the field of EU referendum studies by explicitly examining the conditioning impact of political awareness on patterns of voting behaviour.

This chapter has tested the hypotheses derived from the voting behaviour model presented in Chapter 2. First, it has tested the proposition that issue proximity considerations are the most important determinants of voting behaviour in EU referendums. In other words, voters' attitudes towards European integration are the key explanatory variable influencing voting behaviour. The analyses of eighteen individual referendums and a pooled referendum dataset corroborated this hypothesis. These analyses also showed that elite cues matter. Party recommendations are important determinants of voting behaviour, as well as other 'second-order' factors, such as satisfaction with the government's performance and trust in politicians. Second, this chapter examined the conditioning effect of an individual's knowledge of politics. By estimating interaction effects, this chapter has assessed how political awareness influences the relative impact of political attitudes on vote choice in EU referendums. The analyses of voting behaviour in the eighteen referendums give fairly conclusive results: political awareness has a positive impact on the relative importance of attitudes on voting behaviour. The higher a voter's political awareness, the more she will rely on her EU attitudes when deciding in referendums. These results thus generally corroborate the theoretical propositions outlined in Chapter 2. What are the implications of these findings? First, they show that—in contrast to the claim put forward by many scholars and commentators—EU referendums are very much about Europe. That is, attitudes towards the European project play an important role in how voters decide. Second, they show that Europe matters more to those voters who have more information. That does not imply that governments can simply give more information to voters and rely on them to vote yes. Rather, it suggests that underlying sentiments towards European politics matters more to better informed voters. The findings also suggest that these interaction effects may vary between referendums depending on the nature and the intensity of the information provided. In other words, context matters. While this chapter has explored the patterns of voting behaviour that are stable across time and between countries, but vary between segments of the electorate, it is also important to examine how the context of each individual referendum campaign influences behaviour. In the next chapter, the impact of campaign intensity on voting behaviour is examined by addressing the question of how the campaign environment affects the individual's vote choice and aggregate outcomes. The following chapter thus returns to the issue of how variations in the supply of information may affect the behaviour of voters in EU referendums.

## Notes

1. Philip Converse quoting Mark Shields, a political columnist, referring to the American electorate (Converse 2000: 331).
2. It has unfortunately proven impossible to find adequate survey data from the 1987 Irish referendum on the Single European Act.
3. It was not possible to obtain a national survey of the Irish membership referendum in 1972, so the Irish sample of the Eurobarometer 6a survey has been used instead. This survey contains a question item on voting behaviour in the Irish 1972 accession referendum.
4. Details on all variables in the model can be found in table 2.1A in Appendix 2.
5. A separate model with turnout as the dependent variable (including all respondents) has also been evaluated. The results of evaluating this model showed that political awareness has a considerable and significant impact on whether or not an individual votes in EU referendums.
6. Examples of attitude questions include: 'Do you think [your country] should unite fully with the European Union or protect its independence from the European Union?'; 'Do you think the movement towards the unification of Europe should be speeded up, slowed down, or continued as it is at present?'; 'Are you for or against the proposal that defence and security policy becomes a part of the policy areas decided jointly in the European Union?'.
7. By creating a summated rating scale, we transform the individual Likert items into an interval variable. A 21-point scale has been created to include as much nuance as the question items allow for.
8. When conducting principal component analysis (a form of factor analysis) on these items, I extracted more than one factor (component) for most samples, which could suggest that more than one attitude dimension is present. However, the eigenvalues of these second and third components are significantly smaller than the first eigenvalue, thus suggesting that they contribute

little to the explanation of variance in the variables and can be ignored. Chapter 8 examines the effect of such 'secondary' attitude dimensions on vote choice.
9. To check the reliability of the summated rating scale, I also saved the factor (component) scores of the main factor and used them as the attitudes scale, and there was no significant difference between these results and the results presented here where the summated rating scale is used.
10. When estimating the direct impact of political awareness on voting behaviour there is a potential problem of endogeneity, since people who are more supportive of the EU may also be more likely to gain information about the issue. To check whether this is actually the case, I created a separate 'political awareness' scale that excluded all knowledge items that referred to European affairs and only included general knowledge questions. An analysis showed that this scale had a 0.9 correlation with a pure 'European awareness' scale, and hence we can conclude that political awareness is not mainly related to support for the specific issue. It was decided to use the political awareness scale including European integration questions, since many of the factual question items in the surveys relate to European issues.
11. Examples of question items included in the political awareness scale are: 'What is the name of your country's European Commissioner?'; 'How many countries are members of the European Union?' (factual knowledge); 'How knowledgeable are you about European politics?' (subjective knowledge); 'Would you say that you are very interested in European politics?' (political interest question). Measures of education have not been included in this scale.
12. The results are not significantly different when using a party dummy (yes/no) instead of a 4-point scale, but the scale was chosen to better represent actual party cues.
13. This party scale has been created on the basis of party documents as well as information gathered in elite interviews with politicians.
14. Or the alternative question item that most resembles this question. In the Irish 2002 survey, I used the question item, 'Which, if any, of the political parties do you usually support?'.
15. Class has been measured as a 5-point scale from lower working class to upper middle class. A measure of education has not been included in the final model, since it is (weakly) correlated with political awareness. However, a previous test shows that this variable is not significant in any referendum other than the Norwegian 1972 membership referendum.
16. It has unfortunately not been possible to test for the effect of all of the independent variables in each of these referendums, since not all of the post-referendum surveys included the necessary question items.
17. Missing values in the dependent variable (vote choice) have been removed by listwise deleting. Missing values in any of the independent variables have been imputed using multiple imputation technique (with AMELIA software).

18. The following surveys were included: Denmark 1972, 1992, 1993, 2000; Ireland 1972, 2001, 2002; Norway 1972, 1994; Spain 2005; France 2005; the Netherlands 2005; and Luxembourg 2005.
19. These simulations were carried out using the CLARIFY 2.1 software developed by Tomz, Wittenberg and King (Tomz et al. 2003).

# 4

# Campaign Effects in Referendums

*The electorate behaves about as rationally and responsibly as we would expect, given the clarity of the alternatives presented to it and the character of the information available to it.*[1]

—V.O. Key

The campaign leading up to the Danish referendum on the Euro on 28 September 2000 began half a year prior to the actual vote. During these six months of campaigning, the issues of the single currency and European integration became the main item on the news agenda. No one could be in doubt that the stakes were high: most lampposts were covered with campaign posters and national politicians used every opportunity to promote their side of the story. In the period from March to August, the campaign accounted for around 10 per cent of the main evening news and, in the final month of the campaign, 25 per cent of all television news covered the referendum (de Vreese 2004: 54). Daily newspapers carried on average one front-page story and three articles relating to the campaign each day during this period. By the time the referendum day came around, almost 88 per cent of Danish voters turned out to express their opinion. In contrast, the official campaign leading up to Irish referendum on the Nice Treaty on 7 June the following year lasted barely a month. With the next Irish general election just around the corner, most mainstream parties chose to save their campaigning funds for this occasion. As a consequence, there were few posters, little door-to-door canvassing, and relatively limited news coverage of the referendum campaign. After this lax and lethargic campaign, a record low of only 35 per cent of Irish voters turned out to give their say on the Treaty.

In both of these referendums, the ballot proposal was rejected by a small margin of voters, but we would expect that the decision-making processes

## Campaign Effects

that led to these outcomes were different, given the very dissimilar political environments. In the former case, the campaign provided an abundance of information about the ballot proposal, the salience of the issue was high, and the political parties clearly expressed their recommendations. In the latter case, the campaign provided little information about the treaty, issue salience was low, and the parties gave ambiguous signals.

Chapter 3 focused on the individual voter and variations in political awareness. Examining micro-level decision-making yielded a number of insights into how information influences vote choice. In particular, it was shown that voters who pay more attention to politics are more likely to vote on the basis of their opinions about Europe, whereas voters who receive less information about politics will tend to rely more on their feelings about domestic politics. However, information effects depend not only on the individual's ability to receive political messages, but also on the degree to which citizens are provided with the necessary information concerning the issue at stake. We would expect that vote choices are influenced by the context in which they are taken. An examination of the campaign environment is thus important to fully understand voters' decision-making. Based on the model presented in Chapter 2, our theoretical expectation is that when more information is available and issue salience is high, lower levels of uncertainty will increase the utility of voting and reduce abstention. Moreover, high-intensity campaigns provide more information about the location of the alternatives and therefore we expect that people become more capable of employing their issue preferences in their vote choice.

This chapter examines these propositions by addressing the following question: How do variations in the intensity of the referendum campaign affect patterns of voting behaviour? Campaign effects are measured at two levels. First, campaign intensity is measured at the aggregate level and the effect on levels of turnout and 'issue voting' is evaluated. Second, the chapter analyses individual-level variation in exposure to campaign information and assesses the impact on knowledge and voting behaviour. These micro-, macro-, and multi-level analyses reveal that context matters: the campaign environment in EU referendums acts both as an informer and a mobilizer and influences patterns of behaviour. Turnout is higher and issue voting is more prevalent in high-intensity campaigns.

The chapter proceeds as follows. First, it reviews the main theories of campaign and information effects. Second, it discusses the specific role of campaigns in EU referendums and presents testable hypotheses. Third, a measurement of campaign intensity, based on multiple indicators, is applied to the nineteen referendum cases, and the impact of variations in campaign intensity on aggregate levels of turnout and issue voting is evaluated. Finally, the effect of individual-level variations in exposure to campaign information is analysed and the mediating effect of campaign intensity on vote choices is examined.

## 4.1. Theories of campaign effects

The effect of election campaigns on voting behaviour has been studied extensively, especially in the American context (see Shaw 1999 for an overview). Studies of campaign effects have historically found little empirical evidence of election campaigns influencing vote behaviour. Instead, a number of studies has made the strong case that campaigns do little more than activate latent candidate or party preferences and can generally be viewed as having 'minimal consequences' (see Lazarsfeld et al. 1944; Rosenstone 1983; Abramowitz 1988; Gelman and King 1993). This literature typically emphasizes fixed social, demographic, and political determinants of voter behaviour, such as class or partisanship, and controlling for the effect of these stationary characteristics leaves little room for campaigns to make a difference. Yet, despite strong evidence for the 'minimal effects' thesis, the issue of campaign influence remains an open question in the literature. Recent studies have argued that the 'minimal effects' hypothesis is an artefact of conceptual and methodological problems in the literature (see Shaw 1999; Iyengar and Simon 2000; Hillygus 2005). In particular, it has been argued that the existing literature has focused too much on the impact of campaigns on preferences and has consequently overlooked other important effects. As Iyengar and Simon have noted:

Perhaps the most fundamental obstacle to understanding the real-world role of political campaigns is a conceptual limitation of what effects are deemed relevant. Traditional research has looked mainly at persuasion... The single-minded quest for persuasion effects has ignored the transmission of information, the setting of campaign agendas, and the alteration of the criteria by which candidates are judged (2000: 151).

Iyengar and Simon (2000) concede that campaigns might have little direct effect on voters' preferences, since they tend to activate voters' prevailing partisan sentiments. Yet, they argue that campaigns have pivotal effects in the areas of 'voter learning' and 'agenda control', which should be explored further. After all, campaigns decide the quantity and the nature of the information disseminated to voters. Other studies support this argument about the importance of campaigns as *informers*. Franklin's (1991) study of US Senate campaigns found that voters exposed to senatorial campaigns were more competent in their understanding of their incumbent senator's position on a liberal–conservative scale. Alvarez (1997) corroborates this result for a broad array of knowledge and attitude questions in analyses of contemporary presidential elections, and equally Bartels (1988) has found significant information gains during the presidential primaries of 1984. Several scholars have demonstrated that voters exposed to high-intensity campaigns, which make larger volumes of information available, are more engaged and cast more informed votes. According to Kahn and Kenney's (1997) study of US Senate elections, citizens experiencing an intense race use more sophisticated criteria when evaluating the contestants than citizens following less intense races. In his extensive study of Senate elections, Westlye (1991) equally demonstrates that 'issue voting, and voting on the basis of candidates' ideologies, takes place more often among voters who have information about both candidates as a result of exposure to a high-intensity campaign and less among those who have information only about the incumbent' (1991: 16). In short, these studies suggest that campaigns serve to inform voters and, in turn, help to structure vote choices. As Schmitt-Beck and Farrell (2002) point out, the effect of campaigns is highly contingent on the nature of the campaign and the individual voter. In line with the US literature, the comparative studies in Farrell and Schmitt-Beck's (2002) edited volume on campaign effects show that high-intensity campaigns have a greater effect than low-intensity campaigns and that the scope of campaign influence depends on the political interest of voters. Drawing on Zaller's work (1992), they conclude that the influence of campaigns is mediated by political awareness and predispositions of individuals.

Recent studies have also focused on the campaign as a *mobilizer*. Kuklinski et al. (2001) have shown how the political environment affects the quality of citizens' political decision-making by not only acting as a source of information, but also by playing a motivational role of encouraging citizens to invest effort and time in making political judgements. Moreover, a growing body of research has argued that campaign efforts influence an individual's likelihood of voting (for an overview see Hillygus 2005). Experimental research has found consistent and substantial campaign effects on voting turnout (Ansolabehere and Iyengar 1996; Gerber and Green 2000; Lassen 2005). Similarly, some survey research has found a positive correlation between total campaign expenditures and competitiveness of the race on the one hand and turnout in elections on the other hand (Cox and Munger 1989; Franklin 2004).

Building on this literature, this chapter examines the role of the campaign as an *informer* and a *mobilizer* in EU referendums. Rather than focusing on the broad effects of campaigns, including agenda-setting and persuasion, this chapter examines how variations in campaign *intensity*, that is, the quantity of information provided, affect patterns of voting behaviour.

## 4.2. Campaign effects in EU referendums

Only recently has the literature on referendums started to discuss campaign effects in a systematic manner. Yet, the campaign context is crucial to the study of opinion formation in referendums since the degree of uncertainty associated with unfamiliarity with the issue and unclear elite cues make voters especially susceptible to campaign influence in referendums (Magleby 1984; Farrell and Schmitt-Beck 2002; de Vreese 2007). Leduc (2002) argues that since voting behaviour in referendums often exhibits greater volatility than is found in elections, campaigns are likely to play a greater role in the opinion formation process. In the Swiss context, several studies have shown that campaigns can make a difference (Bützer and Marquis 2002; Christin, Hug, and Sciarini 2002; Kriesi 2005). Bützer and Marquis (2002) have shown that, in accordance with Zaller's theory (1992), the division of political elites is of prime importance to opinion formation in referendum campaigns, and Christin, Hug, and Sciarini (2002) also find that Swiss voters can use campaign information, such as party endorsements, to vote competently.

With regard to European referendums, the importance of the information environment during a campaign has been acknowledged in several studies (Siune and Svensson 1993; de Vreese and Semetko 2002, 2004; de Vreese 2004; Gerstlé 2006), but no study has presented a systematic comparative study of its effect on voting behaviour. De Vreese and Semetko (2004) show that the information environment, in particular the media, served to crystallize individual opinion on the vote choice in the Danish referendum on the single currency. In their study of the Dutch referendum on the Constitutional Treaty, Schuck and de Vreese (2008) also found that voters who were more exposed to the pro-Treaty news media were more likely to shift to the yes-side during the campaign. It is not surprising that these studies find that campaigns matter in referendums. Indeed, we may expect that they matter more than they do in elections. Referendums present a different choice to elections. No political parties or candidate names appear on the ballot and voters must choose amongst alternatives that are sometimes unfamiliar. If voters know little about the specific ballot proposal, it is mainly the various information sources available to them over the course of a campaign that provide the basis for their opinion on the ballot question. The campaign can therefore play a crucial role in informing voters about the choices and in disseminating relevant party cues. Hence, as discussed in Chapter 2, the vote choice will depend not only on the characteristics of the individual, but also on the political environment in which vote decisions are taken. People with high levels of political awareness may act differently from people with lower levels of awareness, as shown in Chapter 3. Moreover, electorates that are given extensive information on the ballot proposal can be expected to behave differently from electorates deciding in campaign settings where very little information is provided. More information will reduce uncertainty, and thereby increase the utility of the ballot proposal.

However, sometimes campaign information may be misleading and deceptive. For example, political elites may deliberately set out to mislead the public about the consequences of the ballot or the reversion point. Following Lupia and McCubbins (1998), we can distinguish between two types of information effects: enlightenment (information will help voters to make more accurate predictions about the consequences of their actions) and deception (information will reduce the ability of voters to make accurate predictions). Voters are only likely to be deceived by political elites if they find them trustworthy and knowledgeable; so even if political elites set out to deceive, they are not always successful (Lupia and McCubbins 1998). Voters are thus more susceptible to persuasion by parties that they feel loyalty towards (more on this in Chapter 6). Moreover, attempts of deception can be costly for political elites if they are caught misleading the public. Political parties, in particular, may be reluctant to stray too far from the truth in referendum campaigns since this might damage their reputation more permanently. Deception is thus less likely in high-intensity and polarized campaigns. First, voters will receive more information from both sides, and this will make it easier to detect which messages are trustworthy and credible. Second, in a high-intensity two-sided campaign, the threat of verification and penalties for lying are likely to be higher, and this will make it less likely for elites to adopt a strategy of deception (Lupia and McCubbins 1998). To be sure, some deception will occur during referendum campaigns, but more intense campaigns will generally reduce, rather than increase, the likelihood of this.

Building on the spatial model presented in Chapter 2 and the existing research on campaign effects, we would thus expect that the intensity of the campaign influences patterns of voting behaviour in EU referendums. The intensity of the campaign can be defined narrowly as 'the level of information disbursement' in a given election or referendum (Westlye 1991: 17). More specifically, the intensity of a referendum campaign can be conceptualized as the interaction between the cues emitted by competing political elite actors, media coverage, and the perceived closeness of the outcome (see Kahn and Kenney 1997; Farrell and Schmitt-Beck 2002). The interplay of these factors contributes not only to the quantity of the information available in the political environment, but also to the extent that the environment encourages individuals to process this information. The level of partisan polarization on the issue will influence the intensity and nature of competing elite cues. According to theories of issue evolution, it is mainly polarization among elites that raises the public's awareness of a new issue (see Riker 1982; Carmines and Stimson 1986, 1989). Equally, when parties take different stances on the ballot issues in a referendum, this tends to increase the salience of the referendum issue. This, in turn, may influence campaign strategies and spending, which affect the quantity and type of information available in the public sphere. The competitiveness of the contest is also likely to have an effect on the salience of the campaign and influence the strategies of both partisan and non-partisan groups, and, in turn, citizen participation (Franklin 2004). Finally, these factors will shape the way in which the news media decide to cover the referendum. Higher levels of polarization and a more competitive race will increase the 'newsworthiness' of the story and bring more coverage by the news media. The interaction of these forces determines the type of information available to voters and produces the environment in which they make their vote choices. This is illustrated in Figure 4.1.

According to Figure 4.1, high-intensity campaigns are characterized by a combination of some or all of the following factors: partisan—and perhaps also non-partisan—competition on the issue, a high level of uncertainty about the outcome of the referendum, and extensive news coverage of the issue. High levels of intensity serve both to provide more information and to encourage people to invest time in obtaining information by increasing the salience of the issue at stake in the referendum. Campaign intensity is influenced by partisan polarization, which in turn

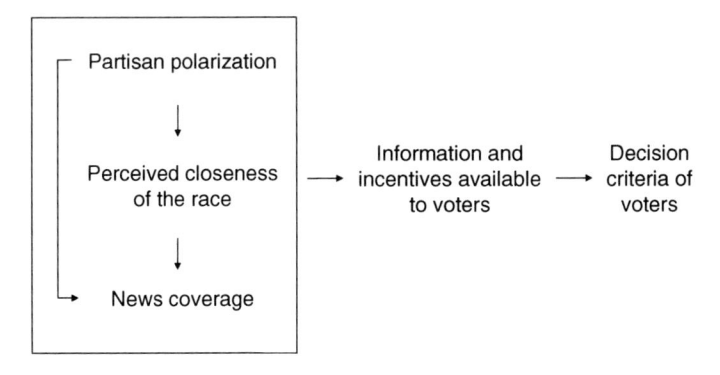

```
┌─────────────────────────────────────────────────────────────┐
│  ┌─ Partisan polarization                                   │
│  │                                                          │
│  │         ↓                  Information and      Decision │
│  │  Perceived closeness  →   incentives available  → criteria of │
│  │     of the race              to voters           voters  │
│  │                                                          │
│  │         ↓                                                │
│  └→ News coverage                                           │
└─────────────────────────────────────────────────────────────┘
```

Figure 4.1. Elements of campaign intensity

will affect the perceived closeness of the race and the coverage afforded to the issue by the news media.

Following the model presented in Chapter 2, our expectation is that more information will increase the expected utility of a particular proposal to the voter (Equation 2.2). If campaigns reduce uncertainty and thus increase expected utility, we would also expect voters to have increased incentives to cast their vote (see Hypothesis 2.3). In the literature, formal models of turnout have predicted that informed citizens are more likely to vote, because information increases the voter's certainty that she is voting for the right candidate, that is, the candidate who yields the highest utility to the voter (see, e.g. Matsusaka 1995). This turnout effect is likely to exist at the aggregate level, where higher intensity campaigns will lead to higher levels of turnout, as well as at the individual level where more exposure to the campaign is likely to increase the individual's probability of voting. We can thus formulate the following hypothesis:

**Hypothesis 4.1:** The higher the intensity of the campaign, the higher the level of turnout in the referendum. At the individual level, citizens exposed to more campaign information are more likely to vote than citizens exposed to less information.

High-intensity campaigns are not only going to affect the likelihood of people voting in the first place, but they will also affect the way in which people make their specific vote choice. When campaign intensity is high, more information is available to individual voters and they are more motivated and more capable of making sophisticated judgements compatible with their underlying attitudes. Put differently, citizens will be more aware of the location of their 'ideal point' on the European integration-continuum and better equipped to relate this to a specific ballot proposition. In contrast, when campaign intensity is low, voters have limited access to easily available information and few incentives to make complicated decisions about the ballot proposal, and they are more likely to vote on the basis of non-issue-specific factors and depend more heavily on cognitive short cuts. High levels of campaign intensity should therefore produce effects similar to high issue salience, and as outlined in Hypothesis 2.5, we thus expect high-intensity campaigns to induce issue voting.

To test these propositions at the aggregate level, the following section develops a measure of campaign intensity, which is applied to the nineteen referendum cases.

## 4.3. Measuring campaign intensity

How do we create a measure of campaign intensity which can be used to compare campaigns across countries and over time? Most studies of campaign intensity employ a single measure to capture the level of intensity. In the American context, a frequently used measure is the summary reports about each election published in the *Congressional Quarterly Weekly Reports* (CQ rating) that classify campaigns dichotomously as intense or not intense (see, e.g. Kahn 1995; Westlye 1991). While the core of this measure, namely the 'competitiveness' of the race, is equally relevant in the context of EU referendums, there is little reason to believe that competitiveness can actually be classified as a binary variable. Another common measure is campaign spending by parties (see Kahn and Kenney 1997; Partin 2001). Campaign spending may be considered a useful proxy of campaign activity, although less so in a cross-national analysis, since spending levels depends significantly on the specific national regulation of campaign funding. Moreover, it is almost impossible to get reliable data on campaign spending in the context of EU referendums, and it has therefore not been possible to use spending as a measure of campaign activity.

Instead, this chapter follows the strategy of using multiple indicators, a method which has been recommended in several recent studies of campaign intensity. Both Kahn and Kenney (1997) and Sulkin (2001) recommend selecting measures that 'go back to the general conception of an intense race—that is, one that is "hard fought" in which both candidates run visible, vigorous campaigns, are successful at raising funds, and attract a good deal of media attention' (Sulkin 2001: 611). On this basis, these studies choose campaign spending, media coverage, and polling data as three indicators of campaign intensity. Adopting a similar approach, this chapter develops a measure of campaign intensity that seeks to capture the multidimensionality of the concept in the context of EU referendums. This measure relies on the following three indicators: partisan polarization, the perceived closeness of the race (uncertainty about the outcome), and media coverage.

*Partisan polarization* on the ballot proposition is the first indicator of the intensity of the campaign, since competing partisan views are likely to lead to increased intensity of the campaign environment. In a situation where there is no partisan opposition to the ballot proposal, the referendum is also likely to be less salient to the news media and voters. Partisan polarization is measured as the percentage of parties who recommend a no-vote in the referendum weighted by these parties' share of the seats in parliament (see also Bützer and Marquis 2002). This measure is then transformed into a 5-point scale depicting the level of polarization.[2] The resulting measure provides an estimation of opposition to the ballot proposal in parliament.[3]

The perceived public stance on the issue—or *the closeness of the race*—is also likely to influence the campaign environment. If the public is perceived to be equally divided on the issue, the intensity of the campaign is likely to be higher than if there is a large majority in favour of the proposal. The perceived closeness of the race is measured as the average difference between intended yes- and no-voters in the opinion polls during the six weeks leading up to the referendum. This average figure is transformed into a 5-point scale[4] to form a summated scale of all three indicators of intensity.

Finally, *media coverage* of the referendum issue is a good indicator of the information available to the citizens. Information is mainly disseminated to the public through the media, and voter awareness of a ballot proposition is thus likely to grow with increasing media coverage (Bützer and Marquis 2002; de Vreese and Semetko 2004; Schuck and de Vreese 2008). Moreover, media coverage can be seen as a general indicator of the saliency of an issue. In this study, news coverage has been analysed by measuring the average number of daily articles mentioning the referendum issue during the three months leading up to the referendum in two mainstream daily national newspapers with a high circulation. While not all voters will read the largest circulating newspapers, the news media will tend to respond in a similar fashion to the standard criteria of 'newsworthiness' (Kahn and

Kenney 1997: 1883). Hence, the referendum coverage in two large daily newspapers is a good indicator of the general level of media coverage of the campaign.

In order to make cross-national comparisons possible, however, it is important that similar newspapers are examined in all countries. Newspapers were therefore selected on the basis of criteria of high circulation, quality (mainstream), and national scope (see also Kriesi et al. 1995: appendix). Applying these criteria, the following mainstream daily newspapers were chosen: *Berlingske Tidende* and *Politiken* in Denmark, *Le Monde* and *Le Figaro* in France, the *Irish Independent* and the *Irish Times* in Ireland, *Luxemburger Wort* in Luxembourg, *Aftenposten* (morning edition) and *Dagbladet* as the Norwegian sources, *De Volkskrant* and *De Telegraaf* in the Netherlands, and finally, *El Mundo* and *El Pais* in Spain. The coding was carried out by trained coders fluent in the respective languages and the reliability of the results is very high with an inter-coder reliability score of above 0.90. The news coverage measure was calculated as an average of daily coverage in the two national newspapers. As with the other indicators, this measure is transformed into a 5-point scale.[5] Employing these indicators, the overall intensity of the referendum campaigns are shown in Figure 4.2.

Figure 4.2 shows considerable variation in the level of campaign intensity on this scale which ranges from 3 to 14. The campaign environment was most intense in the second Norwegian referendum on membership (14), followed by the Danish referendum on the Euro (13), the first Norwegian referendum on membership (12), and the French referendum on the European Constitution (12). The campaigns leading up to the two Danish referendums on the ratification of the Maastricht Treaty were also highly salient. In general, the Irish referendums were the least intense, although we do find some variation. The campaign leading up to the Amsterdam Treaty has the lowest intensity; partly because it was overshadowed by the Good Friday Agreement ballot held on the same day. The salience of the issue of the Amsterdam Treaty was so low that the Irish newspapers did not even report the results of this referendum on the front-page in the days following the referendum. Equally, the campaign in the first Nice Treaty referendum was a lacklustre event, while the campaign leading up to the second referendum on the Nice Treaty was considerably more intense (as will be discussed in greater detail in Chapter 7), as was the campaign prior to the more recent Lisbon Treaty referendum. Interestingly, there was great variation in the four referendums on the European Constitution held in 2005. The votes in Spain and Luxembourg

## Campaign Effects

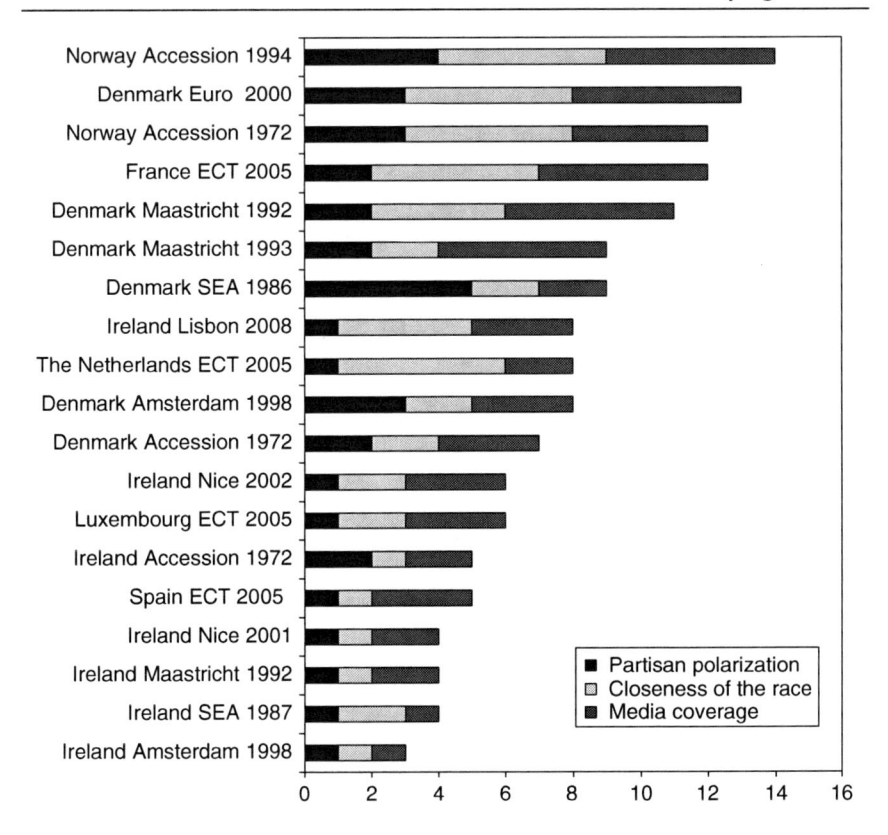

**Figure 4.2.** Campaign intensity in EU referendums
*Source*: National newspapers, opinion polls, official parliamentary documents and elite interviews.

were relatively lacklustre events when contrasted with the impassioned campaign in France (see Chapter 8). In the remainder of this chapter, our measure of campaign intensity will be employed to examine the impact on participation and vote choices.

### 4.4. Evaluating the impact of campaign intensity

In this section, we examine the relationship between campaign intensity and voting behaviour at the aggregate level. In the first instance, we evaluate the theoretical propositions by presenting descriptive plots of aggregate patterns of voting and campaign intensity. While these descriptive statistics cannot be regarded as a formal statistical test of

# Europe in Question

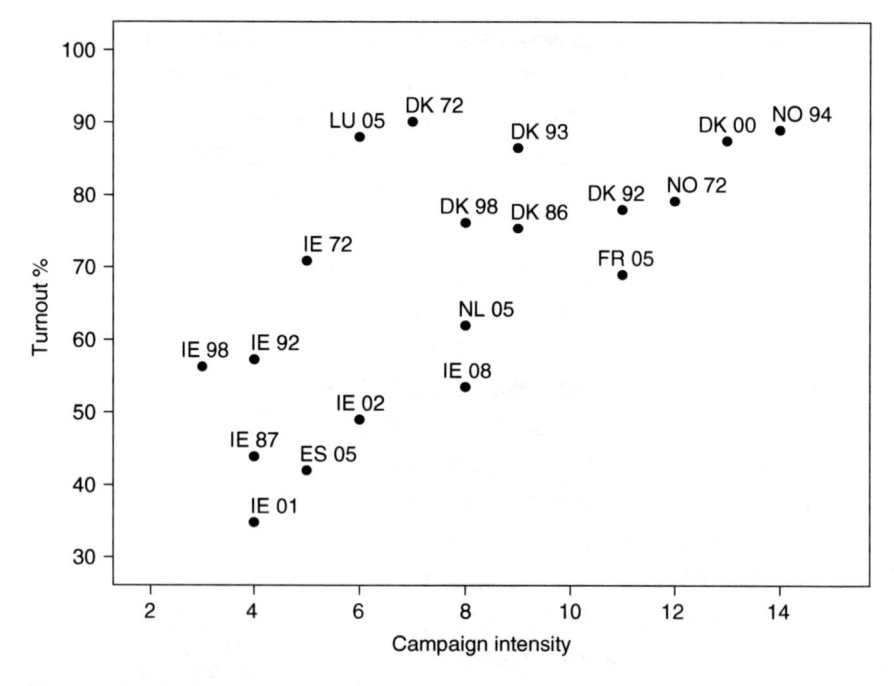

**Figure 4.3.** Campaign intensity and turnout

the hypotheses presented above, they nevertheless suggest the presence of a strong relationship between campaign intensity, turnout, and issue voting.

### 4.4.1. *Campaign intensity and turnout*

According to Hypothesis 4.1, more intense campaigns would lead to higher levels of turnout. To evaluate this hypothesis, Figure 4.3 plots the relationship between turnout and the levels of campaign intensity. This clearly indicates a strong relationship between campaign intensity and turnout. The Pearson correlation between the two measures is 0.69. Generally, turnout is highest in referendums with high-intensity campaigns, such as the Norwegian vote on accession in 1994 and the Danish Euro referendum in 2000. Yet, there are also some outliers, such as the Luxembourgian referendum on the Constitutional Treaty where turnout is very high at 89 per cent despite low campaign intensity, but this is most likely due to compulsory voting laws in Luxembourg.[6]

Of course, we know that turnout varies significantly cross-nationally and this may partly drive the strong correlation, but in a simple bivariate

## Campaign Effects

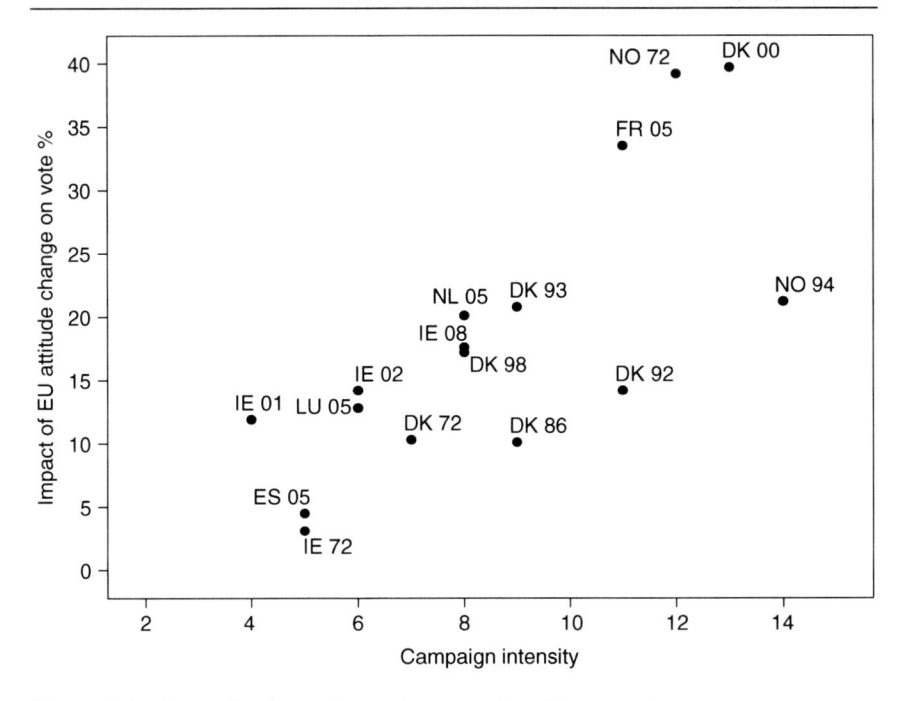

Figure 4.4. Campaign intensity and country-level issue voting

analysis it is not possible to account for country-specific factors. In Chapter 7, we look in more detail at within-country variation in campaign intensity and turnout. The case study of the two Irish referendums on the Nice Treaty illustrates that the more intense campaign leading up to the second referendum vote most probably brought more voters to the polling stations. In support of Hypothesis 4.1, Figure 4.3 thus provides some suggestive evidence that high-intensity campaigns motivate people to go to the polls.

### 4.4.2. Campaign intensity and issue voting

We would also expect that high-intensity campaigns activate attitudes, and that these attitudes play a greater role in the vote decision itself. According to Hypothesis 2.5, a highly salient campaign environment will encourage voters to rely more on their attitudes towards the ballot proposition when deciding. In order to allow easy comparison of the impact of attitudes in different referendums versus the campaign intensity, Figure 4.4 provides an overview of the predicted impact on the yes-vote of a change in the EU attitude variable in each of the referendums. When the

97

impact of attitude changes is higher, it implies that issue voting is more pronounced in a particular referendum. This calculation of predicted probabilities is based on the logistic regression model of voting behaviour discussed in Chapter 3, and calculated by simulating a change in yes-votes calculated by simulating a half of a standard deviation change in the EU attitude variable, keeping all the other independent variables at their mean. Thereby, we can compare how much attitudes influence the probability of voting yes in different referendum contexts.[7]

Figure 4.4 shows that the impact of attitudes was greatest in the referendums with the most intense campaigns: the Danish Euro referendum, the Norwegian membership referendums, and the French ECT referendum. For example, a half standard deviation increase in EU attitudes in the France referendum (a move from 11 to 13 on a 20-point scale) would increase the probability of voting yes by an amazing 34 per cent, whereas the same change in attitudes in Spain would only increase the probability of voting yes by 5 per cent.

The correlation between campaign intensity and the impact of attitudes on vote choice is 0.76. Hence, this figure corroborates the proposition that as campaigns become more intense, citizens will be more likely to draw connections between their own ideological and issue positions and the ballot proposal. While these descriptive statistics do not allow us to reach firm conclusions, the findings in this section do suggest that high-intensity campaigns increase turnout and enhance the impact of attitudes on vote choices. We can explore these relationships further by examining whether we find similar patterns at the individual level.

## 4.5. Testing the effect of campaign exposure

To substantiate the link between campaign environments and patterns of voting behaviour illustrated above, this section examines how individuals respond to variations in campaign exposure and intensity. We expect that citizens in polities with high-intensity referendum campaigns are more likely to vote, more knowledgeable about the ballot issue, and more likely to vote on the basis of issue attitudes. To examine the impact of the campaign environment on individual-level participation and vote choices, we first analyse how exposure to campaign information affects participation. *Campaign exposure* is a measure of the degree of campaign information that the individual has received in the period leading up to the referendum. Campaign information includes campaign

# Campaign Effects

posters, house visits from campaigners, official brochures and leaflets, and television programmes and newspaper articles covering the referendum. Our expectation is that variation in the degree of campaign exposure will have a similar effect to variation in the campaign environment. Second, we analyse the interaction between the campaign context and individual behaviour in a multi-level model that includes both individual-level (micro) and contextual (macro) variables. We expect high-intensity campaigns to induce issue voting.

## 4.5.1. Turnout in referendums

As Downs (1957) noted, the decision to participate in any given election or referendum is affected by the information available to each individual. Information may increase the benefits of voting by helping citizens to make decisions that maximize their utility, but information is also inherently costly. Hence, according to the Downsian model of 'rational abstention', the acquisition of information plays an important role in the decision to vote, since rational citizens will only vote if the returns outweigh the costs. The informational demands of voting led Downs to predict that certain types of citizens are more likely to participate in elections than others. In particular, he argued that high-income (and highly educated) voters would be more likely to vote, because the voting and information demands would be less costly:

> There are two reasons to suspect that the proportion of low-income citizens who abstain is usually higher than the proportion of high-income citizens who do so. First, the cost of voting is hard for low-income citizens to bear; therefore, even if returns among high- and low-income groups are the same, fewer of the latter vote. Second, the cost of information is harder for low-income citizens to bear; hence more of them are likely to be uncertain because they lack information (Downs 1957: 273).

Downs' theoretical predictions have been corroborated by several studies of voter turnout in North America and Europe. These studies tend to show that better educated, wealthy, and older individuals participate in elections more frequently than others (Lijphart 1997; Wolfinger and Rosenstone 1980; Dee 2003). Though there are some notable exceptions, studies of voter turnout thus tend to emphasize relatively fixed demographic and socio-economic determinants. Yet, as discussed in Chapter 2 (Hypothesis 2.3), it seems equally reasonable to expect that exposure to campaign information will reduce the informational costs associated with voting and increase the utility of voting, thus making individual citizens less likely to abstain (see also Hillygus 2005).

To evaluate whether campaign exposure actually influences turnout in referendums, we are interested in estimating the extent to which campaign exposure has an effect on the probability of voting. It is often argued that campaign research at the individual level suffers from an endogeneity problem, since a person's information acquisition may be endogenous to the outcomes that we are interested in examining, such as participation and knowledge (see, e.g. Lassen 2005). Yet, what is referred to as an endogeneity problem may also be seen as an omitted variable problem (Rosenstone and Hansen 1993; Hillygus 2005). In other words, while it is true that people who intend to vote are also more likely to follow the campaign coverage, this may not be because their vote intention causes them to acquire more campaign information, but rather because of some other factor that influences both, e.g. political interest or education level. Hence, while the problem of endogeneity is certainly a concern, it can be partially alleviated by estimating a multiple regression model and controlling for other factors that are likely to influence both campaign exposure and vote intention, such as education and income levels. Hence, in order to examine the effect of campaign exposure, we estimate a multiple logistic regression model with the turnout decision as the dependent variable. The key independent variable is the individual's level of exposure to the campaign. Campaign exposure is measured by analysing survey responses to question items on campaign information, such as whether the respondent had been exposed to advertisements, leaflets, canvassing, television and radio programmes about the referendum, newspaper articles, or posters.[8] On the basis of these question items, a scale of individual campaign exposure was created.[9] The control variables include a Likert scale of the individual's education level[10] and social class,[11] as well as age (see Appendix 2). Given the consensus in the literature, these variables are all expected to have a significant impact on turnout. Finally, we have included controls for region (urban or rural) and gender that may also have an influence on the propensity to vote.[12] The results of estimating this model using a pooled dataset are shown in Table 4.1.

As Table 4.1 illustrates, our key independent variables are all positive as we would expect, yet only campaign exposure, social class, gender, and age are significant. Older middle class citizens are most likely to turn out in EU referendums, just as we would expect in elections. Being female and living in a rural area is negatively correlated with turnout. Importantly, Table 4.1 also indicates that campaign exposure is positively

Table 4.1. Predicting turnout in EU referendums

| Independent variables | Logit | Robust S.E. |
|---|---|---|
| Campaign exposure | 0.30** | 0.11 |
| Education | 0.13 | 0.12 |
| Social class | 0.14* | 0.06 |
| Region (urban) | −0.24 | 0.17 |
| Gender (female) | −0.24** | 0.08 |
| Age | 0.21** | 0.07 |
| Constant | −1.58** | 0.43 |
| % correctly predicted | 78 | |
| McFadden R Squared | 0.11 | |
| N | 30,721 | |

* Significant at 0.05
** Significant at 0.01
Note: This logit model has been adjusted for clustering within each referendum sample.

and significantly related to the likelihood of voting, even when we control for the relevant socio-economic determinants of voting. To get a more intuitive sense of the magnitude of the impact of campaign exposure on turnout, it is useful to present this relationship graphically. Since social class and age are two of the most powerful predictors of turnout, Figure 4.5 shows the predicted probability of voting in an EU referendum for individuals exposed to low, medium, and high levels of campaign information[13] given their class and age.

As we can see from the predicted probabilities plotted in Figure 4.5, the level of campaign exposure has a very considerable impact on the likelihood of voting. Working class respondents have a probability of 0.39 of turning out when their exposure to campaign information is limited, but this increases to a probability of 0.94 when they receive large amounts of information about the campaign (Figure 4.5a). Similarly, citizens in the 18–24 age group only have a 0.32 probability of voting when they receive little campaign information, but a 0.93 probability of voting when they are exposed to large amounts of information (Figure 4.5b). What is also noteworthy is that, whereas class and age clearly affect the probability of voting for people who are exposed to low and medium levels of campaign information, this effect disappears when individuals are exposed to very high levels of information (as the flatness of the 'high exposure' slope indicates). This is partly a 'ceiling effect' as the probability of voting yes approaches 1, but it could also suggest that campaign exposure tends to even out social and age differentials in the electorate.

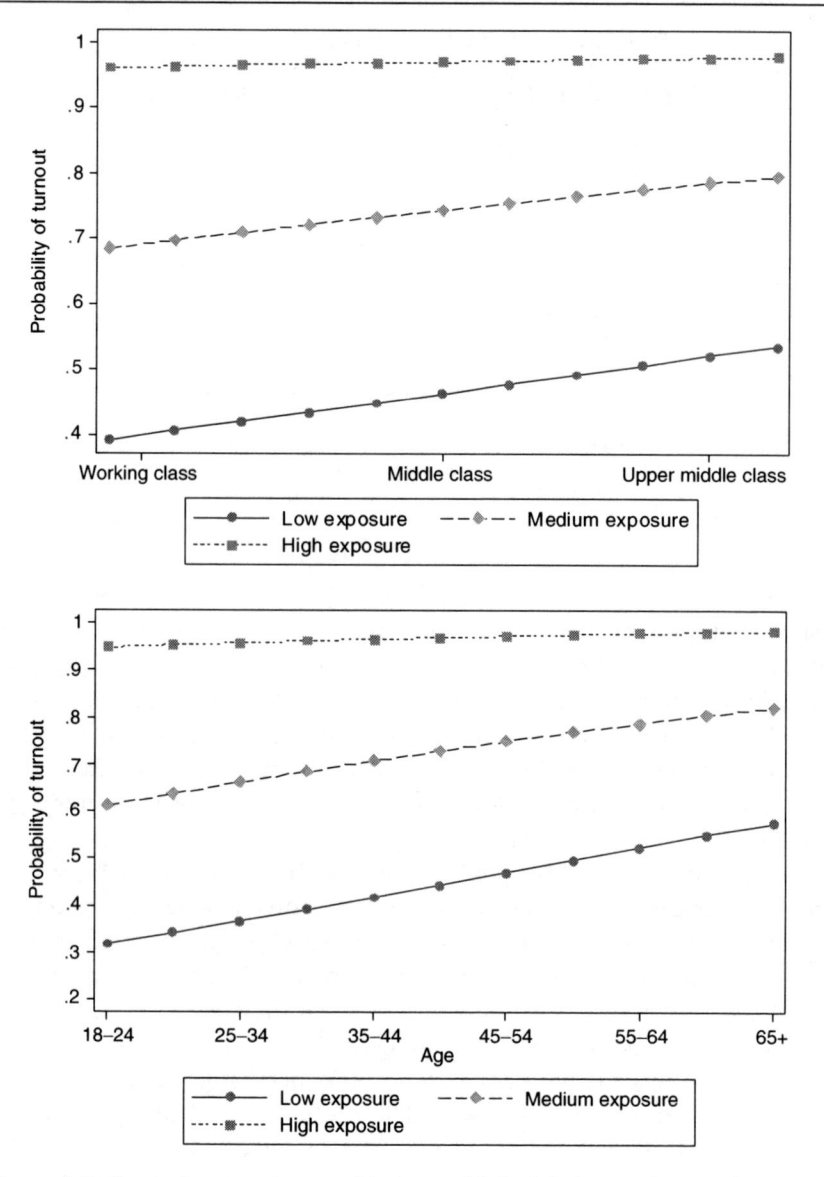

**Figure 4.5.** Campaign exposure and turnout. (*a*) Social class and campaign exposure; (*b*) age and campaign exposure

We should interpret these findings with some caution, since it is difficult to disentangle the direction of causality in these individual-level observational studies, where it is unclear whether exposure to campaigns leads people to vote, or whether individuals choose to be exposed to the campaign because they have an interest in voting. Notwithstanding the potential problem of endogeneity, these results suggest that exposure to campaign information makes it far more likely that an individual votes in a referendum, even when controlling for education levels. The results are robust across each of the referendums included in the analysis. In Chapter 5, we examine the effect of information on vote intention in two experimental studies. The experimental design allows us to clearly disentangle cause and effect, and the results from these studies confirm the findings in this chapter: exposure to information makes individuals more certain about their attitudes and more likely to vote.

### 4.5.2. Ballot-specific knowledge

One of the reasons that we expect campaign exposure to increase turnout is because campaigns inform voters about the available choices, thereby increasing the utility of voting. As stressed by Matsusaka (1995) and others, it is the voter's subjective belief about her information level that guides participation. Hence, formal models suggest that voters who *feel* more confident about their knowledge of the alternatives derive higher utility from voting. If referendum campaigns inform voters in a way that makes them feel more knowledgeable, we expect higher exposure to campaign information to be positively associated with voters' perception of their ballot-specific knowledge. To evaluate this proposition, we can estimate a model where subjective knowledge of the ballot is the dependent variable. The measure of subjective ballot model is a 4-point Likert scale where the respondent is asked to rate her understanding of the issue involved in the referendum (e.g. the Maastricht Treaty) from 'no understanding' to a 'very good understanding'. In addition to campaign exposure, the independent variables include education level, EU attitude scale (as described in Chapter 3), class, gender, and age. This model has been estimated using ordinary least squares,[14] and the results are reported in Table 4.2.

As expected, campaign exposure is positively and significantly related to perceived knowledge of the ballot. Perhaps surprisingly, the magnitude of this effect is greater than that of education level, which is insignificant in this pooled model. Women tend to report that they know less about the issue than men, as do younger people. Interestingly, attitudes towards the EU have no effect on the perceived knowledge of the ballot. We assume that these information effects have an impact not only on individuals'

**Table 4.2.** Predicting ballot-specific knowledge

| Independent variables | Coeff. | Robust S.E. |
|---|---|---|
| Campaign exposure | 0.10** | 0.01 |
| EU attitudes | 0.01 | 0.01 |
| Education | 0.06 | 0.07 |
| Social class | 0.06 | 0.04 |
| Gender (female) | −0.14* | 0.05 |
| Age | 0.06* | 0.02 |
| Constant | 1.47** | 0.39 |
| R Squared | 0.13 | — |
| N | 18,826 | — |

* Significant at 0.05
** Significant at 0.01
*Note*: This OLS model has been adjusted for clustering within each referendum sample.

likelihood to vote, but also on the criteria they employ when they do vote.

### 4.5.3. *Issue voting and campaign exposure*

As discussed above, we expect high campaign exposure to induce issue voting, because campaigns inform the voter about the available alternatives and increase the salience of the issue. Figure 4.4 illustrated a strong relationship between campaign intensity and issue voting at the aggregate level. We want to examine whether this relationship also exists at the individual level. In other words, are individuals in intense campaign environments more likely to vote on the basis of their attitudes? To examine this question, we estimate a multilevel logistic regression model with respondents at level one and referendums at level two.[15] This allows us to examine how campaign intensity interacts with vote choices. Our dependent variable is the binary vote choice (1 = yes) and our key independent variables are EU attitudes, partisan recommendation, and government satisfaction (see descriptive statistics in Appendix 2). As in Chapter 3, EU attitudes is a summated rating scale (21-points) capturing citizens' attitudes towards European integration. Party recommendation measures whether the respondents' preferred party recommended a yes- or a no-vote, and government satisfaction is a 4-point scale ranging from 'very dissatisfied' with the government's performance to 'very satisfied'. We also include controls for education, class, age, and gender. Moreover,

Table 4.3. Issue voting and campaign intensity

| Independent variables | Logit | S.E. |
|---|---|---|
| EU attitudes | 0.33** | 0.02 |
| Party recommendation | 0.76** | 0.03 |
| Government satisfaction | 0.62** | 0.04 |
| Education | 0.05* | 0.02 |
| Social class | 0.07** | 0.02 |
| Age | 0.17** | 0.02 |
| Gender | 0.03 | 0.04 |
| Campaign intensity | −0.10** | 0.00 |
| Campaign intensity * EU attitudes | 0.02** | 0.00 |
| Constant | −6.28** | 0.45 |
| *Variance component* | 1.12** | — |
| −2* *Log likelihood* | 16716.05 | — |
| N (groups, individuals) | 17,23,433 | — |

\* Significant at 0.05
\*\* Significant at 0.01
Note: This is a random intercept logistic regression model where level 1 is individual and level 2 is referendums.

the model includes campaign intensity (as in Figure 4.2) as a level 2 independent variable. To test for the mediating effect of the campaign context on issue voting, we include an interaction between EU attitudes and campaign intensity. The results are shown in Table 4.3.

As also shown in Chapter 3, this table indicates that EU attitudes, party endorsements, and satisfaction with government performance are the most powerful predictors of vote choice. In this model, we can also see that campaign intensity has a negative effect on yes-vote. The direction of causality is not clear-cut, however. More intense campaigns may make it more likely that voters reject the ballot, or perhaps conversely, when the race is very close and the ballot is likely to be rejected, campaigns become more intense. As we know, the rejected ballots on the Euro in Denmark, the Constitutional Treaty in France, and accession in Norway were among the most intense, and this was at least partly because public opinion was so divided. More interesting is the positive and significant interaction between campaign intensity and EU attitudes. While the magnitude of the effect is small, it nevertheless suggests that voters rely more on opinions on Europe in intense campaigns than in less-intense campaigns. To get a better sense of the actual magnitude of the direct and conditioning effect of campaign intensity, we plot the predicted effect of attitudes on the probability of voting yes at three levels of campaign intensity. The plot is shown in Figure 4.6.

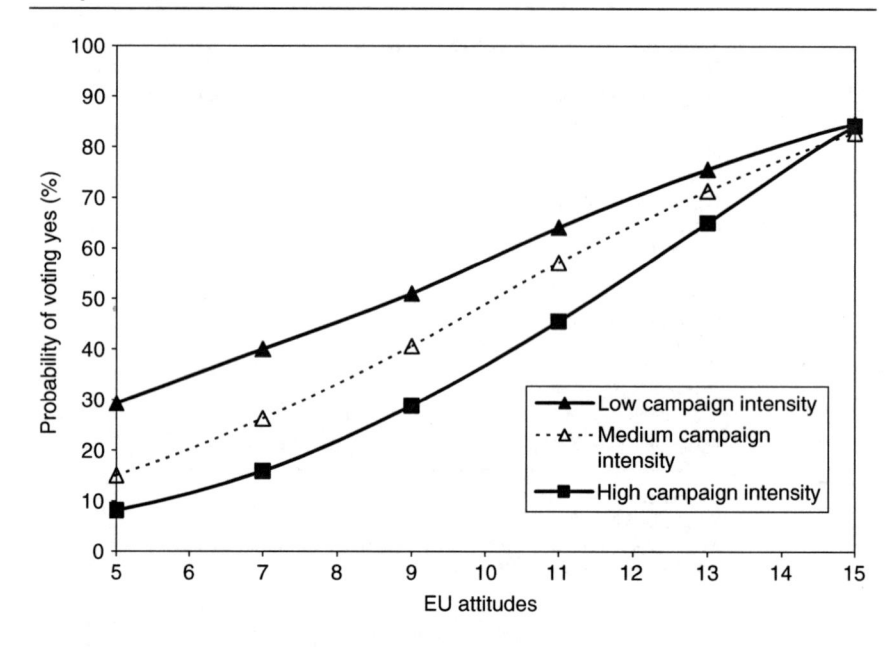

**Figure 4.6.** Issue voting and campaign intensity

Figure 4.6 shows that vote choice overwhelmingly depends on voters' attitudes towards European integration, especially at the extremes, yet that the campaign environment also makes a difference. In more intense campaigns, the probability of voting yes is generally lower. But attitudes also matter more in these campaigns. A shift in attitudes in an intense campaign environment thus has a greater effect on vote choice than in more subdued campaigns. In sum, the evidence presented in this section suggests that the campaign environment is important when it comes to advancing issue voting and turnout.

## 4.6. Conclusion

In response to the rejection of the Constitutional Treaty in France and the Netherlands in 2005, the European Commission launched *Plan D* for Democracy, Dialogue and Debate (European Commission 2005). At the heart of this proposal was the idea that more debate and dialogue about Europe would lead to greater public support for the project. It may be the case that an intensified debate on Europe could have a positive effect on attitudes. But the investigation of the effect of information on vote choices in European referendums in this book reveals that information effects are more subtle than policy-makers and politicians often assume. Chapter 3 showed that knowledge about the EU does not necessarily guarantee a positive vote in referendums on EU question. Rather, it implies that people are more likely to rely on their own convictions and less likely to follow the recommendations of national elites. This chapter has shown that campaigns with vigorous debate and arguments tend to induce higher levels of popular participation and more sophisticated decision-making, but they do not necessarily result in an affirmative vote. Exposure to campaign information also makes citizens feel more knowledgeable about the issue at stake. Moreover, there is some indication that more intense campaigns foster more issue voting. These findings support the theoretical propositions outlined in the spatial framework of Chapter 2: more information reduces uncertainty and thus increases the likelihood of people voting (Hypothesis 2.3). Higher campaign intensity makes voters more likely to rely on issue preferences (Hypothesis 2.5).

Hence, the *quantity* of information is important when it comes to advancing issue voting and turnout, but it does not guarantee the outcome desired by national and European elites. It was not the lack of debate and information which led to the rejection of the Constitutional Treaty in France in 2005. It is perhaps the nature of the debate that may have affected vote choices as much as the quantity of debate. As Kuklinski et al. (2001: 412) have noted, 'rather than the volume, it is the diagnostic value of information that influences how well citizens are able to cope with policy choices. Information has a high diagnostic value when it clearly and fully conveys the central considerations relevant to a decision or a judgement task'. This chapter has focused on how the quantity of information influences vote choices. In the next chapter, we look more closely at how different types of information and 'frames' generate different responses from people. Using survey experiments we explore how particular types of campaign information—elite framing and elite endorsements—influence opinions on EU ballot questions. This allows us to present a much more detailed analysis of how citizens respond to different types of information and to more clearly distinguish between cause and effect.

In Chapter 6, we focus on the 'quality' of information. When we refer to 'quality' in the context of vote choices, we move beyond the empirical investigation of patterns and explanations of political behaviour presented in the previous chapters and we address important normative questions: what is a competent vote choice in the context of EU referendums; how do we measure the 'quality' of voting behaviour; an which factors can influence levels of voter competence? These normative and empirical questions are addressed in the Chapter 6, which examines how different types of information may advance the competence of voters in EU referendums.

## Notes

1. Key (1966: 7).
2. The measure of polarization is calculated on the basis of the mean party position, weighted by the vote share of the party. The actual measure ranges from 0 (no opposition) to 52 per cent (majority opposition in Parliament). These numbers are transformed into a 5-point scale in the following manner: less than 10 per cent (weighted) opposition gives 1; 10–20 per cent gives 2; 20–30 per cent gives 3; 30–40 per cent gives 4; and more than 40 per cent opposition in parliament gives the score of 5 points.
3. This measure does not account for the level of polarization that can be found outside the parliamentary arena. Non-parliamentary organizations, such as Eurosceptic public movements, have played an important role in many of these referendums, notably in Denmark and Norway. This effect will be discussed in more detail in Chapter 7. The measure of media coverage is likely to capture high levels of extra-parliamentary activity during a campaign.
4. The difference between the yes- and the no-side is transformed into a 5-point scale in the following manner: an average lead of the yes-side of more than 15 per cent gives 1; a lead of more than 10 per cent gives 2; a lead of more than 5 per cent gives 3; a lead between 0 and 5 per cent is transformed to a score of 4, whereas a lead for the no-side (on average over the period) is given the score of 5 (maximum uncertainty for the yes-side). This scale reflects that the government as the agenda setter in these referendums always recommends a yes-vote, and hence any lead of the no-side is likely to enhance the intensity of the campaign.
5. The 5-point scale of media coverage is created as follows: less than half an article a day on average equals a 1-point score; 0.5–1 gives 2; 1–2 gives 3; 2–3 gives 4, and more than 3 gives a 5-point score.
6. The correlation between campaign intensity and turnout is 0.74 if Luxembourg is excluded from the sample.
7. The country-specific estimations are based on the same models shown in Chapter 3 (Tables 3.1–3.3). The same models, but without the interaction terms, are used to calculate the first differences shown in Figure 4.4.
8. In some of the surveys, the respondents were asked to rate the usefulness of these sources of information, but our measure merely recorded whether or not the respondent had been exposed to/was aware of the information sources.

9. The 13-point summated rating scale was based on a minimum of six question items and Cronbach alphas for each of the scales were in the range between 0.75 and 0.95.
10. Education level is measured as a 5-point scale ranging from 'leaving school before 15' to 'university education'.
11. This is a 5-point social class scale ranging from 'unskilled manual worker' to 'professional/manager'.
12. Given the number and type of explanatory variables, one might expect that this model could suffer from multicollinearity, but the diagnostic tests showed that this is not the case for any of the results presented in this section.
13. These three levels of campaign exposure have been created on the basis of the scores on the campaign exposure scale: the quarter of respondents with the lowest scores (i.e. they were exposed to only very limited campaign information) were placed in the 'low' campaign exposure group and the quarter of respondents with the highest score were in the 'high' campaign exposure group, while the remaining half were allocated to the 'medium' campaign exposure group.
14. The dependent variable is an ordinal 4-point Likert scale, but I have chosen to report OLS estimates rather than ordered logistic regression estimates, since the results are very similar in this case and the former are easier to interpret.
15. Hierarchical (or multilevel) modelling is one method which allows us to explicitly model differences in voting behaviour according to the national context. Such models also correct for dependence of observations within a particular referendum (intra-class correlation) and make adjustments to both within and between parameter estimates for the clustered nature of the data (Snijders and Bosker 1999; Raudenbush and Bryk 2002). Since we are not interested in the individual referendums per se, but rather wish to draw general inferences about the effect of individual and contextual variables on voting behaviour, a random effects model would seem more appropriate (see Snijders and Bosker 1999: 43). When estimating the model as a three-level model (respondent, referendum, country), the estimates of the coefficients are virtually identical. We have also estimated the models as simple binary logistic regressions (correcting the standard errors for clustering within countries), and the results are very similar to the multilevel estimates.

# 5

# Framing Effects in Referendums: Experimental Evidence

> *Framing is an essential feature of public discourse on matters of political import. Every public issue is contested in a symbolic arena, where advocates attempt to impose their own meaning on the issue.*[1]
>
> —Nelson and Kinder

Public opinion and electoral behaviour often depend on which 'frames' elites choose to use. Frames provide

a central organizing idea or story line that provides meaning to an unfolding strip of events, weaving connection among them. The frame suggests what the controversy is about, the essence of the issue (Gamson and Modigliani 1987: 143).

Frames are never entirely neutral. By defining what the heart of matter is, they suggest how people should decide on an issue.

Given the volatility of voters in referendums and the relative unfamiliarity of most citizens with the issue of European integration, framing should matter more than in other electoral situations. The previous chapter examined how the intensity of the campaign affects patterns of voting behaviour in EU referendums. It was shown that campaigns with vigorous debate and competing arguments tend to induce higher levels of popular participation and more sophisticated decision-making by voters. The purpose of this chapter is to examine the micro-mechanisms of public opinion formation in referendums by exploring the principal ways in which elites can influence individual attitudes towards EU ballot proposals: by supporting or opposing the proposals (elite cues) and by emphasizing certain aspects of the proposal (issue framing). Specifically, we look at the effect of government endorsements on partisan and non-partisan voters (*government endorsement*) and the effect of emphasizing different consequences of the two possible outcomes (*consequences frame*). By examining these elite cueing and framing effects, this chapter is also testing some of the central claims presented in the theoretical model in Chapter 2, concerning the effect of (un)certainty about the position of the ballot proposal and the reversion point on vote choice. In line with this theory, the central proposition of this chapter is that elite frames matter for vote choices in referendums, but that the effect is mediated to some extent by political awareness and partisan affiliations.

To test these predictions concerning framing effects, this chapter analyses the data from two survey experiments. By using an experimental design, it is possible to determine the specific nature of the frame and make assessments of causal predictions by neutralizing the effect of confounding factors. The experimental evidence presented here complements the analysis of the survey data presented in the previous two chapters by exploring how citizens respond to elite recommendations and how the framing of a ballot proposal influences vote choices.

The chapter proceeds as follows. First, it presents a more detailed discussion of framing theory and outlines the key hypotheses concerning elite cues and framing effects in referendums. Second, it presents two survey experiments designed to test framing effects in referendums: an experiment on a (hypothetical) referendum on the Euro and an experiment on a (hypothetical) referendum on the EU's Lisbon Treaty. This is followed by a discussion of the results of the analyses and their implication for our understanding of referendum behaviour. The findings show that government endorsements have a significant effect on attitudes towards referendum proposals, but that this effect is mediated by partisanship. Consequences frames also have a substantial effect: when negative consequences of the no-vote are highlighted, people are more likely to favour a yes-vote, whereas a negative emphasis on the consequences of the ballot proposal leads people to say no. The chapter thus provides further evidence to suggest that citizens are susceptible to influence by the information provided by elites during a campaign, yet that the effects of such elite frames are moderated by pre-existing attitudes and political awareness.

## 5.1. Theories of framing effects

Citizens' perceptions of political issues are shaped not only by the amount of information they receive, but also by the selection and presentation of information. A ballot proposal on European integration is inevitably a complex and multifaceted issue. A vote on EU treaty ratification may, for instance, be presented as an issue of surrender of national sovereignty, or it may be portrayed as a matter of maintaining essential economic and political ties with European neighbours. In other words, a single proposal may be 'framed' in different ways. Framing refers to the process by which people develop a particular conceptualization of an issue or reorient their thinking about an issue. A framing *effect* occurs when the emphasis on a subset of potentially relevant considerations causes individuals to focus on these considerations when constructing their opinion on an issue (Nelson et al. 1997; Druckman 2001a, 2001b; Chong and Druckman 2007a, 2007b).

The literature suggests two primary ways in which frames operate: 'the importance change model' and 'the content change model' (see Chong and Druckman 2007a; Slothuus 2008). According to the importance change model, frames operate by making certain beliefs more relevant and applicable to the issue at stake (Nelson and Kinder 1996; Nelson et al. 1997).[2] Frames 'affect opinion simply by making certain considerations seem more important than others; these considerations in turn, carry greater weight for the final attitude' (Nelson et al. 1997: 569). A less prominent interpretation of the framing process is the content change model, which stresses that frames introduce new arguments and information that the individual had not previously thought about (Chong and Druckman 2007a; Slothuus 2008). According to this model, framing changes the content of the underlying considerations, whereas the former model emphasizes changes in the importance of pre-exiting considerations. In the political psychology literature, framing effects have been expressed formally by way of a conventional expectation value model of individual attitudes. Here, individual attitudes can be portrayed as $Attitude = \sum v_i w_i$, where $v_i$ is the evaluation of the object on attribute $i$ and $w_i$ is the salience weight associated with that attribute (Nelson et al. 1997; Chong and Druckman 2007a). For example, an individual's overall attitude towards a referendum proposal will consist of a combination of positive and negative evaluations of the proposal, $v_i$, on different dimensions $i$. An individual may believe that the treaty will result in further surrender of national sovereignty ($i = 1$), but that European integration is essential for her country's economy ($i = 2$). The overall evaluation of the project will therefore depend on the relative magnitudes of $v_1$ and $v_2$ discounted by the relative salience weights $w_1$ and $w_2$. (Nelson et al. 1997; Nelson and Oxley 1999). Framing can thus operate by influencing the relative

# Framing Effects

salience of different evaluations $w_i$ (*importance change*) or by introducing new dimensions $i$ in the minds of voters (*content change*).

This model highlights a conceptual distinction between framing effects and persuasion (or *belief change*), which involves changing people's minds about the particular attributes of the project $v_i$ (Nelson and Oxley 1999). Whereas changing people's fundamental beliefs is a tall order for most politicians, they can more easily attempt to mobilize voters behind or in opposition to a proposal by encouraging them to think about the proposal along particular lines. Framing effects thus constitute one of the primary means by which elites influence citizens' opinion. Elites will, of course, not limit themselves to the framing of issues, but will also generally try to influence public opinion by more openly speaking in favour or against an issue. Such elite cues can also be very effective, but they tend to be strongly conditional on individuals' feelings about the elites in question (Lupia and McCubbins 1998; Sniderman 2000). In other words, elite cues, such as party endorsements, will primarily have an effect on those citizens who are positively disposed towards a party that gives the endorsement, whereas framing effect may work as a more subtle way of increasing the salience of certain considerations in the minds of citizens.

We can easily relate this conventional framing model to the theoretical model presented in Chapter 2. Framing can influence attitudes towards ballot proposals by influencing individuals' perceptions of the positions of the ballot proposal and the reversion point, by affecting the certainty of these positions, and finally, by influencing the relative salience of issue-specific attitudes. Elite cues equally provide citizens with information about their own positions in relation to the ballot and reversion point, and the certainty of these opinions. Hence, a close examination of framing effects and elite cues allows us to explore the micro-mechanisms of opinion formation in referendums suggested in our theoretical framework.

### 5.1.1. *Framing effects and elite cues in referendums*

Framing effects and elite endorsements are highly relevant in the context of referendums on European integration where the multifaceted nature of the proposals, coupled with the uncertainty of voters, provides plenty of scope for elites to offer competing interpretations of the issue at stake. Following our theoretical framework, we are specifically interested in two types of elite framing. The first is the framing of the position of the proposal and the reversion point. The second type of framing is elite cues, or party endorsements.

Recall the theoretical model in Chapter 2, which suggests that a voter's evaluation of a proposal depends on the distance between her own 'ideal point' and the relative position of the ballot proposal and the reversion point (Hypothesis 2.1). Moreover, the evaluation also depends on the certainty associated with these positions (Hypothesis 2.2). In line with this theory we expect that citizens' evaluations of a proposal are influenced by the manner in which the proposal and reversion point positions are framed. We refer to this type of frame as *consequences frames*, since they emphasize the potentially negative or positive consequences of the two possible outcomes. Consequences frames are closely related to what is known as 'valence frames' in the framing literature, that is, frames that evaluate political issues or situations in either positive or negative terms (de Vreese and Boomgaarden 2003) or in terms of risk and opportunity (Schuck and de Vreese 2006). In the context of referendums, such frames can emphasize the potentially negative (or positive) consequences of either outcome, and therefore influence how voters think about the choice set. More specifically, we would expect that a frame that highlights the most extreme consequences of the proposal will lead more people to oppose the proposal, since this frame increases the salience of the potentially negative attributes associated with the proposal rather than with the reversion point. Equally, we expect that a frame highlighting the negative aspects of the reversion point—the consequences of a no-vote—will encourage more people to evaluate the proposal positively. Thinking about this spatially, the former frame emphasizes that the proposal's position is far from the median voter, whereas the latter frame emphasizes the extreme position of the reversion point (see Figure 2.3). Of course, some individuals may favour the more extreme positions, but such voters who hold a strong anti- or pro-European position are unlikely to be swayed either way, as we have seen in Chapter 3. Hence, we can formulate the following hypotheses:

**Hypothesis 5.1:** Frames that emphasize the potentially negative consequences of a ballot proposal will make individuals more likely to oppose the proposal.

**Hypothesis 5.2:** Frames that emphasize the potentially negative consequences of a no-vote (reversion point) will make individuals more likely to favour the proposal.

Framing effects also influence the level of certainty associated with voters' perceptions of the ballot proposal/reversion point. By providing information on their positions, frames can increase voters' utility of either the proposal or the reversion point and make voters less likely to be undecided (and abstain) in a referendum (Hypothesis 2.3). In a competitive context, citizens will be exposed to competing frames and as such the information flow is likely to increase the certainty about both the proposal and the reversion point. In a highly competitive campaign, voters are more likely to rely on their prior issue attitudes when voting and they are also less likely to abstain, as we have seen in Chapter 5. When we present voters with one-sided frames, we also expect them to be more decisive, given that frames provide additional information.

**Hypothesis 5.3:** Individuals who are exposed to elite framing of the proposal are more likely to have an opinion on the proposal than individuals who are not exposed to framing.

Frames that focus on a particular aspect of a policy issue are often referred to as 'issue frames' or 'frames in communication' (Druckman 2001a; Chong and Druckman 2007a; Slothuus 2008). They influence political opinion and behaviour, by defining and constructing a political issue. Another related way in which elite communication can influence public attitudes towards an issue is through elite endorsements. Elite endorsements do not generally focus on a particular aspect of the issue and are consequently not normally interpreted as 'framing effects' in the literature,[3] but just like issue frames, endorsements are one of the principal tools that elites use to influence public opinion (see Lupia 1994). Elite endorsements provide information to the voter about the position of the proposal, and indeed the position of the voter's own ideal point, and thus persuade her to vote a certain way. As Lau and Redlawsk (2001: 953) have pointed out, elite endorsements have an obvious heuristic value as 'all that is necessary is to learn the candidate endorsed by a group and one's own attitude towards the group, and an obvious cognitively-efficient inference can be made' (see also Sniderman et al. 1991). In European referendums, the endorsements of political parties are arguably the most visible elite cues. Kriesi (2005: 139) has referred to the partisan heuristic as 'the quintessential shortcut in direct democratic votes'. Hence, we expect that endorsements by elites, such as governments, will influence the way in which people think about a proposal. Overall we expect that government endorsements will make voters more positively disposed towards a proposal:

**Hypothesis 5.4:** A government endorsement of a ballot proposal will make people more likely to favour the proposal, all other things being equal.

It is unlikely that government endorsement will have the same effect for all voters, however. Sniderman (2000) and others have referred to elite endorsements as the 'likeability heuristic', implying that voters infer their own position on the basis of whether it is endorsed by a group they like or dislike. We expect that citizens who are positively disposed towards the government will be more likely to be swayed by their endorsement than citizens who oppose the government. This brings us to the more general question of *framing moderators,* that is, individual-level attributes that condition framing effects.

### 5.1.2. Moderators of framing effects

As emphasized in the theoretical chapter, we expect opinion formation processes to vary across different types of individuals. Chapter 3 showed that political awareness mediates the extent to which individuals rely on issue attitudes in referendums. We also expect that individual attributes will condition the effect of framing (see Druckman and Nelson 2003; Chong and Druckman 2007a; Slothuus 2008). Specially, we focus on two types of moderators: political awareness and partisanship.

Studies of the mediating effect of political awareness on framing effects have produced mixed results. On the one hand, some scholars have argued that more politically aware (and knowledgeable) individuals possess more strongly held prior opinions and therefore they are less susceptible to framing effects (Kinder and Sanders 1990; Haider-Markel and Joselyn 2001). On the other hand, it has been argued that frames will have a greater effect on more knowledgeable people, because such people are likely to comprehend the considerations presented in a frame and be capable of integrating them in their utility calculation (Zaller 1992; Nelson et al. 1997; Druckman and Nelson 2003; Slothuus 2008). Given that both arguments are likely to hold some truth—individuals who possess prior opinions will exhibit less susceptibility to new frames, and knowledge will facilitate the response to frames—it may be difficult to disentangle the moderating effects of political awareness. Chong and Druckman (2007a: 112) recommend that scholars control for prior attitudes when estimating frame effects, in which case they predict that 'knowledge enhances framing effects because it increases the likelihood that the considerations emphasized in a frame will be available or comprehensible to the individual'.

The existing literature on framing has, however, tended to ignore that the moderating effect of political knowledge may also depend on the *type* of frame that individuals are exposed to. More specifically, we can distinguish between issue frames and equivalency frames. As described above, issue frames are concerned with emphasizing a subset of potentially relevant considerations, whereas equivalency frames examine how the use of 'different but logically equivalent words or phrases causes individual to alter their preferences' (Druckman 2001*a*: 228). An example of an equivalency frame is the Kahneman and Tversky (1984) study, which provided two frames of the effectiveness of a programme to combat 'an unusual Asian disease' by stating either that 200 out of 600 people 'will be saved' or that 400 out of 600 'will die'. The two framings are logically indistinguishable in real terms, but Kahneman and Tversky found a significant difference in support of the programme depending on which frames subjects were exposed to. We expect that more knowledgeable people will be less likely to be swayed by such equivalency frames which are essentially based on framing information in a positive or negative light without any real change of content. On the other hand, knowledgeable people will be more likely to respond to issue frames that require integration of new information into their overall evaluation. Hence, we put forth the following hypothesis:

**Hypothesis 5.5:** Politically aware citizens are less susceptible to equivalency frames, but more responsive to issue frames compared to less politically aware individuals.

As already mentioned above, we also expect that citizens will respond differentially to elite endorsements, depending on their partisanship. For example, if the government expresses support for a particular proposal, this is likely to have an effect only on people who support the government, whereas people who oppose the government will be no more likely, or perhaps less likely, to support the proposal. Hence, it follows that:

**Hypothesis 5.6:** Government endorsements have a stronger effect on the opinions of people who support the government than on those who do not.

These propositions are tested using two survey experiments, which will be described in greater detail in the next section.

## 5.2. Two survey experiments

We use data from two survey experiments in order to test framing effects in referendums. In each of these experiments voters were asked how they would vote in a (hypothetical) referendum. The first experiment related to a referendum on joining the European single currency, the euro, and the second concerned the ratification of the Lisbon Treaty. Both survey experiments were carried out in Britain. The experimental aspect of these two surveys implies the random assignment of respondents to 'control' and 'treatment' conditions. The control group simply received the vote intention question, whereas the 'treatment groups' were also exposed to survey items manipulated to represent different 'consequence' and 'elite endorsement' frames. By comparing the vote intention of respondents in the treatment groups to those in the control group, we can evaluate the causal effect of these frames.

There are several advantages in using survey experiments to examine our propositions. First, the experimental method allows us to design and control the frames that respondents are exposed to. Second, experiments enable us to make clear causal predictions through random assignment of respondents to frames (treatments). Finally, these survey experiments—unlike most laboratory experiments—were carried out using a representative sample of the population, and hence they allow us to draw more accurate inferences about real-world opinion formation processes (Gaines, Kuklinski, and Quirk 2007). One of the criticisms levelled against experimental research is that the external validity is low. When seeking to infer to the real world, an important task of the researcher is therefore to create an experimental context that closely resembles a real-world environment. In our survey experiments, respondents were asked about how they would vote in two hypothetical referendums. Given that these questions were not asked during actual referendum campaigns, this may appear reduce the 'real-world resemblance' of the design. However, in both cases the experiments were carried out at a time when such referendums were a real possibility.[4] Moreover, the fact that they were not carried out during an actual referendum campaign makes it easier to interpret the results, since the respondents were less contaminated by actual campaign effects (Gaines, Kuklinski, and Quirk 2007). We describe each of the experiments in greater detail below.

### 5.2.1. *The Euro referendum experiment*

The Euro referendum experiment was designed by the British Election Study as a part of their 2001 campaign study and was conducted using a random-digit-dialling telephone sample by Gallup (see Clarke et al.

**Table 5.1.** Euro referendum split-sample experimental treatments

| | |
|---|---|
| Treatment 1: Control | When the referendum on British membership in the European Monetary Union, the EURO, is held will you vote to...?<br>• give up pound and join euro<br>• keep pound and reject euro |
| Treatment 2: Euro frame | When the referendum on British membership in the European Monetary Union, the EURO, is held will you vote to...?<br>• join euro<br>• reject euro |
| Treatment 3: Government support cue | When the referendum on British membership in the European Monetary Union, the EURO, is held and the British government recommends entry, will you vote to...?<br>• give up pound and join euro<br>• keep pound and reject euro |
| Treatment 4: Government support and Euro frame | When the referendum on British membership in the European Monetary Union, the EURO, is held and the British government recommends entry, will you vote to...?<br>• join euro<br>• reject euro |

2005).[5] There were four groups of respondents which represent the split sample experiment. Each treatment went to just under 1,000 respondents and the treatments were framing both the question and the answers. These treatments are shown in Table 5.1.

As Table 5.1 shows, respondents in the control group[6] were asked how they would vote in a referendum on the Euro and were given the option to 'give up the pound and join the euro' or 'keep the pound and reject the euro.' The second group was given a different set of options, which only mentions the euro. This can be regarded as an 'equivalency frame' since the answer categories of group 1 and 2 are logically equivalent (joining the euro implies giving up the pound); yet, the two answer categories also highlight the implications of the proposal in different manners. The first set of answer categories puts emphasis of the negative consequences of a yes-vote ('give up the pound and join the euro') to a greater extent than the second set of answer category ('join the euro'). We would thus expect that fewer voters would support the proposal when presented with the first set of answer categories compared with the latter (Hypothesis 5.2). The second type of treatment includes a government support cue ('the British government recommends entry') in the question wording for each of the two answer categories (treatments 3 and 4). As hypothesized above, we expect individuals exposed to this frame will be more likely to

**Table 5.2.** Lisbon Treaty referendum split-sample experimental treatments

| | |
|---|---|
| Treatment 1: Control group | Last December, governments across the EU signed a new treaty, the Treaty of Lisbon. This treaty replaces the draft EU Constitutional Treaty. Some countries will hold a referendum on the new treaty [*Introduction*]. If there were to be a referendum in Britain, how would you vote? |
| Treatment 2: Government support | [*Introduction*]. The British Labour government is strongly in favour of the treaty. If there were to be a referendum in Britain, how would you vote? |
| Treatment 3: Reversion point frame | [*Introduction*]. If Britain rejects the treaty, some experts have warned that this will result in Britain leaving the EU. If there were to be a referendum in Britain, how would you vote? |
| Treatment 4: Proposal frame | [*Introduction*]. If Britain accepts the treaty, some experts have warned that Britain will surrender further powers to the EU. If there were to be a referendum in Britain, how would you vote? |

support the proposal, conditioned by their pre-existing attitudes towards the government and partisanship.

### 5.2.2. Lisbon Treaty referendum experiment

Another experiment was designed by this author specifically for the purposes of testing the theoretical propositions outlined above. This experiment was carried out in January 2008 by the internet survey company YouGov, as a part of their Omnibus survey answered by a nationally representative sample of 2,000 British adults. As shown in Table 5.2, this experiment involves the random assignment of respondents to one control condition and three treatment conditions.

All respondents were asked how they would vote in a referendum on the Treaty of Lisbon. Respondents in the first treatment group were also provided with a government endorsement: 'the British Labour government is strongly in favour of the treaty'. Again, we would expect that respondents exposed to this endorsement to be more willing to favour the proposal, especially those who are Labour supporters. The two other treatments frame the consequences of rejecting the proposal ('some experts have warned that this will result in Britain leaving the EU') and accepting the proposal ('some experts have warned that Britain will surrender further powers to the EU'). We expect that the individuals exposed to the former frame will be more likely to vote yes, whereas those exposed to the

## Framing Effects

Table 5.3. Framing effects in the Euro referendum experiment

|  | Yes | No | Undecided | Difference in yes-vote |
|---|---|---|---|---|
| Control group ($N = 909$) | 24 | 62 | 14 | — |
| Euro frame ($N = 937$) | 32 | 50 | 18 | 8*** |
| Government support frame ($N = 934$) | 30 | 57 | 14 | 6*** |
| Government support and Euro frame ($N = 941$) | 33 | 53 | 14 | 8*** |

Note: Table entries are percentages for each treatment group.
*** Significant difference between control and treatment with $p < .01$ (two-tailed).

latter will be more likely to vote no. These propositions, as well as the moderating factors, are examined in the next section.

### 5.3. Results

Given the experimental design, it is quite simple to test whether the consequences frames and government cues have an effect on public opinion. All we need to do is to compare the vote intention of the treatment groups with the control group and test whether they are statistically different in the expected direction. Table 5.3 shows the result from the Euro referendum experiment.

We can see that each of the frames have worked as expected. Respondents who were asked to 'join the euro' were 8 percentage points more likely to say that they would vote in favour of the proposal, compared with those who were asked to 'give up the pound and join the euro'. Equally, the government endorsement had a significant effect: respondent receiving this cue were 6 percentage points more likely to say they would vote yes. Respondents in the final group, which combined the two frames, were unsurprisingly the most likely to favour the proposal. The Euro referendum experiment thus lends support to our expectations concerning framing effects in referendums. Interestingly, the frames do not make people less indecisive, but this is surprising given that equivalence frames provide limited additional information. In fact, the Euro frame, which provides the least information about the consequences has the highest number of undecided respondents (18%), as we would expect.

Table 5.4 shows the results from our Lisbon Treaty experiment and paints a similar picture.

Again, we can see that all three frames have a significant effect on vote intention. As in the previous experiment, respondents exposed to

**Table 5.4.** Framing effects in the Lisbon Treaty referendum experiment

|  | Yes | No | Undecided | Difference in vote[†] |
|---|---|---|---|---|
| Control group ($N$ = 522) | 17 | 41 | 42 | — |
| Government support ($N$ = 511) | 24 | 36 | 40 | 6*** |
| Reversion point frame ($N$ = 433) | 23 | 43 | 34 | 6** |
| Proposal frame ($N$ = 487) | 16 | 59 | 25 | 19*** |

*** Significant difference between control and treatment with $p < .01$; ** $p < .05$ (two-tailed).
[†] For treatments 2 and 3 we measure the difference in yes-vote, for treatment 4 (proposal frame) we measure the difference in no-vote.

the government endorsement are also about 6 percentage points more likely to support the proposal. The reversion point frame—warning about Britain's exit of the EU as a possible consequence of rejecting the treaty—has a similar effect on the yes-vote. Interestingly, respondents exposed to this frame are also, on average, slightly more likely to reject the proposal, which suggests that Britain's exit from the EU is not perceived as a negative frame by all voters. Indeed, we would expect that issue frames provide more information about the position of the proposal/reversion point and that people exposed to such frames are less likely to be undecided as a consequence (Hypothesis 5.3). It is not surprising that the issue frames in this experiment provide more information, and in turn more certainty of opinion, than the equivalency frames in the Euro experiment. We see the same pattern for respondents exposed to the proposal frame (warning of the surrender of powers to the EU). This frame has by far the largest effect on intended no-votes: individuals receiving this frame are almost 19 percentage points more likely to reject the proposal. The difference is caused by a shift from undecided to no-voters, which implies that the proposal frame gives voters the certainty about the position of the proposal that enables them to reject it rather than be uncertain (the number of undecided respondents drops from 42 to 25%). This finding is in line with the results presented in the previous chapter, which showed that individuals exposed to more campaign information have more ballot-specific knowledge and are more likely to vote.

Overall, both experiments confirm that frames can have significant effects on public opinion. Framing the consequences of the proposal or reversion point will change voters' minds as expected, and equally government endorsement make voters more likely to accept the proposal. Yet, as discussed above, we also expect that these frames may work differently depending on the political awareness and the partisanship of the individual respondents. This is examined in further detail below.

### 5.3.1. Effect of individual-level moderators

To examine the conditioning effect of individual-level attributes, we estimate a multinomial logit model[7] with vote intention (yes, no, undecided) as the dependent variable, and the treatment effects as well as individual-level attributes as the independent variables. By interacting the treatment effects with the relevant individual level variables, we can establish whether framing effects are conditioned by these attributes. For each of our experiments we estimate three models. The first model is a base model with a dummy for each of the treatments (with the control group as the reference category). The second model examines the moderating effect of political awareness. Recall that we expected political sophisticates to be less susceptible to equivalency frames, but more susceptible to issue frames. Finally, our third model examines whether the effect of government endorsements is mediated by partisanship.

Table 5.5 examines the Euro referendum experiment. For the sake of simplicity, we only look at two of the three treatment conditions: Euro frame and government support cue (treatments 2 and 4 in Table 5.1).[8]

As we saw in Table 5.3, both frames have a positive effect on yes-vote, whereas only the euro frame has a significant effect when we compare undecided with a no-vote intention. Model 2 examines the conditioning effect of political awareness. Political awareness is measured in terms of how much attention the respondent pays to politics.[9] We control for EU attitudes,[10] since politically aware respondents are expected to have stronger prior attitudes (see Druckman and Nelson 2003; Chong and Druckman 2007a). Unsurprisingly, attitudes towards EU membership have a significant and quite substantial effect on intended vote choice. The table also shows that people who are politically aware are more likely to favour the proposal to join the Euro, even when controlling for attitudes. The analysis of the conditioning effect of political awareness in model 2 shows that politically aware respondents are less likely to be affected by the frame. This result is as we expected, since political sophisticates ought to be less susceptible to equivalency frames such as this one.

Model 3 also conforms to our expectations. It shows that the elite endorsement cue only has an effect on the vote intention of Labour party identifiers whereas respondents identifying with other parties do

Table 5.5. Multinomial logit of vote choice in the Euro referendum

|  | Model 1: Frames | | Model 2: Political attention | | Model 3: Partisan | |
| --- | --- | --- | --- | --- | --- | --- |
|  | Yes Log odds (SE) | Undecided Log odds (SE) | Yes Log odds (SE) | Undecided Log odds (SE) | Yes Log odds (SE) | Undecided Log odds (SE) |
| Government support cue | 0.29*** (0.09) | 0.15 (0.12) | 0.40*** (0.11) | 0.21* (0.12) | 0.14 (0.13) | −0.03 (0.17) |
| Euro frame | 0.34** (0.09) | 0.46*** (0.11) | 0.59*** (0.14) | 0.36** (0.16) | 0.41*** (0.09) | 0.52*** (0.11) |
| Attitudes towards EU membership | — | — | 2.06*** (0.08) | 1.23*** (0.08) | — | — |
| Political attention | — | — | 0.54*** (0.10) | 0.21* (0.12) | — | — |
| Partisanship (reference = no party) |  |  |  |  |  |  |
| Labour partisan | — | — | — | — | 0.72*** (0.11) | 0.21 (0.13) |
| Conservative partisan | — | — | — | — | −1.30*** (0.15) | −1.19*** (0.17) |
| Liberal Democrat partisan | — | — | — | — | 0.65*** (0.14) | 0.05 (0.17) |
| Political attention* Euro frame | — | — | −0.40** (0.19) | 0.23 (0.22) | — | — |
| Labour* Government cue | — | — | — | — | 0.43*** (0.16) | 0.48** (0.21) |
| Constant | −0.78*** (0.05) | −1.47*** (−0.07) | −6.82*** (0.25) | −4.82*** (0.25) | −1.00*** (0.10) | −1.32*** (0.12) |
| N | 3721 |  | 3715 |  | 3715 |  |
| McFadden's R squared | 0.004 |  | 0.16 |  | 0.07 |  |

Source: BES Euro referendum experiment *** $p < .01$; ** $p < .05$; * $p < .10$.

Table 5.6. Multinomial logit of vote choice in the Lisbon Treaty referendum

| | Model 1: Frames | | Model 2: Political att. | | Model 3: Partisan | |
|---|---|---|---|---|---|---|
| | Yes Log odds (SE) | Undecided Log odds (SE) | Yes Log odds (SE) | Undecided Log odds (SE) | Yes Log odds (SE) | Undecided Log odds (SE) |
| Government support cue | 0.41** (0.17) | 0.06 (0.14) | 0.37 (0.24) | 0.05 (0.18) | 0.21 (0.22) | 0.08 (0.16) |
| Reversion point frame | 0.23 (0.18) | -0.27* (0.15) | 0.06 (0.32) | -0.57** (0.24) | 0.25 (0.19) | -0.28* (0.15) |
| Proposal frame | -0.48*** (0.18) | -0.90*** (0.15) | -1.12*** (0.33) | -1.49*** (0.22) | -1.01*** (0.19) | -0.95*** (0.15) |
| Attitudes towards European unification | — | — | 1.05*** (0.05) | 0.64*** (0.03) | — | — |
| Political attention | — | — | 0.26 (0.24) | -1.55*** (0.19) | — | — |
| Partisanship (reference = no party) | | | | | | |
| Labour partisan | — | — | — | — | 1.38*** (0.20) | 0.39** (0.17) |
| Conservative partisan | — | — | — | — | -1.01*** (0.19) | -1.24*** (0.13) |
| Liberal Democrat partisan | — | — | — | — | 1.12*** (0.22) | 0.36* (0.19) |
| Political attention* Reversion point | — | — | 0.47** (0.17) | 0.50 (0.35) | — | — |
| Political attention* Proposal | — | — | 0.43 (0.33) | 0.58* (0.32) | — | — |
| Labour* Government cue | — | — | — | — | 0.73** (0.34) | 0.22 (0.33) |
| Constant | -0.85*** (0.13) | 0.03 (0.09) | -4.69*** (0.29) | 1.52*** (0.52) | -1.06*** (0.18) | 0.37*** (0.13) |
| N | 1953 | — | 1953 | — | 1953 | — |
| McFadden's R squared | 0.02 | — | 0.37 | — | 0.10 | — |

*Source*: Lisbon Treaty referendum experiment *** $p < .01$; ** $p < .05$; * $p < .10$.

not respond to this treatment.[11] The Labour government, which was in power at the time of the survey, was in favour of joining the Euro (when certain conditions were met). Entry into the Euro-zone was also supported by the Liberal Democrats, whereas the Conservatives strongly opposed it. We can also see that party identification generally has the expected effect vote intention: Labour and Liberal Democrat supporters are more likely to vote yes than no, whereas Conservative identifiers are much more likely to vote no. These results are thus similar to those presented in Chapters 3 and 4, which illustrated that people who identify with parties recommending a yes are more likely to support a referendum proposal. By using experimental methods, we are able not only to examine the effect of partisanship on vote choice, but also to explicitly model how citizens respond to elite cues, without concerns about endgeneity.

The relationship between vote choice, government evaluations and partisanship can also be illustrated graphically. In Figure 5.1, we show the vote intention of respondents who were exposed to the government endorsement cue, using data from the Euro referendum experiment. The figure shows vote intention as a function of respondents' evaluation of the government's performance as well as their partisanship.[12]

Figure 5.1 shows that citizens' vote decision is dependent not only on their partisan affiliation, but also on how they evaluate the government's performance at a particular point in time. Labour supporters who are exposed to the elite endorsement, are likely to support the ballot proposal when they feel that the government has done a good job, but they are far more likely to reject it when they are dissatisfied with the government's performance. Unsurprisingly, Conservative supporters have less than a 25 per cent probability of supporting the Euro proposal, regardless of what they feel about the government's performance. As shown in Table 5.5, voters' responsiveness to government cues and government performance is thus strongly mediated by partisanship.

Table 5.6 illustrates the results for the same models applied to the Lisbon Treaty referendum experiment.

Again, the first model shows that government endorsements make respondents more likely to vote yes, but they do not make potential no-voters significantly more uncertain. In model 2, we estimate the conditioning effect of political attention, controlling attitudes towards European unification.[13] Unlike the previous experiment, the proposal and reversion frames are not 'equivalency frames', and we therefore expect that politically attentive respondents will be more likely to pick up on the information provided in these frames. As expected, we find that the

**Framing Effects**

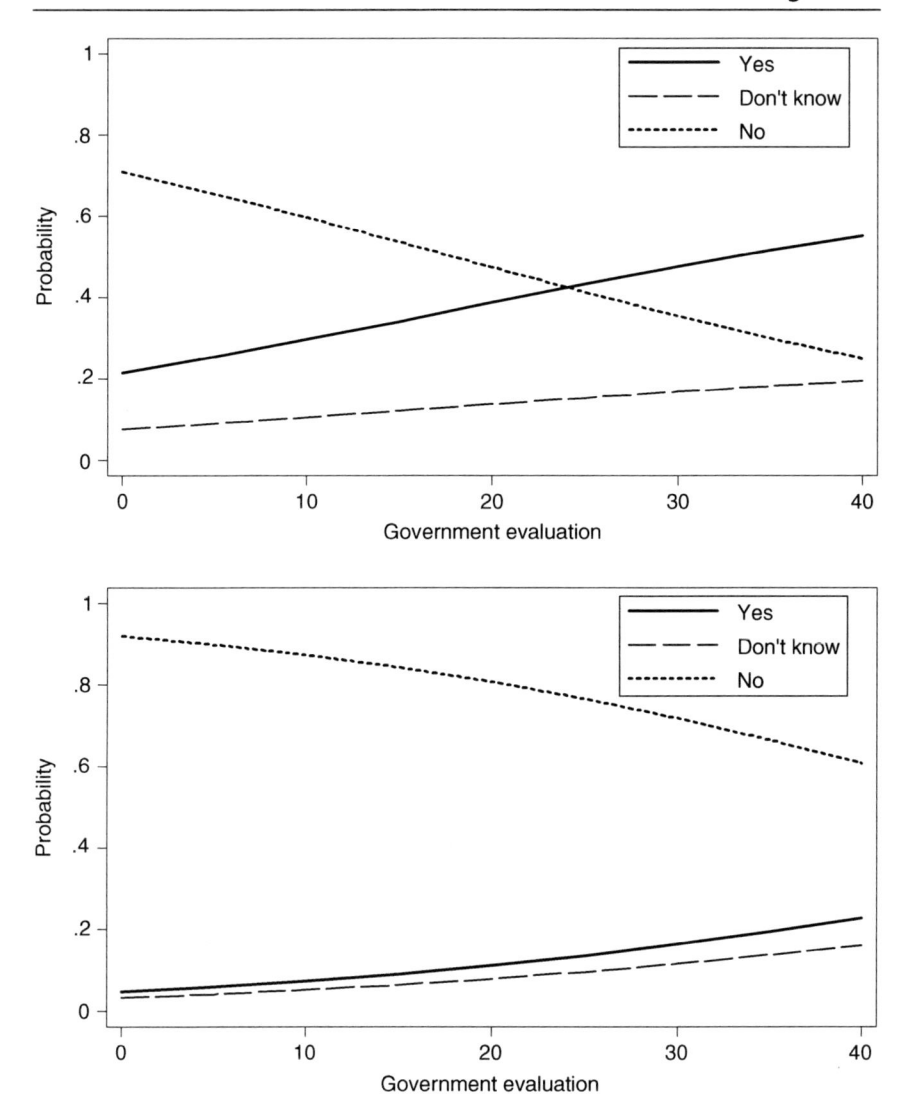

**Figure 5.1.** Effect of government evaluation and cues on Euro vote. (*a*) Labour supporters; (*b*) Conservative supporters.

*Note*: The figures show predicted probabilities of vote choice for Labour/Conservative party identifiers with mean EU attitudes who were exposed to a government endorsement frame.

*Source*: 2001 BES campaign study.

interaction between the reversion point frame and political awareness is positive and significant. This suggests that more politically aware citizens are more likely to respond to this frame. However, none of the other interactions are significant at the 95 per cent level. These mixed results lend some support to our hypothesis, but also echo the disagreement in

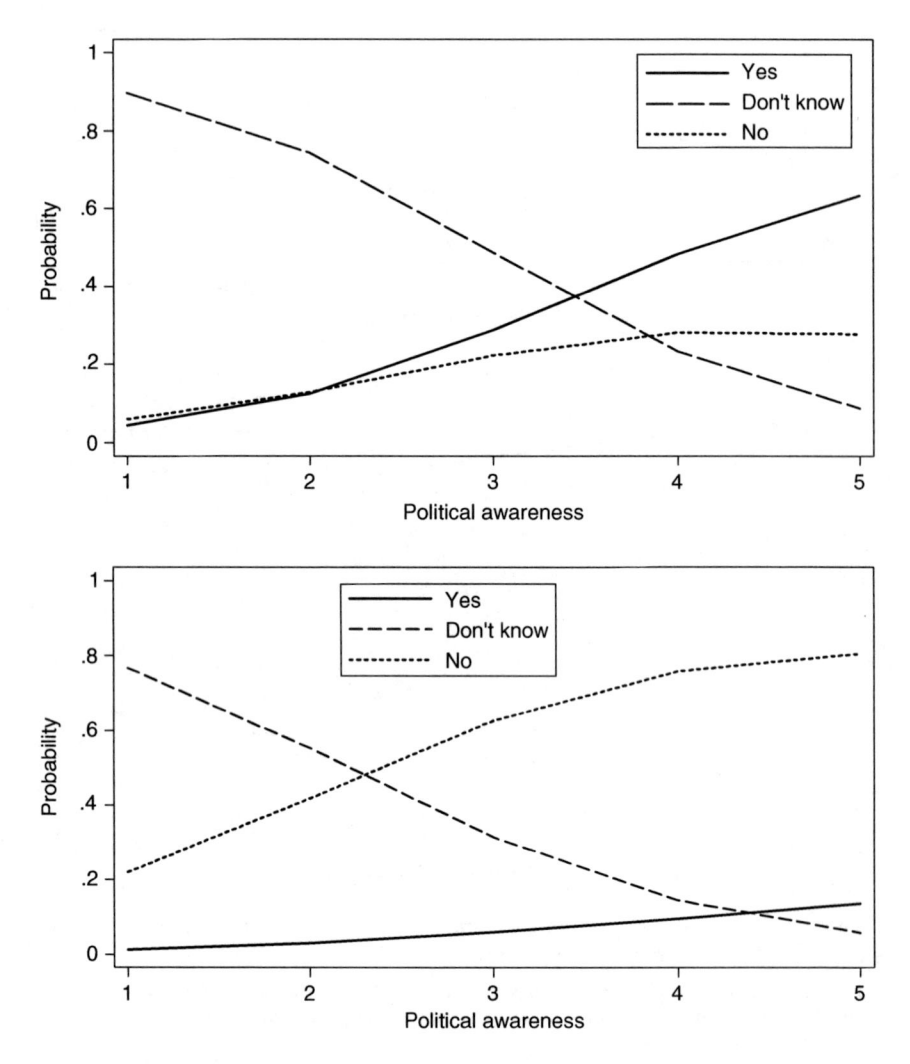

**Figure 5.2.** Effect of political awareness on Lisbon Treaty vote. (*a*) Labour supporters, (*b*) Conservative supporters

Note: The figures show predicted probabilities of vote choice for Labour/Conservative party identifiers with mean EU attitudes who were exposed to issue frames.
Source: Lisbon Treaty referendum experiment, 2008.

the literature concerning the effect of political awareness as a moderator of framing effects. On the one hand, political sophisticates hold stronger prior attitudes and are thus less likely to change their mind. On the other hand, they are more likely to pick up on frames, given their knowledge, and integrate it into their utility calculation. To illustrate the effect of political awareness on vote intention, we plot the vote intention of those respondents exposed to either of the two issue frames in Figure 5.2. We plot the vote intention of both Labour and Conservative Party identifiers.

Figure 5.2 shows that lack of political awareness is likely to lead to indecision for both groups of party supporters. Yet, it is interesting to note that as awareness increases, Labour supporters are more likely to favour the proposal, whereas Conservative supporters are more likely to reject the proposal as they become more knowledgeable. These figures thus illustrate that political awareness, combined with issue frames, makes people more likely to have an opinion on the ballot proposal, yet this opinion is tempered by pre-existing attitudes and loyalties.

As illustrated in Figure 5.2, the final model in Table 5.6 shows that partisanship operates as a reliable moderator of framing effects: as in the previous experiment, we find that only Labour supporters respond to the government endorsement cue. We also find the same main effects: Labour and Liberal Democrat partisans are more likely to support the treaty, whereas Conservative supporters are less supportive.

## 5.4. Conclusion

This chapter has employed survey experiments to investigate framing effects in referendums. The experimental evidence has clearly shown that issue frames and elite endorsements can sway public opinion. We have found that frames that emphasize the consequences of a yes- or a no-vote in the referendum influence citizens' vote intention. When the negative consequences of a no-vote are highlighted, more people favour the proposal, and when the negative consequences of a yes-vote were presented to respondents, more people decided to oppose the proposal. Put in spatial terms, these frames can be seen to push either the proposal or the reversion point to a more extreme position, further away from the ideal point of most voters. Moreover, this chapter has shown that endorsements by governments make citizens who are positively disposed towards the government more likely to support a ballot proposal.

But in real-world campaigns, voters are exposed to competing elite cues and conflicting frames, highlighting both negative and positive consequences of the proposal and the reversion point. So what, if any, inferences can we draw from these one-sided experiments? First, our results imply that issue frames provide information to voters, which makes them more likely to express an opinion on the issue at stake. This echoes the findings in Chapter 4, which showed that individuals who were more exposed to the campaign information were more likely to rely on their issue attitudes when voting and less likely to abstain. Second, the fact that referendum campaigns are competitive environments does not imply that issue frames have no effects. Chong and Druckman (2007*b*: 640) have found that in competitive environments, 'strong frames will dominate weak frames because strong frames will be considered more applicable to the issue'. The 'strength' of a frame is determined by a number of factors, including the quality of the argument, the saliency of the message, and the credibility of the source. Perceptions of credibility will vary across contexts and across individuals. In Chapter 7 we explore how the 'frames' employed by the elites in two Danish and two Irish referendums were more or less successful depending on such factors. A third, and related, point is that the effectiveness of frames depends in large part on individual abilities and pre-existing attitudes and loyalties. The analyses in this chapter have clearly shown how government endorsements only have an effect on those citizens who are already positively disposed towards the government. In a competitive campaign environment, party endorsements are thus likely to have an effect, but they will be mediated by voters' feelings towards the party as well as their pre-existing attitudes. The analysis of the mediating effect of political awareness presented a more mixed picture, which suggests that politically aware voters are more responsive to information provided by issue frames, but less susceptible to 'equivalency frames'.

This chapter has thus shown that citizens do respond to the messages provided by elites. Yet, their responses are tempered by pre-existing attitudes and partisanship and mediated by their knowledge of politics. This raises the important question of citizen competence: are voters too easily manipulated by elites, too fickle and uninformed, to make competent decisions in referendums? Framing effects have often been described as a sign of 'citizen incompetence,' but this may not necessarily be the right inference to make. The evidence in this chapter has shown that while public opinion is swayed by the information provided by frames, this information also provides them with more firm opinions on the

# Framing Effects

proposal and these opinions are broadly in line with pre-existing attitudes and loyalties. As Druckman (2001a: 246) notes, 'citizens appear to consciously weigh the considerations suggested by elite frames, compare these consideration to their predispositions and information, and contemplate the source of the frame. This all suggests that citizens deal with elite frames in a relatively competent and well-reasoned manner'. The question of citizen competence in referendums is examined in more detail in the next chapter.

## Notes

1. Nelson and Kinder (1996: 1057).
2. This model is related to the so-called 'accessibility model', which stresses that frames operate by making a person's pre-existing considerations more accessible in the minds of voters and hence more important in the opinion formation process (Kinder and Sanders 1996; Slothuus 2008; Zaller 1992).
3. Druckman (2001a, 2001b), however, has examined how the credibility of elites influences the effectiveness of their frames. He finds that perceived source credibility is a prerequisite for successful elite framing.
4. When the Euro experiment was conducted in 2001, there was a real possibility that the Labour government would hold a referendum on the single currency during that parliamentary period. Equally, there were strong pressures on the Labour government to hold a referendum on the Lisbon Treaty in 2008 due to the party's manifesto pledge to hold a referendum on the Constitutional Treaty. Hence, in both instances the questions on vote intention were not entirely hypothetical.
5. Interviews were carried out by telephone using a CATI system. The data and supporting documentation are available from the UK Data Archive at the University of Essex. See Appendix 1.
6. It is not clear that this experiment was designed with a clear control group in mind. The investigators do not compare with a specific control group in their analysis of this experiment, but compare treatment groups instead (see Clarke et al. 2005). However, with no explicit baseline, it is more difficult for the researcher to evaluate which treatments shape attitudes (see Gaines et al. 2007). Hence, in this analysis I designate the first treatment group as the 'control' and compare the other groups with this baseline. In the design of the second experiment, I explicitly included a control group as a baseline for testing the effectiveness of each of the frames.
7. Diagnostic checks on both experiments failed to indicate that the multinomial logit analyses suffered from violations of the IIA (independence from irrelevant alternatives) assumption, and re-estimating the analyses using

multinomial probit produced results very similar to those presented in Tables 5.5 and 5.6.
8. The main findings are the same when we estimate the effects of treatments 3 and 4 separately.
9. Attention to politics is measured using the following question: 'On a scale from 0–10 where 10 means a *great deal of attention* [emphasis in original] and 0 means *no attention* [emphasis in original], how much attention do you pay to politics and public affairs?'
10. Attitude towards the EU is measured by asking respondents whether they strongly disapprove, disapprove, approve, or strongly approve of Britain's membership of the EU.
11. The party identification data are gathered using the question: 'Generally speaking, do you think of yourself as Conservative, Labour, Liberal Democrat or what?' We coded three dummies for Labour, Conservative and Liberal Democrat identifiers. Other party supporters and respondents with no party identification were coded as the reference category. For the sake of simplicity, we only include the interaction between government supporters and government cue in model 3. When we also include the interaction between opposition supporters (Conservatives and Liberal Democrats) and government cue in the model the coefficient on the government interaction remains significant and positive, but the opposition interactions are insignificant. We find the same results in the Lisbon Treaty experiment.
12. To measure evaluations of government performance, respondents were asked to use 11-point scales to rate how well the incumbent government had performed in four policy areas: (i) health care, (ii) taxation, (iii) education, and (iv) crime. The question is: 'How many marks out of 10 would you give the Government for its performance in each of the following areas: (a) the National Health Service, (b) taxation; (c) education; (d) the level of crime in Britain'. On the basis of these questions, we created an additive scale of government performance, ranging from 0–40.
13. EU attitudes are measured using the question: 'Some say European unification should be pushed further. Others say it already has gone too far. What is your opinion? Please indicate your views using a 10-point-scale. On this scale, 1 means unification "has already gone too far" and 10 means it "should be pushed further". What number on this scale best describes your position?'.

# Part III

# Case Studies

# 6

# Voter Competence: What do Voters Need to Know?

> *Democracy is based upon the conviction that there are extraordinary possibilities in ordinary people.*[1]
> 
> —Harry Emerson Fosdick

The above quote implies a possible tension between the capabilities of ordinary citizens and the requirements of democratic governance. Nowhere is this tension more apparent than in referendums, where citizens are asked not merely to choose delegates or caretakers who can make policies on their behalf, but rather to cast judgements on important and often complex policy questions. In the case of European integration referendums, citizens are asked to determine the future of European economic and political integration with consequences that reach beyond their own nation. Faced with this juxtaposition between *ordinary* citizens and *extraordinary* choices, it is important to ask: Are citizens sufficiently competent to vote in referendums?

The previous chapters have examined *how* voters behave in referendums and the ways in which political information affects patterns of behaviour. This brings us to the question of how voters *ought to* behave. Only by explicitly addressing the normative issue of whether voters are capable of taking reasoned and competent decisions in referendums, can we shed light on some of the key issues in the debate on EU referendums, such as how to interpret the public rejections of ballot proposals and whether direct democracy should be encouraged as a device for involving and engaging citizens in democratic governance in Europe. Hence, this chapter addresses the following questions: How do we define competent voting in European integration referendums; and How can voter competence be measured; More specifically, the chapter focuses on the types of information that are necessary and sufficient to induce competent voting. In other words, it considers the question: What do voters need to know?

One of the criticisms often levelled against the use of direct democracy concerns the lack of voter competence. Since voters are struggling to make informed choices in normal elections, scholars have questioned whether they will be able to make competent decisions when asked to vote directly on unfamiliar and complex issues (Bowler and Donovan 1998; Christin, Hug, and Sciarini 2002). What is missing from this debate, however, is a systematic exposition of what exactly we mean by *competent voting* in referendums and how this can be measured. This chapter proposes a framework for evaluating voter competence in referendums. First, it proposes the normative expectation of issue proximity voting, arguing that voters are expected to make decisions on the basis of preferences relevant to the task at hand. Second, the chapter considers the type of information required for voters to accomplish this task. The previous chapters have shown that issue voting requires a certain amount of knowledge. This chapter examines in greater detail how different types of information can impede or promote competent voting. In particular, the analysis focuses on the highly visible 'endorsement heuristics' provided by political parties in referendum campaigns and examines whether these cues can function as substitutes for detailed knowledge of the ballot proposal. The main findings suggest that partisan endorsements can aid competent behaviour, but only to the extent that voters are sufficiently knowledgeable about party positions on the European integration dimension.

This chapter proceeds as follows. After a brief evaluation of knowledge and information levels amongst European citizens, a conceptualization of voter competence in EU referendums is presented. Secondly, it discusses the extent to which partisan endorsements can be expected to provide reliable substitutes for detailed information. Finally, the theoretical propositions are evaluated empirically in a detailed analysis of the 1994 Norwegian referendum on membership.

## 6.1. Information and knowledge

> *If most American voters lack factual information, a constraining ideology, and an ability to deal with issues in highly publicized candidate races, how can they be expected to sort through the complex policy choices they face in the low information setting of direct democracy?*[2]
>
> —Shaun Bowler and Todd Donovan

Table 6.1. Public knowledge of national and European politics

|  | Correct answer (%) |
|---|---|
| *National political knowledge (1993)*\* | |
| National capital | 90 |
| Head of national government | 87 |
| National legislative authority | 42 |
| Members of national government | 42 |
| *EU political knowledge (1993)*\* | |
| Capital for EU institutions | 71 |
| Commission president | 42 |
| Legislative authority in EU | 19 |
| Members of EU Commission | 7 |
| *EU political knowledge (2007)*\*\* | |
| Number of member states | 57 |
| Presidency of the EU | 49 |
| Method of electing MEPs | 45 |
| Feeling informed about European politics | 30 |

Sources: \*Eurobarometer 39.0, fieldwork conducted in 1993.
N: 14,039 (respondents from 12 member states and Norway).
\*\* Eurobarometer 67.2, fieldwork conducted in May 2007.
N: 29,222 (respondents from 27 member states, and Croatia and Turkey).

As Bowler and Donovan suggest, it seems reasonable to question the ability of voters to make reasoned decisions under direct democracy, given the findings of voter ignorance in representative processes of democracy. Despite the democratic ideal of an informed electorate, numerous studies have shown that most people have very limited knowledge about policy issues and party platforms (see, e.g. Campbell 1960 et al.; Delli Carpini and Keeter 1991). Studies have also shown that European citizens tend to know considerably less about politics at the European level than about domestic matters. Eurobarometer survey data[3] allow us to compare citizens' knowledge of European and national political affairs.

Table 6.1 indicates that, while generally having little knowledge of political affairs, voters are more ignorant about political affairs at the European level than at the national level. Whereas a majority of Europeans can correctly identify Brussels as the 'capital' for EU institutions, they are unable to answer basic questions about the Union's political system, such as the final legislative authority (only 19% answered correctly) or identify members of the Union's executive (only 7% could identify a member, while 42% could name the president). The results from a more recent survey conducted in 2007 give no more reason for optimism about citizens' knowledge about the EU. When asked whether the statement that 'The

EU currently consists of fifteen Member States' is true or false, only 57 per cent of respondents could correctly identify this claim as false. Perhaps even more surprisingly, less than half of respondents knew that Members of the European Parliament are directly elected, despite the six EU-wide elections to the European Parliament held since 1979. Half of respondents were also unfamiliar with the rotating presidency in the EU and only 30 per cent felt that they were 'fairly well informed about European political affairs'.

These findings of public ignorance have been used as a justification for avoiding plebiscites altogether. In the words of Belgium's former Foreign Minister, Erik Derycke: 'I'm glad that we have no referendums. How for God's sake are you going to explain a complicated thing like the Euro in a yes-and-no question to voters?'[4] Similar concerns have been voiced by politicians in countries that hold frequent referendums on European questions. The former EU spokesperson of Denmark's governing Liberal Party, Charlotte Antonsen, has observed that, 'Denmark has chosen to consult the public on the most complicated area in politics. In all other areas, we are happy for Parliament to decide. But the EU, which is perhaps the most complicated of all, we subject to referendums. That's a little absurd'.[5]

But how much detailed information do voters need to make competent choices in referendums? Are voters required to have a detailed understanding of the intricacies of the Euro or to know the names of all of the members of the European Commission in order to make a competent decision in an EU referendum? As described in Chapter 2, the basic idea of recent research on the relationship between information and voting is that limited information need not prevent people from making competent vote choices. This strand of literature defines competent voting as voters choosing the same way as they would have done if perfect information were available (see for example Lupia 1994, 2001, 2006; Lau and Redlawsk 1997). To achieve this, voters can use various types of information shortcuts as substitutes for detailed factual knowledge about politics. Heuristics are also a useful tool for voters to arrive at competent decision in referendums. In particular, party endorsements may offer a type of judgement shortcut that allows citizens to infer their own position on a ballot issue without detailed information about the proposal itself (Sniderman 2000; Lau and Redlawsk 2001). However, as the critics of the heuristics literature have pointed out, it is not reasonable to simply assume that such heuristics can work and substitute for domain-specific knowledge (Bartels 1996; Kuklinski and Quirk 2000). In his empirical analysis of information effects in American presidential elections, Bartels (1996) finds that fully informed voters act very differently from less informed voters. This suggests that information differentials are not entirely overcome by the use of heuristics. These findings, however, are not surprising given that some contextual knowledge is needed to employ heuristics effectively. Bartels examines differences across levels of political sophistication, but he does not examine whether different types of information have similar effects on patterns of behaviour. Yet, if we want to examine the effectiveness of cues in aiding competent decision-making, the latter is as important as the former. Hence, this chapter examines whether certain types of information—in particular, party endorsements—can work as effectively as detailed information about the ballot proposal. But first, we need to define the concept of competent voting in the specific context of EU referendums.

## 6.2. Conceptualizing voter competence

When we study voting behaviour, we make inferences about what causes people to act in a certain way: How do voters decide between candidates, parties, or issues? Examining voter competence is somewhat different because we are not only interested in understanding how people decide how to vote, but we also have certain *normative expectations* about how they ought to behave. How do we decide on these normative criteria? This question is seldom answered explicitly in empirical studies of voter competence. Part of the reason lies in the inherent difficulty in establishing competence measures in politics where there are no objective standards of better and worse, right and wrong: 'there is no single right way to vote, no single right position on an issue, no single right set of beliefs. From the standpoint of studying citizen competence, this observation is bad news' as Kuklinski and Quirk (2001: 285) have noted. Yet, while we cannot establish a universally agreed-upon conceptualization and measurement of voter competence, we can make an attempt to engage in a systematic debate about these issues by setting out explicit theoretical propositions and empirical measures that can be evaluated.

Kuklinski and Quirk (2001: 287) suggest that the first step in evaluating civic competence should be to 'identify the *task* that the actor is asked to undertake'. Competence, then, concerns the ability of individuals to accomplish this specific task. The task of a voter in a referendum is to choose between two policy alternatives, the ballot proposition, and the reversion point. But would it be regarded as normatively desirable for voters to answer the question in any way they see fit? Would we consider it competent behaviour if voters simply pick the first option on the ballot, or if they, for example, answer on the basis of the number of red lights that they crossed on the way to the polling station, their feelings about the state of the national economy, or their evaluation of the performance of the government of the day? While the latter two reasons, at least, cannot be dismissed as entirely *irrational* behaviour, they may be seen as normatively undesirable. Why? Because our normative expectation is that there is a clear link between the question asked (the ballot proposal) and the answer provided by the individual voter (the vote choice). Hence, while a *rational* choice may simply imply 'one that is based on reasons, irrespective of what these reasons may be' (Lupia et al. 2000: 7), a *competent* choice is related to the accomplishment of a specific task and it should thus be based on preferences pertaining to that task. As Druckman (2001: 232) notes, democratic competence 'concerns the expression of [citizen] preferences to which governors can and should respond'. But governors can only respond appropriately to the expression of voter preferences if these expressions relate to the question posed.

This chapter thus proposes a narrow conceptualization of competence that, unlike the broader notions of reasoning or rationality, refers to the accomplishment of a specific task. A competent vote in referendums can thus be defined as one that is based on preferences specific to the issue on the ballot and which would be the same if full information were available. Note that this definition differs from the more generic version presented in the heuristics literature, since voters are not merely expected to vote 'as if' they were fully informed, but they are also expected to rely on 'proximity considerations' related to the ballot proposal. Issue voting is normatively desirable because of the specific *objective of the task* posed to citizens. This will be discussed in more detail below.

### 6.2.1. *Issue-specific versus second-order voting*

To understand how citizens can competently accomplish a political task, we need to consider the specific objective of that task. To be precise: What is the purpose of asking people to decide on a proposition concerning

European integration? From the perspective of democratic theory, the broad objective may be to ensure an element of 'government by the people'. More specifically, the purpose of holding referendums on aspects of European integration, at least from a normative perspective, is the public legitimization or veto of an EU-related policy proposal. In the context of European integration, public veto power can be seen as particularly important since these proposals involve the surrender of national sovereignty to a supranational body; that is, the transfer of powers from national representatives to European (elected and non-elected) officials.[6] But to achieve the politically desirable outcome of legitimizing a transfer of sovereignty, it is vital that voters decide on the issue posed to them. As van der Eijk and Franklin have noted in their study of elections to the European Parliament:

The logic of democratic elections presupposes that the political verdict of electorates can be construed as emanating from the political preferences of voters, preferences that are relevant to the decision-making arena concerned (van der Eijk and Franklin 1996: 6).

The same is true for EU referendums, where we expect voters to base their choice on preferences related to the European question, so the outcome of the referendum can be seen as a democratic mandate for (or against) a particular policy option. Yet, we know from the literature and the empirical evidence presented in Chapter 3 that voters in reality often base their choices on 'second-order' factors that are not based on issue-specific preferences. Some scholars have pointed to the potentially negative consequences of second-order voting (see, for example, van der Eijk and Franklin 1996; Norris 1998; Garry, Marsh, and Sinnott 2005). Garry, Marsh, and Sinnott (2005: 205) have reasoned that while issue voting, 'assumes a rational and reasoned calculation by the voter based on his or her views on EU matters... (t)he second-order approach sees voting in EU referendums simply as a chance for voters to express their domestic political preferences'. A common interpretation thus suggests that second-order voting is less rational and reasoned than issue-specific voting (see also van der Eijk and Franklin 1996: 28). Yet, the conceptualization presented here does not suggest that 'second-order' voting is necessarily irrational, but rather that it lacks competence from a normative perspective. We can thus make a distinction between *rational* and *competent* voting. For example, it may be rational (i.e. based on strategic reason) for a British voter to reject an EU ballot proposal, such as the (hypothetical) ballot on the Lisbon Treaty described in Chapter 5, because she wants to punish the

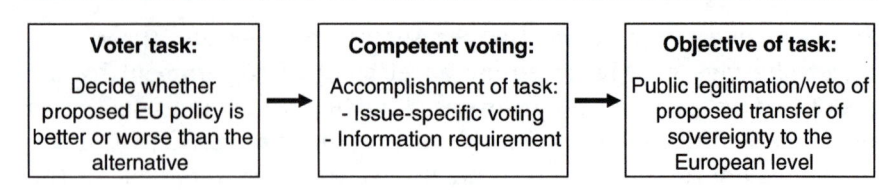

| Voter task: | Competent voting: | Objective of task: |
|---|---|---|
| Decide whether proposed EU policy is better or worse than the alternative | Accomplishment of task:<br>- Issue-specific voting<br>- Information requirement | Public legitimation/veto of proposed transfer of sovereignty to the European level |

Figure 6.1. Voter competence in EU referendums

Labour government for going to war in Iraq. This vote choice, however, is not *competent*, because it does not accomplish the specific task, namely to choose the better of the two alternatives: the Lisbon Treaty or the reversion point. As Garry, Marsh, and Sinnott (2005: 206) note: 'if the second-order model is correct, we should beware of inferring, in the event of a 'yes' vote on EU treaty changes, that the electorate was in favour of the substantive content of the treaty in question'. The conceptualization of voter competence in European referendum can be summarized in a graphical chart.

Figure 6.1 illustrates that voter competence, as it has been conceptualized here, is related to the specific task facing the voters and the objective of that task. Competent voting is thus based on issue-specific proximity considerations. As discussed in Chapter 2, issue proximity voting requires voters to have a certain knowledge of how their issue preferences relate to the specific ballot proposal and the reversion point, that is, competent voting requires information. But while some information is certainly needed, issue proximity voting does not necessarily demand voters to have detailed and 'encyclopaedic' knowledge about European integration, since voters can rely on shortcuts to overcome their information shortfalls. Given the limited knowledge that most voters have about European politics, they will, to a large extent, rely on such cues. But heuristics, such as elite cues, may not always enable voters to act competently. To enhance competent behaviour, cues should signal to the voters where they are located in relation to the two alternatives on the ballot. For voters to be able to rely on this information, they also need information about the interests and location of the information provider. In other words, 'competence-enhancing' cues should convey the relative utility of the ballot proposal versus the reversion point. The nature of such cues will be discussed below, but first we need to address the question of how voter competence can be measured.

## 6.2.2. Measuring voter competence

According to Kuklinski and Quirk (2001), the conceptualization of civic competence should be followed by the selection of empirical *indicators* that allow us to measure competence empirically and *standards* that enable us to categorize performance. As mentioned above, it has been common practice in studies of civic competence to focus on *information levels*, and this type of measurement of competence levels tends to involve some analysis of people's factual knowledge of political affairs (Luskin 1987, 1990; Delli Carpini and Keeter 1996). As the heuristics school moved away from the focus on information levels to an emphasis on information processing, they also adopted a different approach to the measurement of competence. Rather than setting certain standards for factual knowledge levels, many researchers have focused on whether voters can act 'as if' they were fully informed. Competent behaviour can thus be examined by comparing voters across different levels and types of information; or what Kuklinski and Quirk (2001: 296) have referred to as the 'well-informed-proxy group comparison'. Applying this method involves selecting a group of well-informed citizens and comparing their behaviour with that of the voters who are less informed. If the less-informed approximate the behaviour of the well-informed, then their behaviour is seen to be competent, and the presumption is that competency is achieved by relying on informative heuristics (see, e.g. Lupia 1994). Hence it is assumed in the literature that the more informed voters are the competent voters.

As was shown in Chapter 3, higher levels of knowledge of European affairs lead to more issue voting in EU referendums. These findings are thus consistent with the expectations of the literature on information effects, but what do they actually tell us about voter competence? People with higher levels of factual knowledge may be more competent voters, yet we also know from the literature that voter competence can be achieved by using cues rather than having detailed knowledge of EU affairs. Hence, in the empirical examination of voter competence, we compare voter competence across both *levels* and *types* of information to establish what type of heuristic information is sufficient for competent performances. Before proceeding to the analyses of voting behaviour, the next section addresses the issue of party endorsements as cues in referendums in greater detail.

## 6.3. Party endorsements as cues

The endorsements of political parties are arguably the most important 'informational shortcuts' provided in EU referendums. Parties are the key actors articulating and aggregating political interests and simplifying political choices for voters. The analysis of media coverage during referendum campaigns[7] corroborates this thesis: party endorsements receive far more attention than the endorsements provided by interest organizations, NGOs and public personas. The contest is framed by the media mainly by referring to the arguments provided by different political parties.[8] Moreover, as the *setter* of the referendum, the governing party (or parties) has considerable signalling power in terms of deciding the specific timing and wording of the referendum proposal (Lupia and Johnston 2001). Since political parties are likely to provide the most important—albeit not the only—informational cues to voters about how to vote, it is important to understand the nature of these cues and how they are processed.

Partisan endorsements can enhance competence by signalling to voters where their ideal point is located in relation to the two alternatives on the ballot; that is, by informing the voter which choice is better for them. Relying on the party endorsements of the preferred party seems an obvious choice for most voters, since voters are generally aware of their own proximity to the party (Zaller 1992). By structuring the 'choice set' for citizens, parties may allow them to make choices approximately coherently, despite their informational shortfalls (Sniderman 2000). The experimental evidence presented in Chapter 5 illustrated that citizens are more susceptible to be influenced by endorsement when they think highly of the endorser. Other experiments on framing have shown that party cues can help citizens overcome framing effects, since cues provide information about the credibility of the information provided (Druckman 2001*a*, *b*). Despite these potential advantages of endorsements, we need to consider two important caveats. First, while heuristics can help voters overcome information shortfalls, the effective use of endorsements also requires information (Kuklinski and Quirk 2000). Second, under certain circumstances party endorsements may in fact mislead citizens. Even advocates of the heuristics approach acknowledge that some information is needed to take advantage of the heuristic shortcuts. As Sniderman (2000: 72) has pointed out, '[I]t takes smarts to take advantage of smart moves'. It is reasonable to assume that partisan cues will only work effectively if they give reliable information about the specific task at hand. As Lau and Redlawsk (2002) have observed, endorsements can work

## Voter Competence

against voters when the question at hand is not structured in the typical manner.

Ballot proposals in EU referendums will often cut across traditional dimensions of contestation. The Left-Right cleavage remains the main dimension structuring political contestation in most European countries. In national elections most voters choose a preferred party based on where they are located on the Left-Right dimension (Evans 2000). Voters can therefore rely on partisan cues to give them information on how their preferences relate to a specific policy proposal based on this knowledge. In EU referendums, however, voters are asked to vote on issues related to European integration, and the question is whether the EU positions of political parties can be read from their position on the left-right dimension. Whereas European integration engages national sovereignty and mobilizes territorial groups, the Left-Right dimension involves the allocation of values among class and functional interests (Marks and Steenbergen 2004). If these two dimensions are orthogonal, then partisan endorsements may be misleading and fail to enhance competence in EU referendums. Several studies have shown that the European integration and Left-Right dimensions are in fact independent of each other (see, e.g. Hix 1999).[9] Moderate parties tend to be predominantly pro-European, whereas parties on the extreme left and extreme right are more Eurosceptic (Hooghe, Marks, and Wilson 2002). Van der Eijk and Franklin have even argued that, 'the democratic deficit in European elections is due to the lack of correspondence between the dimensions of competition among national parties and the dimensions of conflict within the European arena' (1996: 381).

Using the Chapel Hill party expert survey 2002 (see Appendix 1), this nonlinear relationship between party positions on the Left-Right and the EU dimensions can be illustrated graphically.

Figure 6.2 depicts the positions of parties in the EU-27[10] and illustrates a curvilinear relationship between the Left-Right position and the European integration position of parties, resembling an inverted U-curve. Parties on the extreme of the political spectrum tend to be more anti-European than parties located around the centre. Hence, we find a strong and significant relationship when fitting a quadratic regression curve. However, this relationship disappears when we only examine the mainstream parties—that is the Socialist/Social Democratic, Liberal, Christian Democratic, and Conservative party families—which dominate national governments and represent approximately 80 per cent of electoral votes across the EU. This is illustrated in Figure 6.3.

**Europe in Question**

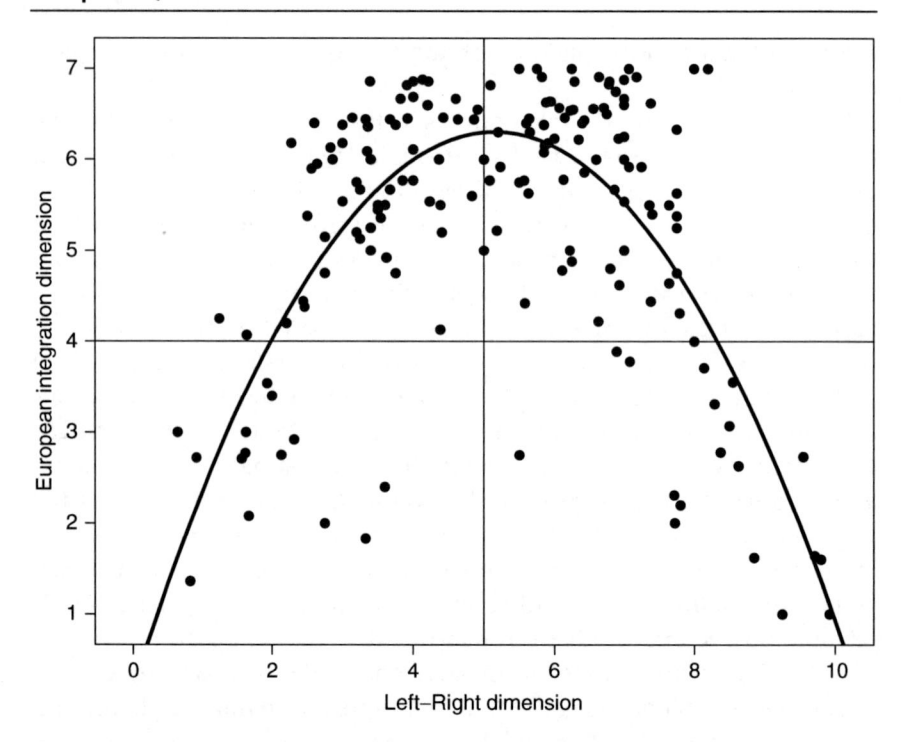

**Figure 6.2.** European party positions on Left–Right and European dimensions

*Note*: EU dimension (1–7): 'Overall orientation of the party leadership towards European integration in 2002'. 4 = neutral.
Left–Right dimension (0–10): Ideological position of the party in 2002, where 0 = extreme left; 10 = extreme right; and 5 = centre.
*Source*: Chapel Hill Party Dataset 2002.

As we can see from Figure 6.3, there is no apparent relationship between the Left-Right and the European positions of mainstream parties. Apart from the British Conservative Party (Cons) and the minor Slovenian National Party (SNS), all of the European mainstream parties are broadly pro-European. It is not possible to discern a party's more exact location on this dimension from any knowledge of its Left-Right position. We can therefore hypothesize that, since partisanship mainly relates to proximity on the left-right dimension, party endorsements can enhance competent voting in EU referendums only when voters have basic knowledge about the positions of parties on the EU dimension. This proposition will be examined empirically using a post-referendum study from the 1994 Norwegian accession referendum.

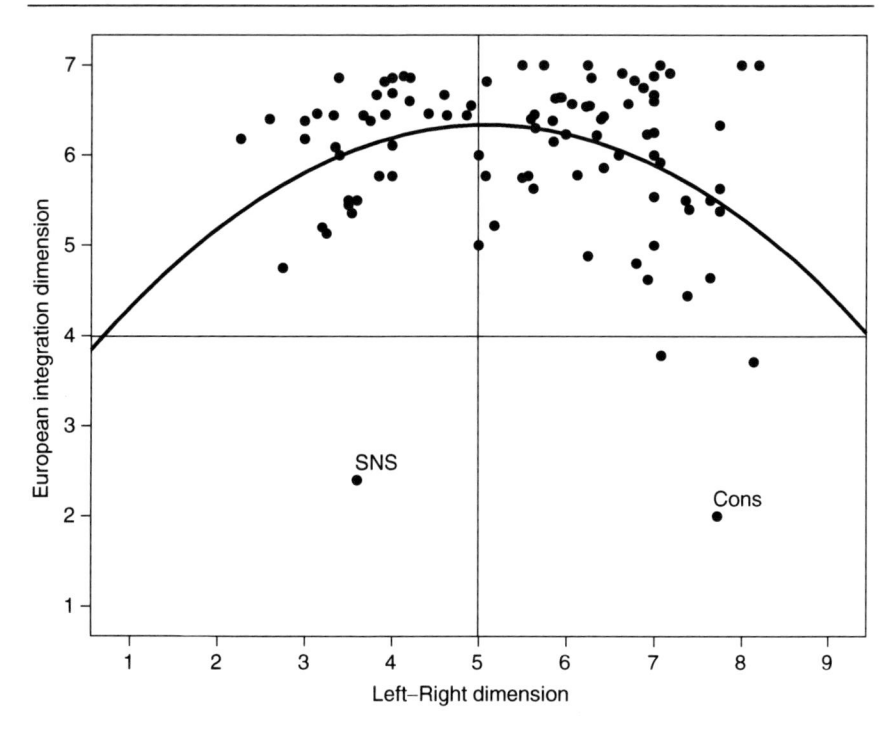

**Figure 6.3.** Positions of European mainstream parties

*Note*: Included in this analysis are parties belonging to the four major party families: Socialist, Liberal, Conservative, and Christian-Democratic.
*Source*: Chapel Hill Party Dataset 2002.

## 6.4. The Norwegian accession referendum

The 1994 referendum was the second Norwegian referendum on accession to the EU. In 1972, a small majority of voters (53.5%) rejected membership. In 1994, 89 per cent of Norwegians turned out to reject the accession for a second time by an even smaller majority of 52.2 per cent. The Norwegian 1994 referendum is an apposite case for examining voter competence in EU referendums, because the quality of the survey data allows us to examine the effect of different types of information in depth. Moreover, it provides a critical test of our examination of voter competence and cue-taking. European integration has been more politicized in Norway than in most other countries and all political parties have taken a clear stance on the issue (Aardal and Valen 1997; Midtbø and Hines 1998; Saglie 2000). Due to the high salience of the European issue we

**Europe in Question**

would expect voters to be more certain of their own issue preferences and better equipped to judge how the ballot proposal and the reversion point relate to these preferences. Moreover, party competition on the issue ought to make party endorsements more reliable cues in the referendum. In other words, if we find that voter competence is low and that partisan endorsements provide inadequate information in this referendum, we would expect even greater problems in EU referendums held in low-salience and low-information environments. On the other hand, if we find that voter competence is high among certain voters, this can teach us important lessons about the circumstances under which voters can act competently and the type of information necessary to achieve this. The Norwegian case makes it possible to examine these information effects because the post-referendum survey from the 1994 referendum contains a number of questions on the respondents' views on European integration and other political issues, as well as their perception of party positions and processing of informational cues.[11]

### 6.4.1. *Party endorsements and voter preferences*

The Norwegian debate on membership had begun already in November 1992, when the Labour government applied to join the EU, and it intensified after membership negotiations were launched in April 1993. The proposal of membership was initiated by the governing party, Labour (*Arbeiderpartiet*), which is by far the largest party in the Norwegian Parliament, *Stortinget*.[12] In addition, the main opposition party, the conservative *Høyre*, also supported membership, as did the populist right-wing party, the Progress Party (*Fremskrittspartiet*). Altogether these pro-EU parties made up 65 per cent of seats in *Stortinget*. Hence, on the basis of this information alone, we would predict that the membership proposal would pass. But only 60 per cent of the voters who identified with the pro-EU parties actually followed their recommendation. In comparison, 76 per cent of voters who identified with the anti-EU parties voted no. EU membership was opposed by *Senterpartiet*, an Agrarian centre party, as well as two small parties on the far left and two small centre-right parties. Hence, while Norwegian party politics is structured along the Left-Right dimension, the European integration issue had split the traditional blocs and created new political alliances (Aardal 1995; Saglie 2000). Figure 6.4 shows the location of the parties on the European and the Left-Right dimension, using data from Ray's party expert survey (see Appendix 1).[13] This figure also includes the mean position of the voters on these dimensions.[14]

Voter Competence

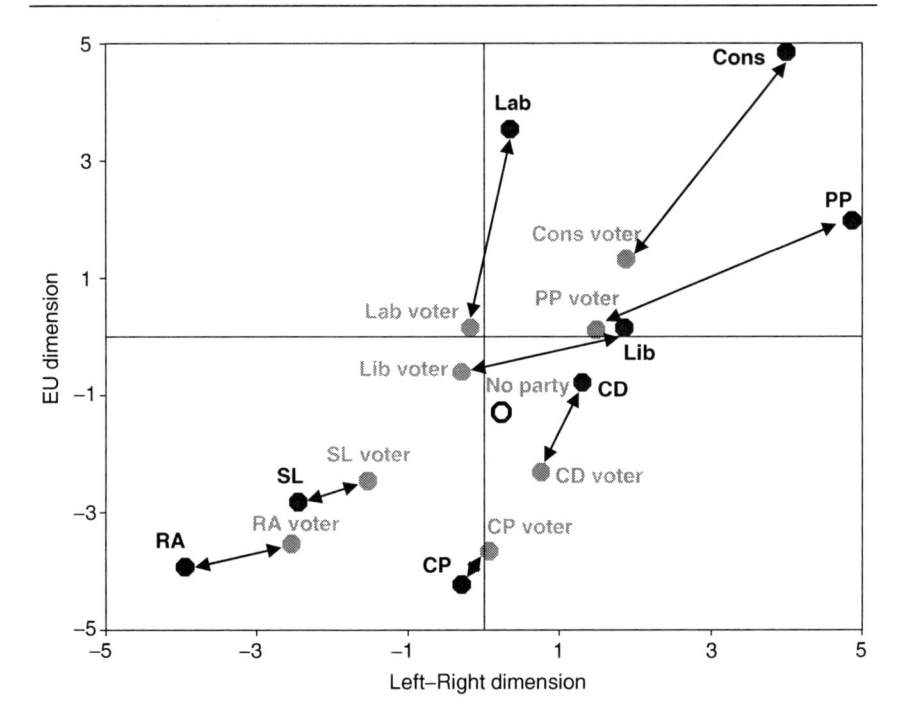

**Figure 6.4.** Party and voter positions in Norway on two dimensions

*Note*: Lab: Labour Party (*Arbeiderpartiet*); PP: Progress Party (*Fremskrittspartiet*); Cons: Conservative Party (*Høyre*); CD: Christian Peoples' Party (*Kristelig Folkeparti*); RA: Red Alliance List (*Rød Valgallianse*); CP: Centre Party (*Senterpartiet*); SL: Socialist Left Party (*Sosialistisk Venstreparti*); Lib: Liberal Party (*Venstre*) *No party*: voters who did not vote in the 1993 *Storting* election.

*Source*: EU-avstemningen 1994 and Leonard Ray's party expert survey. See Appendix 1.

As Figure 6.4 illustrates, there is an ambiguous relationship between the Left-Right dimension and the EU dimension in Norway. The extreme left tends to be very anti-EU, but not more so than the Centre Party. Another important finding is that voters tend to be closer to their parties on the Left-Right dimension than on the European dimension. This is particularly true for voters of the two largest parties, *Arbeiderpartiet* and *Høyre*. As argued above, these orthogonal dimensions may potentially reduce the ability of voters to act competently, since adhering to the endorsements of preferred parties based on proximities on the Left-Right dimension may give them little accurate information on where they are located on the European dimension. The important question is therefore not only the distance between voter and preferred party positions on the EU dimension, but also whether voters are aware of this distance.

**Table 6.2.** Distances between voters and parties

| Distance measure | All | Low political knowledge | Medium political knowledge | High political knowledge |
| --- | --- | --- | --- | --- |
| | Mean (S.D.) | Mean (S.D) | Mean (S.D) | Mean (S.D) |
| EU distance (ideal—actual party position) | 2.8 (2.3) | 3.4 (2.2) | 2.8 (2.3) | 2.6 (2.4) |
| EU distance (ideal—perceived party position) | 2.0 (2.5) | 2.0 (2.4) | 2.1 (2.4) | 1.9 (2.5) |
| Difference between actual and perceived proximity | 0.8 | 1.4 | 0.7 | 0.7 |
| Left-Right distance (ideal—actual party position) | 1.6 (1.3) | 1.6 (1.7) | 1.6 (1.6) | 1.6 (1.3) |
| Left-Right distance (ideal—perceived party position) | 0.8 (1.2) | 0.8 (1.2) | 1.2 (1.2) | 0.8 (1.2) |
| Difference between actual and perceived proximity | 0.8 | 0.8 | 0.8 | 0.8 |
| N | 3332 | 891 | 1540 | 901 |

*Note:* Absolute values indicate the numerical value of the distance on the scale without regard to its sign. Standard deviations in brackets.
*Sources:* 'EU-avstemningen 1994' and Ray's Party Expert Survey. See Appendix 1.

Voters are known to project their own views onto parties they support, thereby enhancing the appearance of consistency in their positions. Since the Norwegian post-referendum survey contains questions on both self-placement and the perceived position of parties on different policy dimensions, we can compare the 'perceived' distance between voters and parties with the 'actual' distance, based on party expert survey data. Table 6.2 shows the results for both dimensions.

Table 6.2 shows the mean distance in absolute values, since the real numbers would underestimate its magnitude when averaging over negative and positive numbers.[15] This table illustrates that the distance between parties and voters on the EU dimension is greater than on the left-right dimension. Using party expert survey data, the actual distance between voters and parties on the EU dimension is 2.8. This is a considerable distance on a 10-point scale. In comparison, the distance between voters and parties is only 1.6 on the Left-Right dimension. There is, however, no difference in the extent to which voters project their own views onto their preferred party. On both dimensions, voters perceive themselves to be on average 0.8 points closer to their party than the expert evaluation. It is interesting to note that, if we divide these results by level of political knowledge, voters with very limited knowledge of politics are

# Voter Competence

far more likely to 'project' (report a smaller distance than the experts) on the EU dimension than voters with higher level of political awareness, but these differences are not found on the Left-Right dimension. This indicates that a higher level of knowledge is required to interpret partisan cues on the European dimension correctly.

Following this we can conjecture that party endorsements may be potentially misleading if people have a very limited knowledge of party politics. On the other hand, clear party positions on this issue may provide useful cues to voters given that they are aware of these positions and how they differ from their own position. Our expectation is therefore that reception of partisan cues will enhance voter competence only if voters have the necessary knowledge to identify how the positions of parties on the EU differ from their own. This proposition will be tested below.

## 6.4.2. The impact of information on voter competence

Voter competence in EU referendums is conceptualized as the ability of voters to choose the alternative (proposal or reversion point) that is closest to their preferences on the issue of European integration. On this basis, how do we measure who voted 'competently' in the Norwegian referendum? It is inherently difficult to establish absolute standards for competent voting in a specific referendum. To get a very rough idea of the distribution of vote choices in the electorate, we present a cross-tabulation of vote choices depending on whether voters followed the recommendation of their preferred party and whether they voted according to their preferences. The difficulty lies in determining whether an individual voted according to his/her preferences, since we need to come up with a rather arbitrary 'cut-off point' on the EU attitude scale distinguishing 'positive' and 'negative' preferences. To get a rough idea of the distribution of vote choices, we can choose the middle value on the European integration scale as the cut-off point. Consequently for anyone choosing a value above the middle value, a yes vote is regarded as the correct choice, whereas for respondents choosing a value below the middle value, a no vote is regarded as the competent choice. The cross-tabulations are shown in Table 6.3.

Table 6.3 shows that for half of the voters, there was no conflict between the recommendation of their preferred party and their own attitudes. Of the remaining 50 per cent of voters receiving conflicting messages,

**Table 6.3.** Voting correctly?

|  | Vote in opposition to party (%) | Vote as party (%) |
|---|---|---|
| Vote against EU preference | 18 | 9 |
| Vote in line with EU preference | 23 | 50 |

*Note*: Cell values indicate percentage of all voters.

23 per cent became defectors and chose to follow their own convictions, 9 per cent opted for the party line, and 18 per cent—perhaps surprisingly—followed neither the party nor their own attitudes. These 18 per cent of voters may have voted on the basis of 'second-order' considerations or some other reasons not related to the ballot proposition or the party line. Hence, if competent voting constitutes voting on the basis of ones EU preferences, we can conclude that 73 per cent of voters in this referendum voted competently.

However, it would be too hasty to judge competence on this basis alone. In order to classify voters into categories of 'competent' and 'not competent', we would need to observe not only their true preferences on the EU dimension, but also the location of the ballot proposal and the reversion point, as outlined in the spatial model in Chapter 2. While we can reasonably argue that accession to the EU is more 'pro-integration' than staying outside the Union, we cannot precisely locate these alternatives on a scale. Since the value we want to observe is how voters would have voted if they were themselves fully informed about these positions, another way of obtaining an approximate idea of competent voting is by comparing groups according to their level of information. By using the method of 'well-informed proxy group comparison' described above, we can compare voting behaviour across types and levels of information. The assumption is that, if you are very knowledgeable about European politics, you will also be better equipped to choose the best alternative according to your own preferences, and you will not be misled by elite cues that are incompatible with your own preferences (Zaller 1992; Kriesi 2005). Hence, we want to examine the extent to which the vote choice is compatible with the voter's EU preferences and how this compares across groups with different types and levels of information.

To examine the effects of information on competent voting, we distinguish between three types of information: cue reception, cue knowledge, and EU knowledge. The 'cue reception' indicator simply measures individual exposure to partisan cues. This scale thus measures the extent to which people have been exposed to and can identify the positions of parties, but it does not measure whether individuals identify these positions *correctly*. The 'cue knowledge' indicator measures whether individuals can correctly identify the positions of parties. This scale is created by calculating the distance between the voters' perception of party positions and their actual position (according to the expert surveys). The smaller the distance, the greater the knowledge of party positions and the higher the score on the scale. The last scale measures detailed knowledge of the EU. This scale is created as a summated 'political awareness' scale by calculating correct answers to factual knowledge questions on the EU, and it is thus similar to the political awareness scale employed in the analyses in Chapter 3.

By examining how these types of information interact with vote considerations, we can arrive at a better understanding of how information may influence voter competence. However, two potential concerns should be addressed. The first concern is that the three measures may capture the same thing and are so highly correlated that any distinction is meaningless. While this is a valid concern, the conceptual distinction between the three measures is very important when examining competence. Moreover, although the indicators are positively correlated, as we would expect, this correlation is very low (below 0.2) in all cases,[16] and the inter-item reliability of each scale is very high.[17] A closer look at the three indicators also reveals that the 'EU knowledge' group seems to capture what is generally referred to as political sophistication or awareness (Zaller 1992). The EU knowledge scale is strongly correlated with measures of education, newspaper reading, political interests, and EU interest, whereas these correlations are much weaker, or non-existent, for the two cue-taking indicators. A second potential problem is that these measures – particularly the EU knowledge measure—are endogenous to our dependent variable. In other words, one could argue that the more people support the integration project, the more likely they are to acquire information about the issue. While this is a valid concern, the empirical evidence shows no correlation between EU knowledge and support for European integration, and only a very low correlation between cue-taking and support. Hence, we have grounds to believe that these indicators are capturing three distinct types of information processing that could have markedly different effects on competent voting.

To test the impact of different types of information on voter competence, we can thus compare the behaviour of voters who differ only in the amount and types of information they possess. Our expectation—as

**Table 6.4.** Information types and vote choice in the 1994 Norwegian accession referendum

| Independent variables | Model 1: Reception of cues | | Model 2: Knowledge of cues | | Model 3: Knowledge of the EU | |
|---|---|---|---|---|---|---|
| | Coeff. | S.E. | Coeff. | S.E. | Coeff. | S.E. |
| EU attitudes | 0.85** | 0.06 | 0.53** | 0.10 | 0.76** | 0.08 |
| Party endorsement | 1.43** | 0.12 | 1.41** | 0.40 | 1.89** | 0.44 |
| Distance to party (EU) | 0.05 | 0.10 | 0.07 | 0.08 | 0.06 | 0.05 |
| Cue reception | 0.02 | 0.09 | — | — | — | — |
| Cue knowledge | — | — | −0.31** | 0.13 | — | — |
| Factual EU knowledge | — | — | — | — | −0.01 | 0.04 |
| *Interaction effects* | | | | | | |
| Cue reception * attitudes | 0.01 | 0.02 | — | — | — | — |
| Cue reception * endorsement | −0.09 | 0.06 | — | — | — | — |
| Cue knowledge * attitudes | — | — | 0.12** | 0.02 | — | — |
| Cue knowledge * endorsement | — | — | −0.16** | 0.05 | — | — |
| EU knowledge * attitudes | — | — | — | — | 0.06** | 0.01 |
| EU knowledge * endorsement | — | — | — | — | −0.07 | 0.08 |
| Constant | −5.34** | 1.00 | −4.11** | 0.85 | −5.72** | 0.81 |
| % correctly predicted | 87 | — | 89 | — | 89 | — |
| McFadden's R squared | 0.58 | — | 0.59 | — | 0.60 | — |
| N | 2832 | — | 2832 | — | 2832 | — |

* Significant at 0.05
** Significant at 0.01

*Note*: The dependent variable is the vote in the referendum (yes). All models are estimated using logistic regression and also include controls for age, income, region, Left-Right ideology and government satisfaction. None of these variables are statistically significant in any of the models.

*Source*: EU-avstemningen 1994. See Appendix 1.

outlined above – is that both detailed knowledge of EU politics and high knowledge of party positions will make issue preferences more important in determining the vote. However, we do not expect that simply *receiving* party cues will have the same effect, since such party endorsements may be potentially misleading without a basic level of information. To test these propositions, we have estimated three logit models including interaction terms for each specific information type and the variables that are expected to be most significant in determining the vote: EU attitudes and partisanship (preferred party endorsement).[18]

Table 6.4 reports the results. These results suggest that the type and the amount of information that people possess affect the way in which they decide in the referendum. We can observe that the interactions between EU preferences and both cue knowledge and factual EU knowledge are significant, but that this is not the case for cue reception. In other words, both encyclopaedic knowledge of the EU and knowledge of party position will make issue preferences a more important determinant of the

## Voter Competence

vote, whereas simply receiving cues makes no difference. In addition, the results illustrate that knowledge of partisan positions mediates the extent to which party recommendations affect behaviour: higher levels of knowledge about party positions (cues) reduces the effect of endorsements on vote choice. The results seem to indicate that, as expected, both 'encyclopaedic' information and knowledge of partisan cues can enhance voter competence (since they augment the effect of issue preferences), whereas exposure to cues has no effect. Analysing the effect of different types of information illustrates that it is not necessarily sufficient that individuals are exposed to large amount of information if they cannot use that information to guide their vote choice.

Since our assumption is that high levels of detailed information about the EU enable voters to correctly identify the choices that maximize utility, our 'proxy group' for competence is the group of citizens with high levels of knowledge of the EU. The easiest way to compare across groups is to illustrate the predicted probabilities graphically. Figure 6.5 shows the predicted change in probability of voting yes for each of the information types (cue reception, cue knowledge, EU knowledge) across three information levels (low, medium, high). This has been calculated by increasing EU attitudes by half a standard deviation, *ceteris paribus*.

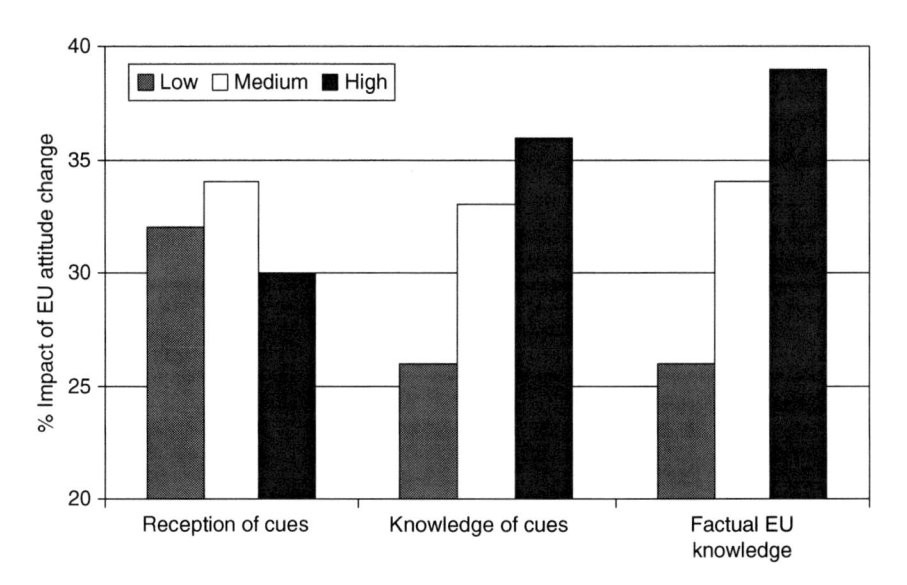

**Figure 6.5.** Issue voting across types and levels of information

155

Figure 6.5 shows that EU preferences have the most significant impact on voting for the 'proxy group' of voters with high levels of factual information; yet information about party cues produces similar patterns of voter behaviour. If a voter is well-informed about party positions on the EU, then issue preferences will matter more. This similarity of patterns across levels for these two types of information suggests that knowledge of party cues can be used as a reliable substitute for detailed knowledge of the EU. On the other hand, we do not detect this variation across levels when we look at 'cue reception', suggesting that simply being exposed to cues is not going to make you better equipped to vote competently.

The models presented in Table 6.4 estimate the effect of different information types separately. But, in reality, some people have knowledge of party cues as well as detailed information about the EU, whereas others will lack both detailed knowledge and an understanding of party positions. To analyse how this combination of information influences voting behaviour, we can simulate the impact of a change in EU preferences on the probability of voting yes (as in Figure 6.5) for a combination of the two information types at each information level (low, medium, high). Table 6.5 reports the predicted impact of a change in EU preferences for each category, including the 95 per cent confidence intervals (in brackets) and the number of respondents in each cell.

As expected, Table 6.5 illustrates that the people who lack knowledge of both cues and the EU are least likely to rely on their EU preferences. But this group only constitutes about 10 per cent of people who voted. The impact of EU preferences increases the higher people score in the factual knowledge category, whereas the evidence is more ambiguous for

Table 6.5. Impact of EU attitude change on the probability of voting yes, across information categories (%)

|  | Factual EU knowledge | | |
| --- | --- | --- | --- |
|  | Low | Medium | High |
| Knowledge of party cues | | | |
| Low | 20 (14–26) N = 290 | 27 (25–29) N = 449 | 35 (27–41) N = 104 |
| Medium | 26 (22–30) N = 343 | 36 (33–39) N = 938 | 60 (42–68) N = 198 |
| High | 26 (14–34) N = 76 | 26 (21–31) N = 346 | *N = 87 |

* Failed to converge because EU preferences > 5 predicts data (yes-vote) perfectly.
Note: Cells include the simulated per cent impact of half a standard deviation change in EU preference variable on the probability of voting yes with 95% confidence intervals in brackets and N = no. of respondents.

## Voter Competence

the 'cue knowledge' category. These findings suggest that extensive EU knowledge makes attitudes more relevant than cue knowledge. While there appears to be little difference between the medium and high 'cue knowledge groups' when combined with factual knowledge, there is a considerable difference between the medium and high 'factual knowledge groups' when combined with cue knowledge. As expected, the people who rely most on their issue preferences are those people with high knowledge of the EU and medium/high knowledge of party positions.

In sum, these comparisons of voting behaviour across types and levels of information provide important insights into our understanding of voter competence in EU referendums. The findings suggest that voters can act competently without detailed knowledge of the EU by relying on party endorsements, if they have a basic knowledge of party positions on the EU. However, the argument that the mere presence of elite cues enhances reasoned voting is not supported by the data.

### 6.5. Conclusion

Many commentators and politicians associate direct democracy with voter incompetence. This assertion is particularly tempting if voters reject a proposal favoured by the elites. Yet, it is notoriously difficult to establish absolute standards for competency in politics. The aim of this chapter has been to establish criteria against which this behaviour can be judged normatively. The chapter has presented the argument that direct democracy rests on the notion that people have meaningful attitudes towards the issues at stake and that they vote on the basis of these attitudes. Hence, voter competence can be conceptualized as issue proximity voting which, in turn, requires information. Assuming that people who are very well-informed about the details of EU politics will vote relatively competently, we can infer how other types of information influence voter competence by comparing patterns of voting across types and levels of information. The findings from the Norwegian accession referendum illustrate that knowledge of party cues has a similar effect on voting behaviour as detailed knowledge of EU politics, although the evidence also suggests that detailed EU knowledge enhances issue voting more than cue knowledge.

These results corroborate and extend the analyses of the information effects presented in the previous chapters. They reaffirm that higher levels of information supply and political awareness induce issue voting.

Moreover, this chapter has shown that information should not be understood narrowly as factual knowledge about the ballot issue, since elite cues can also be used as reliable substitutes for such detailed knowledge. However, the results show that simply being exposed to the cues of political parties has no 'competence enhancing' effect on behaviour. Overall, the findings from the Norwegian referendum give reasons for optimism about voter competence in EU referendums: vote choices seem to be guided mainly by issue preferences, and party endorsements appear to provide reliable information shortcuts provided that voters have basic knowledge of party positions.

The Norwegian case was presented as a 'critical test' of voter competence, since the EU issue has been highly politicized in the Norwegian political debate, and we would thus expect Norwegian voters to be better informed about the issue itself as well as the position of parties. Unfortunately, the available data do not enable us to test these different information effects in other referendums. But we might suppose that voters in countries where the issue is less politicized will act less competently. The findings on the relationship between campaign intensity and issue voting presented in Chapter 4 indicate that this may be the case. Without clear competition on the European dimension, the political environment may fail to enhance voter competence, since the EU dimension does not constitute an integral part of the main dimension of political contestation, and party endorsements may potentially be misleading. The analysis of information effects presented in this book points to the role and responsibility of political parties in providing clear cues and policy alternatives on the issue of European integration. As van der Eijk and Franklin noted in their study of European Parliament elections:

Elections conducted without proper debate of the issues relevant to that arena concerned cannot function as real elections with consequences for the exercise of power in that arena... only by allowing voters to choose alternative visions of the future of Europe can a crisis of democratic legitimacy be averted (van der Eijk and Franklin 1996: 388).

Referendums of European integration may serve to enhance the legitimacy of the integration process, but only if voters are capable of expressing their preferences concerning European integration in these referendums and if politicians, in turn, are responsive to these preferences. The former condition—competent voting—crucially depends on the information and cues provided to citizens by political elites. To examine the interplay between elite cues and public opinion formation in greater detail, the next chapter examines two pairs of referendums in Denmark and Ireland and explores how variations in party cues and campaign information in these referendums led to different patterns of voting behaviour and different outcomes.

## Notes

1. Quoted in Becker and Couto (1996: 116).
2. Bowler and Donovan (1998: 24).
3. This survey was conducted in 1993. More recent Eurobarometer surveys unfortunately do not compare factual knowledge of European affairs with factual knowledge of national political affairs.
4. Quoted in *Humo*, September 2, 1997. See also Cronin 1989.
5. Interview with Charlotte Antonsen, Member of the Danish Parliament and the Liberal Party's EU spokesperson, 1990–2007.
6. As discussed in Chapter 1, some constitutions of European states contain provisions demanding a popular vote in order to change the national constitution and/or to surrender authority to a supranational body.
7. For more details on the newspapers used as sources in this analysis, see Chapter 4 and Appendix 1.
8. In certain referendums, notably the Danish and the Norwegian, issue-specific interest organizations have also played an important role, especially in terms of articulating opposition to the ballot proposal. Yet, they still receive far less attention in the media than political parties.
9. Some studies, however, have found that the Left-Right dimension is related to European integration on a subset of issues, namely those that are concerned with redistribution and regulating capitalism (see, for example, Hooghe et al. 2002).
10. The Chapel Hill 2002 expert survey on party positioning on European integration covers 171 parties in 23 of the current 27 EU member states (not Luxembourg, Estonia, Malta and Cyprus).
11. Unfortunately, the other referendum surveys do not include sufficient question items to allow us to carry out such an analysis.
12. After the election in 1993, *Arbeiderpartiet* held 41% of the seats in the Norwegian Parliament. The second largest party held only 19% of the seats.
13. Unfortunately, there was no party expert survey conducted in Norway in 1994, so for these estimates I used Leonard Ray's party expert survey from 1998 (see Ray and Narud 2000). To ensure that the positions of the Norwegian parties did not shift significantly in the period between the referendum and the survey, I cross-checked the estimation with the party expert estimations from 1992 and 1996, and they show that the Norwegian party positions remained very stable in this period.

14. Voters are classified into groups according to their vote in the 1993 Storting election.
15. The absolute values (numerical values without regard to their sign) inform us about the actual (mean) magnitude of the distance.
16. A factor analysis also shows that the three variables extract three factors with each of the variables loading more heavily on each of the three factors, thus suggesting that the variables can be considered orthogonal.
17. All the information scales have alpha reliabilities in the 0.80 to 0.90 range, and thus have high internal consistency.
18. These measurements are similar, but not identical, to the ones presented in Chapters 3 and 4. First, it was not necessary to rescale the variables in this analysis, as they are not included in a pooled model. Second, in order to include the 'party distance' measure it was necessary to use a single question item for the EU attitudes scale, namely a question where respondents are asked to place themselves on a 10-point European integration scale.

# 7
# From No to Yes: The Danish and Irish Referendums on the Maastricht and Nice Treaties

> *When you have a situation where the government and the political parties representing 96 per cent of the elected representatives say yes, where the main pillars of public opinion—the newspapers—say yes, where the trade union movement says yes-ish, where the business community and farming organisations all say yes, you can be forgiven for being lulled into complacency.*
>
> —Dick Roche, Irish Minister for Europe

> *I was completely certain that it would be a Yes [to Maastricht]. All of a sudden the opinion polls started to change. But no politician had recognised the change. Uffe Ellemann-Jensen said that this was an easy one, because everyone was in favour. Previously it had been difficult, because the Social Democrats were against. He totally misjudged the situation. The polls changed in March and suggested a close race. But I was still certain it would be a Yes. None of us expected this.*[1]
>
> —Holger K. Nielsen, former Chairman of the Danish Socialist People's Party

The above quotes bring us back to the puzzle introduced in the first chapter: Why do a majority of voters reject a ballot proposal on European integration when the elites are almost united in favour? Is it simply a result of random protest voting? A signal of dissatisfaction with the government? Or is the outcome decided by citizens' reasoned choices based on their attitudes towards European integration? The previous chapters have presented the argument that political information conditions the behaviour of voters in referendums and influences the extent to which referendums are 'plebiscites' on the performance of the government or an evaluation of the ballot proposal based on attitudes towards the integration project. To understand the outcomes of EU referendums, we thus need to examine both the supply of information by elites and the processing of information by individuals.

This chapter explores the dynamic interplay between political elites and the public during four referendum campaigns. The specific cases have been chosen as two examples of 'controlled comparisons' where the electorates were asked to decide on the same issue twice: the two Danish referendums on the ratification of the Maastricht Treaty (1992/3) and the two Irish referendums on the ratification of the Nice Treaty (2001/2). In both sets of cases, the ballot proposal was rejected by the electorate in the first referendum, but accepted in the second. What changed between and during the two referendum campaigns that caused the public to behave differently? This chapter provides a detailed analysis of how differences in the political environment—and specifically the information disseminated by political elites—influence the behaviour of citizens in referendums on European integration. Through in-depth analyses of newspapers, campaign material and opinion polls combined with interviews with the key actors in the campaign, this chapter gives a rich description of the dynamics of the campaigns leading up to the referendum votes. To be able to compare within and across cases, each case study is structured around three main questions: What are the strategies adopted by political parties during the referendum campaign—and for what reasons? In what way do elites respond to the opinions and actions of the public during and after referendums? How are the opinions and vote intentions of the public shaped during a referendum campaign—and specifically, how are citizens influenced by elite cues and other available information during campaigns?

This chapter begins with a brief discussion of Denmark's relations to the European Community (EC), followed by a case study of the two referendums on the Maastricht Treaty. It proceeds with a case study of the two Irish referendums on the Nice Treaty. Finally, this chapter concludes with a discussion of the lessons we can learn from the two sets of cases.

## 7.1. Reluctant Europeans: Denmark and the European community

On the eve of the referendum on the Single European Act (SEA) in 1986, the Danish Prime Minister, Poul Schlüter, stated that 'the Union is stone-dead'. He wanted to reassure the Danish public that the EC was not going to extend its supranational powers or move towards a United States of Europe. This reassurance came back to bite the same government in 1992, when it asked the people to vote on the Treaty on European Union, the Maastricht Treaty. In the campaign leading up to the Maastricht referendum, the issue of a 'Union' was firmly on the political agenda. Despite a broad elite consensus in favour of ratification of the Treaty, a small majority of Danish voters rejected the proposal on 2 June 1992, and thus put a temporary stop to the Union project. Yet after being granted several exemptions from the Treaty the Danes voted again, and this time a solid majority accepted the Treaty. This case study examines why a proportion of Danes changed their mind between the campaigns. It also examines the process of the referendum campaign: Which strategies were employed by the political parties? Who set the agenda? How did the campaigns influence opinion formation and referendum outcomes? How did the political elites respond to the public rejection of the ballot proposal?

Before examining the specifics of the two referendums, this section gives a brief overview of the Danish attitudes towards the European project and the Danish EU referendums.

### 7.1.1. *Danish membership of the EC*

Denmark joined the European Communities in 1973, backed by 79 per cent of members of *Folketinget*,[2] the Danish Parliament, and a solid majority of 63 per cent of Danish voters in the 1972 accession referendum. The long campaign leading up to the referendum was dominated by mainly economic arguments.[3] Membership was not only supported by most political parties, but also by the media, trade unions and business organizations. Opposition to membership came from small left-wing parties, including the Socialist People's Party represented in Parliament, together with the very active, non-partisan People's Movement Against the EEC.

After joining the Community, successive Danish governments adopted a minimalist and 'intergovernmentalist' approach to the European integration project (Laursen 1994; Petersen 1996). During the debates in the 1970s and 1980s, Danish governments argued that institutional reforms were unnecessary and that the Council of Ministers should retain its central position in the EC. The question posed in one of the anti-EEC 1972 posters, 'Common Market—EEC?—Federal State', was telling: while the Danes were clearly in favour of the former, there was little support for the latter among elites and citizens. Denmark had joined the EEC for mainly economic reasons and most Danes had little desire to become part of a political union or a federal state.[4]

The Danish government voted against calling an Intergovernmental Conference (IGC) in 1985.[5] But the summit went ahead regardless and resulted in the first revision of the Rome Treaty, the Single European Act (SEA). After the SEA was signed, the Danish minority centre-right government could not get the necessary majority in the Parliament to ratify the Act, because the Social Democrats—the largest party in Parliament—together with the Socialist People's Party and the Social Liberals announced their intention to vote against the Act. The Social Democrats and the Social Liberals had been in favour of joining the EC in 1972, yet argued that 'if we accept the salami tactics of the European Parliament now, the Union will be carried out step by step'.[6] Many Social Democrats and Socialists were also sceptical about the 'capitalist' single market project, whereas the pacifist Social Liberals were against the plans to extend cooperation to the area of defence. In a tactical manoeuvre, the government decided to bypass Parliament and call a referendum on the SEA. After a very short campaign,[7] dominated by stories of the split within the social democratic movement and the detrimental consequences of a no-vote,[8] 56 per cent of the Danes accepted the Act.

Following the referendum on the SEA, the Social Democrats cautiously moved towards a more pro-integration stance (Petersen 1996; Lawler 1997). This allowed six of the eight parties represented in Parliament to support a Danish cross-party memorandum in October 1990 on further reforms in the EC that formed the basis of the Danish negotiations in the 1991 IGC. While the Maastricht Treaty went further than the Danish memorandum in certain areas, especially on defence policy, the six pro-EU parties voted unanimously for the ratification of the Maastricht Treaty in Spring 1992, with the exception of parts of the small Christian People's Party.[9] The vote represented an overwhelming parliamentary endorsement of a very pro-integration treaty. It was also the first time that the Social Democrats and the Social Liberals managed to present a united party line in a decisive EU vote. Only two parties voted against the Treaty, the Socialist People's Party on the left, and the Progress Party on the right. In May 1992, the Maastricht Treaty was ratified in Parliament by 130 to 25 votes. The political elites were thus moving towards a more consensual pro-European stance on the EC, but what about the public?

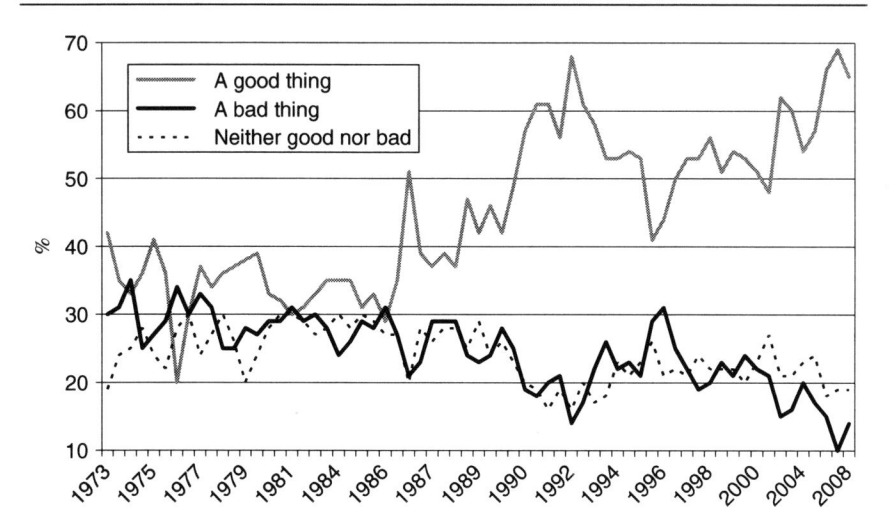

**Figure 7.1.** Danish attitudes towards EU membership
*Source:* Eurobarometer surveys 1973–2008.

### 7.1.2. Public attitudes towards European integration

In the 1972 referendum, 63 per cent of Danish voters supported membership of the EEC, yet during periods in the 1970s and 1980s polls showed that the majority in favour of membership had disappeared. However, as the elites adopted a more pro-integration attitude after the SEA referendum, the public also changed their attitudes towards membership. This trend is evident when Danes are asked to evaluate whether membership of the EU is a good thing, a bad thing, or neither a good nor a bad thing in Eurobarometer surveys.

Figure 7.1 shows a clear upward trend in the positive evaluation of membership in the late 1980s and late 1990s. As a consequence, the Danes are no longer among the most Eurosceptic citizens of the Union. During the last decade, an average of 57 per cent of Danes have expressed that EU membership is a 'good thing' against only 19 per cent who have seen it as a 'bad thing'. As the former Danish Foreign Minister Niels Helveg Petersen has noted, 'public attitudes towards membership have changed. People no longer want to leave the EU. But that hasn't altered the fact that there is a fundamental scepticism towards further integration'.[10]

The results in Table 7.1 show that while there was a large majority in favour of membership and the common market both before and after the

**Table 7.1.** Attitudes towards European integration in Denmark

|  | May 1992 | June 1992 | May 1993 | Sep 2000 |
|---|---|---|---|---|
| Common market | 59 | 74 | 71 | 65 |
| EMU | 46 | 53 | 43 | 48 |
| Common foreign policy | 39 | 38 | 38 | 41 |
| Common defence policy | 37 | 30 | 35 | 46 |
| Single currency | 35 | 34 | 23 | 50 |
| United States of Europe | 23 | 19 | 21 | 16 |
| European citizenship | 15 | — | 14 | 13 |

*Note*: Tables entries denote percentage in favour.
*Sources*: See Appendix 1 and Svensson 2003.

Maastricht referendums, most Danes were opposed to further integration in areas such as foreign policy, defence, and a single currency, and only a small minority of Danes favoured the development towards a United States of Europe. This suggests that the fear of the politically integrated European *Union* and jeopardizing Danish sovereignty may have resonated with the public in 1992, especially since the Maastricht Treaty contained provisions on many of the issues to which a majority of Danes were opposed.

## 7.2. To ratify or not to ratify? The Danish Maastricht referendum

The Maastricht Treaty, which was signed in 1992, officially established the European Union. It included considerable steps towards further economic and political integration, including the commitment of member states to economic and monetary union (EMU); provisions for intergovernmental arrangements for a common foreign and security policy; increased cooperation on justice and home affairs policy issues; and increased the powers of the European Parliament. According to Article 20 of the Danish Constitution, transfer of sovereignty to international authorities, which is not passed by a five-sixths majority in Parliament, shall be subject to a referendum. Since the parliamentary majority ratifying the Maastricht Treaty fell just short of five-sixths, the government was required to call a binding referendum. This section will explore elite positions and strategies and public opinion formation during the campaign leading up to the first Maastricht referendum on 2 June 1992.

## 7.2.1. Elite positions and strategies

From the outset, the government may have expected that the Maastricht referendum would be easier to win than the referendum on the SEA, where it faced opposition from the majority of Parliament and a split trade union movement. In the 1992 campaign, the Treaty proposal was backed by a broad spectrum of parties in Parliament, nearly all interest organizations, and every major newspaper. The most important change since 1986 was the shift in the position of the Social Democrats, since it was mainly social democratic voters who voted against membership in 1972 and the Act in 1986. There are several reasons why the Social Democrats changed their position. First, the experience of 1986 illustrated that it was not an easy task to secure a No to an EC Treaty, and the public had become more positive about membership of the EC (see Figure 7.1). Second, the party leadership reasoned that in terms of electoral support in national elections, it would be relatively costless to adopt a more pro-European stance. As one of the leading Social Democrats, Henrik Dam Kristensen, has noted: 'for the large majority of Danes, our EU position is irrelevant when they vote in local, regional or national elections. They separate domestic politics and EU politics very clearly'.[11] Third, the Community itself had changed in the direction of policies corresponding with traditional social democratic values. In particular, the trade union movement took a great interest in the proposed 'social dimension' in the EU (Petersen 1996). Finally, the position of the Social Liberals had changed dramatically after the end of the Cold War and they had become strong supporters of further integration.[12] Since the Social Liberals were the most likely coalition partner of the Social Democrats, the goal of office-seeking was advanced by adopting a more pro-European position. Hence, for a mixture of policy-seeking and office-seeking reasons, the Social Democrats adopted a policy position of fully endorsing the move towards a European Union.

In contrast to the strong and resourceful yes-side, the no-side was small and lacking in funds. In Parliament, the small Socialist People's Party voted against the Maastricht Treaty, as had been the tradition on the far left in Danish politics. The party opposed 'the tremendous centralization of powers in closed union' and 'the foundation of the United States of Europe'.[13] In addition, the far-right Progress Party, which supported the SEA, opposed the Maastricht Treaty because it went too far in the party's opinion: The EC should remain an economic market, and should not become a military superpower.[14] In addition to these political parties,

**Europe in Question**

there were several extra-parliamentary groups advocating a no-vote. Most important of these groups was the People's Movement Against the EC, which also played a key role in the opposition to membership in 1972. But, the Movement was internally split on the issue of whether to advocate a withdrawal from the EC or to accept membership and fight against the Union.[15]

### 7.2.2. The 1992 campaign

Given the balance of power in elite positions, one cannot blame the Danish Foreign Minister Uffe Ellemann-Jensen for expecting it to be an easy win. Yet, in spite of the apparent position of strength, the referendum campaign became an uphill struggle for the yes-side. The polls quickly made it apparent that this was going to be a very close race. After the yes-side initially had been far ahead in the polls, the two sides were neck and neck during most of the lengthy campaign, and the proportion of voters in favour only started increasing in the ten days up to the referendum (see Figure 7.2).

Figure 7.2 illustrates that before the beginning of the campaign, more than 40 per cent of voters were undecided about how to vote. This suggests that the campaign played an important role in shaping the opinion of a large proportion of voters. But why did the Danish establishment not succeed in convincing a majority of the voters during the campaign? Several explanations have been advanced in the literature, but this

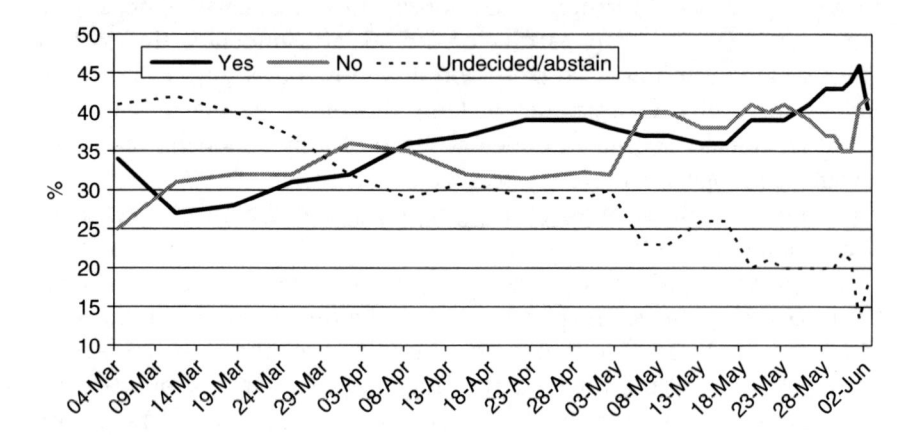

**Figure 7.2.** Vote intentions during the 1992 Maastricht referendum campaign
*Source*: Berlingske Tidende/Gallup and Politiken/Vilstrup.

chapter will focus on four key factors. First, the yes-side appeared weak and divided during the campaign. Second, the referendum agenda was dominated by the issue of political integration, rather than the economic aspects of the integration project. Third, the campaign did not highlight the consequences of a no-vote. Finally, the intensity of the referendum campaign encouraged more people to vote on the basis of their attitudes towards campaign issues, rather than simply following elite cues.

Although the Maastricht Treaty received an overwhelming endorsement by Parliament, the yes-side was neither strong nor united during the referendum campaign. The Social Democrats were preoccupied with a leadership battle between its Chairman, Svend Auken, and his deputy, Poul Nyrup Rasmussen. This internal fight between two party factions was not related to the EU issue, but it nevertheless weakened the capacity of the party to campaign effectively during the campaign.[16] Moreover, instead of presenting a united front, the government and the Social Democrats were openly bickering throughout the campaign.[17] According to one of the leading opposition politicians, Niels Helveg Petersen, the established parties had only themselves to blame for the defeat:

The yes-side made many mistakes during the campaign. It was the yes-side that lost, not the no-side that won. The yes-side was divided. Uffe [Ellemann-Jensen] made the mistake of provoking the Social Democrats by promoting WEU and defence policy. It weakened us that the main players appeared to be in disagreement.[18]

When the elites are weak and internally divided, as was the case in this referendum, it is likely to create uncertainty among voters and this may, in turn, reduce the utility of the proposal, as discussed in Chapter 2. The large number of Social Democrat voters who deserted the party line in the 1992 referendum[19] (compared with the two previous referendums where a majority had followed the party's recommendation[20]) suggests that the party's weak campaign effort may have increased uncertainty amongst voters.

Another important factor during the campaign was the *agenda-setting*. A media analysis of the Danish referendum campaign reveals that the issues related to political integration and the development of a United States of Europe dominated the campaign.[21] Whereas the previous two referendum campaigns had centred on issues related to economic integration and the benefits of a common market, this debate focused on the political aspects of integration, such as the development of a Union with a common foreign and defence policy, loss of national sovereignty, and the democratic deficit in the EU. While the Treaty contained important aspects of economic integration, notably plans for a single currency, the emphasis on the foundation of a European *Union* made it difficult for the yes-side to avoid the discussion of further political integration. As illustrated in Table 7.1, the political aspects of the integration project were far more unpopular than economic integration with the Danish voters, and this agenda thus damaged the yes-side. As a leading EU commentator and Socialist MP, Steen Gade, has noted:

> The traditional message of the yes-side has always been economic self-interest. That was the message in 1972 and 1986. But in 1992 the yes-side couldn't just talk about economics. That is probably why they lost. The political aspects became more and more visible. In 1986, Schlüter said the union was dead, but then it appeared alive and well in 1992.[22]

The predominance of the political integration theme during the campaign was not only a result of the content of the Treaty itself, but also a consequence of the strategic actions of political actors. The Social Democrats launched a campaign for 'an honest yes' by emphasizing the positive aspects of Maastricht, such as the social dimension and provisions for the environment, but this inevitably meant a focus on the political aspects of the integration project (Nielsen 1993: 39–40). To avoid references to the most integrationist aspects of the Treaty, the yes-side played down references to the EMU and defence (Worre 1992, 1995). But, the consequence of this strategy was that the economic aspects of European cooperation were almost forgotten during the campaign. Union opponents seized this opportunity to avert attention from EC membership itself and emphasize the prospects of further political integration by describing the Maastricht Treaty as 'the foundation stone of the United States of Europe'[23] (Siune et al. 1992; Worre 1992; Nielsen 1993). The no-side's strategy appears to have been successful. When asked about the Treaty's content, the most cited theme by respondents is 'political union' (20 per cent) and this mention increased by 10 percentage points during the campaign (Siune et al. 1992: 91). By focusing voters' minds on aspects of political union and further integration, the campaign made the ballot proposal appear far removed from most people's 'ideal point' of European integration. Closely related to this is a third key factor: the interpretation of the 'reversion point'.

One of the key differences between this campaign and the previous referendum campaigns was that the consequences of a no-vote appeared less serious. Put in 'spatial' terms, the reversion point was moved closer to the status quo. This was a result of a combination of 'soft' campaigning by the yes-side that attempted to avoid 'scaremongering' tactics and a new strategy adopted by the no-side: to focus on the dangers of the union while promising voters that they would stay in the EC if they voted no. In support of Hypothesis 2.7, the no-side adopted a campaign strategy of consciously targeting wavering voters, who were in favour of membership of the EC, but were sceptical of more integration (Worre 1992; Nielsen 1993). The campaign message was thus framed as a vote for the EC, but against the Union.[24] Leading members of the People's Movement Against the EC even formed 'Denmark '92'[25] under the slogan 'Yes to Europe, No to the Union'. The former leader of the Socialist People's Party, Holger K. Nielsen, has described his party's strategy in similar terms:

We clearly said during the referendum campaign that if people voted no, Denmark would stay in the EU. That was how we got a no. We were very moderate, and people could feel certain that nothing would happen to Denmark, if we said no. Had we made it a question of yes or no to the EU, then it would have been a clear yes. That's why we chose to be moderate in our argumentation.[26]

The yes-side also contributed to the perception that 'nothing would happen' in case of a no-vote in its own campaign. The Prime Minister, Poul Schlüter, told the media that the Danes would get a 'second chance' if they voted no, and the leader of the opposition, Poul Nyrup Rasmussen, stated that Denmark could work to get a special agreement 'to participate in the EC plus the best parts of the Maastricht Treaty'.[27] For an EC-positive voter sceptical of further political integration, these promises are likely to have been appealing. Certainly the campaign rhetoric moved the 'reversion point' very close to the current status quo, favoured by a majority of voters. A poll prior to the referendum showed that only 13 per cent of voters believed that a No would lead to Danish exit from the EC, whereas half of the voters believed that the Treaty would be renegotiated (Nielsen 1993: 43).

As proposed in Hypothesis 2.1 (Chapter 2), voters are less likely to vote in favour of the ballot proposal if it is perceived to be further away from their ideal point than the reversion point. Moreover, if the voters feel more uncertain about the consequences of the proposal, compared with the consequences of reversion point, this will also make them more likely to vote against the proposal (Hypothesis 2.2). In short, by reassuring voters that a 'no' would have minimal consequences, the elites made it more likely that a larger proportion of voters would say no. In this way, the 1992 campaign differed from the 1972 and 1986 campaigns that were dominated by repeated threats relating to 'the price of a No' and 'the dangers of standing alone'[28] (Worre 1992, 1995). As the leading no-campaigner and Member of the European Parliament, Jens-Peter Bonde, has commented: 'In 1992, people voted against the Maastricht Treaty, and they no longer believed the threat that we would have to leave the EU. They believed the threat in 1986, but not in 1992. That is the reason we had a majority in 1992'.[29] Opinion polls from the campaign suggest that these considerations did play a role in shaping vote choices: whereas only 35 per cent of those who intended to vote yes believed that there could be a renegotiation of the Treaty, 62 per cent of naysayers thought this to be possible. Equally, 75 per cent of intended yes-voters believed a no-vote would mean loss of Danish influence in the EC, compared with 56 per cent of intended no-voters (Nielsen 1993: 43).

A fourth factor that is likely to have played a decisive role is the intensity of the campaign. Unlike in the very short three-week campaign leading up to 1986 campaign, voters had many months to consider the implications of the proposed Union, and the referendum was front-page news during most of the period. The yes-side spent approximately 30 million DKK (approximately 3 million GBP) to persuade the Danes, but this information campaign may have had unintended consequences. As discussed in Chapter 4, more intense campaigns are likely to activate citizens' issue preferences. Certainly, survey data suggest that the Danes became more knowledgeable about the Maastricht proposal during the campaign. In March 1992, only 20 per cent expressed that they felt knowledgeable, but this figure had increased to 55 per cent by May (Siune et al. 1992: 54). Given the framing of the choice in the campaign, it is perhaps not surprising that relying on 'proximity considerations' would have led many people to vote against the proposal. Amongst other things, the intense information campaign may have served to activate issue attitudes and encouraged people to weigh up which of the alternatives was better: the status quo without consequences or an unknown quantity of a Union. On 2 June 1992, 83 per cent of voters turned out to make this decision and a small majority of 50.7 per cent decided to reject the Maastricht Treaty.

The post-referendum survey data suggest that issue voting was an important factor. When voters were subsequently asked why they voted no, their reasons mainly related to their scepticism towards further political integration: surrender of national sovereignty, the federal idea, primacy of EC law, and loss of Danish identity. Table 7.2 also illustrates that

Table 7.2. Reasons for vote choice in the 1992 Maastricht referendum

| Reasons to vote Yes | % |
|---|---|
| Denmark needs the EC | 44 |
| Economic advantages of membership | 19 |
| We should remain members of the EC | 13 |
| Employment | 10 |
| Influence in Europe | 9 |
| **Reasons to vote No** | |
| Surrender of sovereignty | 43 |
| The federal ('union') idea | 14 |
| No common defence policy | 13 |
| EC should not determine Danish law | 11 |
| Danish identity | 11 |

*Note*: Respondents could give multiple answers to this question item. The list of categories presented here is not exhaustive and the figures indicate the percentage of yes/no-voters that mentioned the specific reason.

*Source*: Folkeafstemningen om Maastrichtaftalen, 1992. See Appendix 1.

most yes-voters explained their choice as a necessity—'Denmark cannot stand alone without the EU'—or economic calculation.

The statistical analyses presented in the previous chapters demonstrate that people's attitudes towards the integration project were decisive in determining their vote choices, in combination with their partisanship and feelings about the government and the opposition (see Chapter 3). These analyses also showed that voters who were more aware and more exposed to campaign information were even more likely to rely on proximity considerations (see Chapter 4). But if attitudes towards the integration project—and the framing and information on the Union project presented in the campaign—were the decisive factors in the referendum, why did a sizable proportion of the electorate take a different stance in 1993? What changed before and during the second campaign?

## 7.3. No to the union, but yes to Europe

Although the opinion polls had shown that it would be a narrow vote, the referendum result on 2 June 1992 nevertheless came as a shock to the political establishment in Denmark and in Europe. At a meeting of foreign ministers in EC on 4 June 1992, the other eleven member states made it clear that there would be no renegotiation of the Treaty itself (Laursen 1994). Denmark thus had to find its own solution. The Danish government had lost the initiative and the political situation soon thereafter took a very peculiar turn: in the words of the former leader of the Conservatives, Hans Engell, 'this was an example of where the opposition took over the country's foreign policy. But with the government's acceptance'.[30] The leaders of the three opposition parties, the Social Democrats, the Social Liberals and the Socialist People's Party, came together to formulate the 'National Compromise', interpreting the Danish No. The text was subsequently accepted by all parties in Parliament, except the Progress Party, and laid down the following four exemptions from full Danish participation in the EU: (1) Denmark does not participate in the defence policy dimension (2) Denmark does not participate in the single currency (3) Denmark is not committed in relation to union citizenship; and (4) Denmark cannot accept the transfer of sovereignty in the area of justice and police affairs (Folketinget 2002). The voters' verdict had thus been taken to mean a No to the United States of Europe, but a Yes to European cooperation. This national compromise formed the basis of the Danish governments' negotiations with the EC in December 1992, where the Edinburgh summit adopted a 'decision' that essentially satisfied Denmark's requests.[31]

With the national compromise and the Edinburgh Agreement, the Danish political elites had interpreted the people's verdict and created a compromise, which they hoped would be acceptable to the voters in a second referendum. For this strategy to be successful, it was essential that the new Agreement was perceived as credible by the voters and not just an attempt to make them accept something they had already rejected. A vital component of this strategy was the endorsement of the Socialist People's Party, because it was the only party supportive of the National Compromise that had unanimously recommended a no-vote in the first referendum. Niels Helveg Petersen has noted that the yes-parties were very aware that to win a second referendum, they 'needed a no-party to interpret the No. It would have lacked credibility if the yes-parties interpreted the No. So, it was essential to get an agreement with the Socialist People's Party'.[32]

It was very understandable that the government and the major opposition parties would advocate an agreement that meant Denmark could stay within the EU Treaty framework, yet included opt-outs which might secure public acceptance; a 'Maastricht without thorns'. But what was the incentive of the Socialist People's Party to endorse this compromise? The Socialist People's Party had recommended a no-vote in every EU referendum and more than 90 per cent of its voters had supported the party line in each one, so why would the party risk taking such a major policy U-turn? Apart from sincere policy reasons,[33] an alternative explanation is that the party hoped that by shifting its EU position and making a major policy deal with the Social Democrats and the Social Liberals, they would enhance their chances of being a part of a coalition government. The aim of the party was to form a centre-left government with the Social Democrats and the Social Liberals, and the National Compromise provided the opportunity to show that the party was fit to govern. The party's former political spokesperson, Steen Gade, has corroborated this explanation:

Holger [K. Nielsen] took the initiative to form the National Compromise. We were very conscious to make it with the Social Democrats and the Social Liberals. We wanted to have an "alternative majority" in opposition to the centre-right government. That way we wanted to signal to the other parties that the Socialist People's Party was a party suitable for government.[34]

Hence, with the backing of the entire Parliament, except the far-right Progress Party,[35] the Maastricht Treaty as supplemented by the Edinburgh Agreement was sent to a second referendum on 18 May 1993.

### 7.3.1. The second campaign

The campaign leading up to the second Maastricht referendum was headed by a new minority government, consisting of the Social Democrats and the Social Liberals. The previous government had been forced to resign in January 1993, because of the so-called 'Tamil affair', involving the processing of asylum applications from Tamils.[36] Hence, without dissolution of Parliament, the Social Democrats, led by Poul Nyrup Rasmussen, assumed the leadership of government after ten years in opposition. The former governing parties were, of course, weakened by this affair, yet many commentators reckoned that a social democratic government would be more capable of convincing voters in a second referendum, given that the centre-left voters were the most Eurosceptic. Furthermore, the yes-side was strengthened in the second referendum by the support of the Socialist People's Party and the small Christian People's Party.

The strategy of the yes-side was to argue that the Edinburgh Agreement differed substantially from the proposal presented in 1992. Furthermore, they clearly emphasized that a second no would have serious

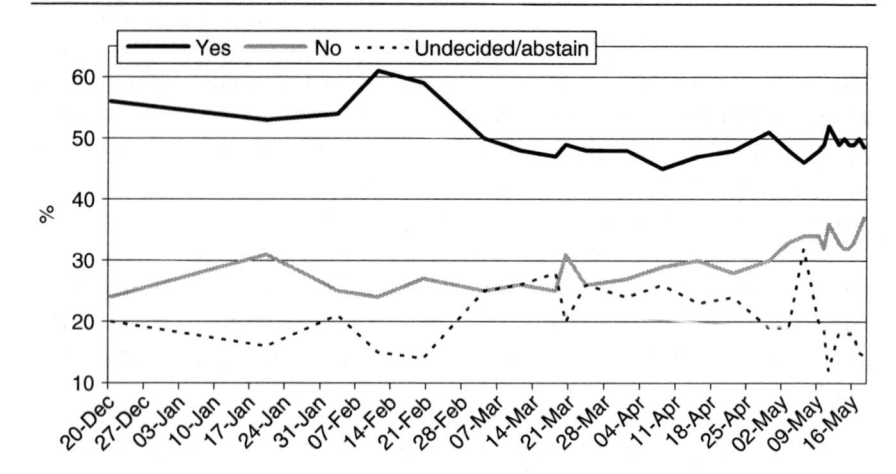

**Figure 7.3.** Vote intentions during the 1993 Maastricht referendum campaign
*Source*: Berlingske Tidende/Gallup and Politiken/Vilstrup.

consequences for Denmark, since it was unrealistic to expect that the other EC members would offer any further concessions. The chief campaign strategist and foreign minister, Niels Helveg Petersen, has described the government's strategy:

It was a successful campaign. The fundamental issue was that we said that the Edinburgh Agreement had created a new basis for a referendum. That was the core of the victory. We had to convince people that they were voting about something else than what they had rejected.[37]

The main argument put forward by the no-side was that Edinburgh was like the 'Emperor's new Clothes': It did not represent anything new and the electorate was therefore being asked to vote on the same thing twice. In addition to the far-right Progress Party, the no-campaign was run by the People's Movement Against the EC, and a splinter group, the June Movement.[38] But the yes-side was far ahead in the opinion polls from the outset. As Figure 7.3 illustrates, more than half of the voters had decided to vote yes before the official campaign started (but after the Edinburgh Agreement had been reached) and only around a quarter of respondents had decided on a no-vote. Moreover, there were far fewer undecided voters than in the first Maastricht referendum campaign.

Figure 7.3 shows that while the yes-side lost some of their voters during the campaign, the outcome was never really in doubt. On 18 May 1993, 56.7 per cent of the Danish electorate gave their yes to the Maastricht Treaty and the Edinburgh Agreement, while 43.3 per cent voted no.

Turnout had increased from 83 to 87 per cent compared with the first Maastricht referendum. What had changed between the two referendums that made a significant proportion of the electorate change their minds?

### 7.3.2. From a no to a yes

A number of studies have attempted to explain the behaviour of voters in the two Maastricht referendums. As mentioned in Chapter 2, the most prominent explanation in the literature is the 'second-order election' theory which emphasizes that people vote on the basis of domestic political concerns rather than European issues in EU referendums and, in particular, that the satisfaction with the government plays an important role. Following this, the two different outcomes in the Danish Maastricht referendums have been interpreted as a result of the change of government between the two referendums: 'it is surely of the utmost significance that during the period since the first referendum an unpopular government (which had proved ineffective in turning diffuse support for the Treaty into actual votes) had been replaced by a much more popular government that was apparently able to prevent an equivalent erosion of support' (Franklin, Marsh and McLaren 1994: 468; Franklin, Marsh and Wlezien 1994: 120). The analysis of voting behaviour presented in Chapter 3 shows that satisfaction with government did influence voting behaviour in the 1992 referendum, but that does not necessarily imply that this is the main factor which caused some people to change their mind between referendums. In fact, many of these studies seem to overstate the unpopularity of the government in 1992, given that the Gallup surveys show that the government had increased its electoral support from 31.8 (in 1990 election) to 34–35 per cent in the Spring of 1992 (Svensson 2002: 740). More significantly, the analyses presented in Chapter 3 show that attitudes and partisanship were more important than government satisfaction in determining voting behaviour in the two referendums. Since we do not have panel data, we unfortunately cannot determine more precisely what made certain voters change their minds. But we can come closer to an answer by examining the characteristic of the group of respondents who voted yes in 1993 and reported a no-vote in 1992 (the 'switchers'). How does this group compare with the voters who did not switch?

Table 7.3 shows the key characteristics (mean values) of five groups of voters: those who abstained, those who voted no in both referendums

**Table 7.3.** Who switched in the Maastricht referendums?

| Mean values for each group of voters | Abstain | No–No | Switched to No | Switched to Yes | Yes–Yes |
|---|---|---|---|---|---|
| Attitudes | | | | | |
| EU attitude scale (1–21) | 10.1 | 6.9 | 8.1 | 10.6 | 13.6 |
| Political union (0–10) | 3.3 | 1.7 | 2.0 | 3.8 | 5.6 |
| Elite cues | | | | | |
| Party endorsement (0–1) | 1.0 | 0.7 | 0.7 | 0.8 | 0.9 |
| Trust in politicians (0–3) | 2.0 | 2.0 | 2.0 | 2.2 | 2.3 |
| Knowledge | | | | | |
| Political awareness (0–10) | 3.5 | 4.6 | 4.0 | 3.9 | 4.9 |
| Knowledge of the EU (1–4) | 2.2 | 2.7 | 2.4 | 2.3 | 2.8 |
| Campaign exposure (0–10) | 3.3 | 5.1 | 3.2 | 5.2 | 6.0 |
| N | 43 | 346 | 29 | 134 | 398 |

Source: Folkeafstemningen om Edinburghaftalen.

(NN), the voters who switched to no in 1993 (YN), those who switched from no in 1992 to yes in 1993 (NY), and those who voted yes in both referendums (YY). It is clear from Table 7.3 that the key factor differentiating the three groups is their attitude towards European integration. Whereas the consistent no-voters are clearly Eurosceptic and the consistent yes-voters are somewhat pro-integration, the 'switcher groups' are almost exactly in the middle of the EU attitude scale in between the two groups. Equally, when we look at the mean values on the response to whether the respondent is in favour of a political union in Europe on a 10-point scale, the consistent naysayers score 1.7, the switchers 3.7, and the yes-voters 5.6. In contrast, there is no significant difference between the three groups when it comes to trust in politicians,[39] as we would have expected following the 'second-order' explanation. Party preferences do differentiate the groups. Figure 7.4 presents a graphical illustration of the differences between the groups in terms of attitudes and political awareness. It clearly shows that 'switchers' and abstainers are situated in between the YY and the NN group on the political integration scale and have slightly lower levels of political awareness.

This comparison across groups, combined with the analysis of voting behaviour presented in Chapter 3, suggests that attitudes towards the EU have played the most significant role in determining who switched vote choice between the two referendums. But this still does not answer the question of *why* people decided to change their vote based on these attitudes. The argument of this chapter is that voters were faced with

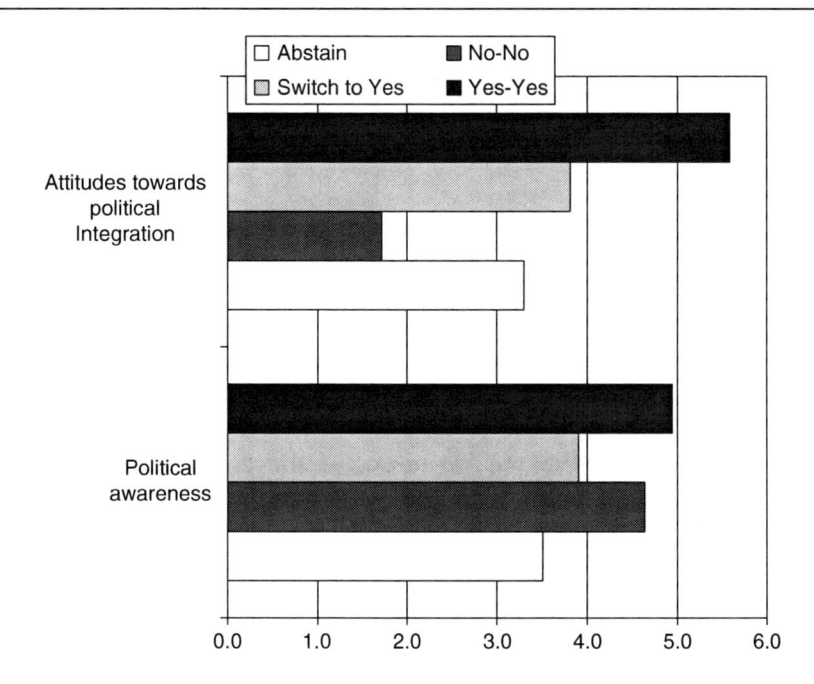

Figure 7.4. Comparing groups of Danish voters: attitudes and awareness

a different choice in the second referendum: not only did the ballot proposal change, due to the exemptions laid down in the Edinburgh Agreement, but the reversion point also changed, because the potential consequences of a second vote were likely to be more severe. The yes-side made it clear that if Danish voters had voted No a second-time, a different arrangement with the EU would be the consequence. In other words, Denmark would have to leave the EC (Nielsen 1993). Hence, if we recall the spatial model presented in Chapter 2, the ballot proposal moved closer to the position of the 'switchers', who are located roughly in the middle on the EU dimension (see Figure 7.4) and the reversal point moved further away from the switchers.

In Figure 7.5, this explanation for the change in behaviour between the two referendums is illustrated in a simple spatial model. The horizontal line represents a policy dimension of more and less European integration, where $r$ is the reversion point, $q$ is the status quo and $x$ is the ballot proposal (see also Figure 2.3). There are three groups of voters with different 'ideal points' on this dimension: NN are the sceptical Europeans, NY are the reluctant Europeans, and YY are the keen Europeans. In the first referendum scenario, the reversion point $r$ is located very close to

# Europe in Question

```
            NN              NY    YY
       r'           r       q     x'    x
    ├────┼────┼────┼────┼────┼────┼────┤
   -3   -2   -1    0    1    2    3
Less European                      More European
 integration                        integration
```

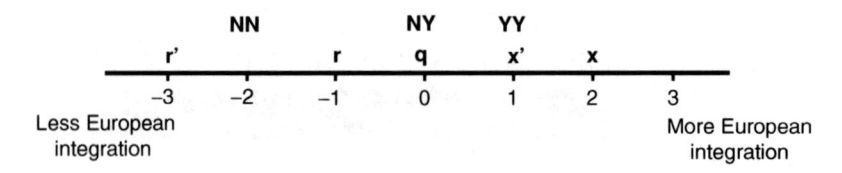

**Figure 7.5.** A spatial illustration of two referendum scenarios

the status quo and the proposal is located at +2. In this scenario, NN and NY voters would both reject the proposal, if they rely on proximity considerations, whereas YY would accept the proposals. However, in the second scenario the reversion point is moved to $r\prime$ and the ballot proposal to $x\prime$ and NY voters thus decide to accept the proposal, since this is closer to their ideal point than the more extreme consequences of a no-vote.

This spatial model is a plausible illustration of why the group of voters with mildly Eurosceptical attitudes (NY) switched between the two referendums. But what caused the proposal and the reversion point to change positions? The change in the position of the proposal was brought about by the exemptions in the Edinburgh Agreement, which took out the most 'integrationist' elements of the Treaty. Franklin, Marsh and Wlezien (1994: 120) have argued that the attitudes towards the Edinburgh Agreement could only have played a negligible role in the change of people's voting behaviour, since voters were 'remarkably ignorant about the details'. But according to polling data, 62 per cent of Danes claimed to have 'some' or 'great' knowledge of the Edinburgh Agreement and only 5 per cent of voters had 'no knowledge' (Siune, Tonsgaard and Svensson 1994: 123). When asked what the most important aspect of the Edinburgh Agreement was only 29 per cent of Danish voters were not able to mention one or more components of the Agreement (Siune, Tonsgaard and Svensson 1994: 140). Moreover, as previously discussed, voters may not need encyclopaedic knowledge in order to vote competently, as they can often rely on cues. The shift of the Socialist People's Party and the Christian People's Party offered highly visible and reliable cues to the voters that the position of the ballot proposal had indeed changed. So, even if a large proportion of voters did not know the minute details of the Edinburgh Agreement, the shift in party positions provided an informative signal of the change in the position in the proposal. Table 7.4 shows the percentage of yes-vote by party preference. It illustrates that the Socialist People's Party had little success in persuading their voters

Table 7.4. Yes-vote by party preference in the two Maastricht referendums

|  | 1992 | 1993 |
|---|---|---|
| Socialist People's Party | 10 | 19 |
| Social Democrats | 35 | 48 |
| Social Liberals | 68 | 61 |
| Centre Democrats | 70 | 62 |
| Christian People's Party | 8* | 13* |
| Conservatives | 74 | 80 |
| Liberals | 87 | 84 |
| Progress Party | 43 | 32 |

Note: Party preference is based on vote in 1990 election.
* N < 20

to adopt a new stance. More than 80 per cent of party supporters voted against the party recommendation in the 1993 referendum. This is hardly surprising, given that these voters are located on the very Eurosceptical end of the integration–dimension (NN). Hence, a small shift in the proposal and the reversion point would not be sufficient to change the behaviour of these voters if they relied on proximity consideration. On the other hand, the cue sent by the Socialist People's Party may have been sufficient to move some of the reluctant Europeans (NY), such as certain Social Democrat voters. Support among Social Democrat voters, who are normally more Eurosceptical than their party, increased from 35 to 48 per cent between the two referendums. Support also went up among Conservative and Christian Democrat voters, whereas it was in fact slightly reduced among Liberal and Social Liberal voters, as well as among supporters of the only remaining no-party, the Progress Party.

Hence, the Edinburgh agreement made a qualitative difference to voter perceptions of the proposal, either directly or indirectly through a change in party cues. As Siune et al. (1994*b*) have explained:

> For a small—but decisive—group of switchers from No to Yes, the Edinburgh Agreement meant that the political aspects of the Treaty became less daunting, and as a consequence, the priority of economic benefits versus political sovereignty changed between 1992 and 1993 (Siune et al. 1994*b*: 135–6).

Moreover, the position of the reversion point changed between the two referendums. In the second campaign, the yes-side strategically abandoned the 'softly-softly' approach and forcefully argued that a second 'no' would have detrimental consequences for Denmark in the EC (see Laursen

1994; Worre 1995). The yes-side emphasized that Denmark could not expect any further concessions from the EC and that a second no could have a high price tag for Denmark. In a television broadcast the week prior to the vote, the governing parties argued that a No would mean a 'looser' association with the EC (Nielsen 1993: 46). Hence, as suggested in Hypothesis 2.7, the yes-side made a great effort in the second Maastricht referendum to emphasize that the choice was no longer between the Union and the status quo, but between the Union and an uncertain situation for Denmark in the EC, possibly an exit. This strategy appears to have been at least somewhat successful given that the proportion of people who believed that Denmark would have to exit the EC after a No doubled between the two referendums (Nielsen 1993).

To conclude, the evidence presented here suggests that Danish voters relied mainly on issue preferences when they changed their vote from no to yes between the two referendums. The campaign thus brought about a change in behaviour by presenting a different choice to the voters in the second campaign. This case study of Danish Maastricht referendums corroborates the finding in previous chapters: when the European issue is highly salient and campaign intensity is high, then issue voting is pronounced. Political elites endeavour to influence the interpretation of the ballot proposal and the reversion point during the campaign. This *issue framing* plays a decisive role in determining the outcome, and government popularity, party cues and other 'second-order' factors are less important. Mark Franklin (2002: 752) has conceded that 'if any European electorates would have based their referendum votes on well thought-out preferences rather than on the positions taken by their parties, it would certainly have been the Danes'. But if the Danish case exemplifies patterns of voting behaviour when issue salience is high and information is abundant, what would be the situation in a political environment where the European issue is less salient? To address this question, the ensuing sections examine the two referendums on the Nice Treaty in Ireland.

## 7.4. Ireland in Europe: a success story

The Irish voters' defeat of the Nice Treaty[40] on 7 June 2001 was met by surprise and dismay all over Europe. In the foreign press, there was a sense of disappointment that a country which had benefited so much from European integration, both in terms of direct subsidies and benefits from trade, would stand in the way of further enlargement to the East.

In the days following the referendum, the Italian *La Repubblica* wrote that 'Europe had been stabbed in the back by its favourite son', the British *Independent* noted that the 'no' 'was a hefty political blow for Brussels, coming from a country where support for the EU has been strong—and one that has benefited hugely from European financial aid' and that the decision 'has given the country an instant reputation as Europe's most ungrateful nation', whereas the Danish *Politiken* suggested that 'the Danish disease had spread to Ireland'. According to many of these newspapers, the no-vote marked hostility to enlargement and deeper integration in Europe among the Irish. But was the Irish 'No to Nice' really a sign of growing scepticism towards integration and of opposition to enlargement in Ireland? And, if so, why did a large majority of voters accept the same Treaty in a subsequent referendum? This case study examines the referendum campaigns leading up to the two Nice referendums and proposes an explanation for why a majority of voters said no in the first referendum, and yes in the second. To begin with, this section gives a brief overview of Irish attitudes to European integration and of previous EU referendums.

### 7.4.1. Enthusiastic Europeans

Ever since Ireland, Britain, and Denmark joined the EC in 1973, both Irish elites and Irish citizens have been regarded as far more pro-European than their counterparts in Britain and Denmark. Successive Irish governments have been successful at dovetailing Irish and Community interests, and Ireland has thus been regarded as a firm supporter of further integration, 'provided the economic benefits will be fairly shared' (Scott 1994: 8). Ireland has, over the years, benefited from generous EU structural funds and Common Agricultural Policy subsidies that have helped boost its economy. From being the poorest member state when it joined the EC, Ireland is today one of the countries with the highest GDP per capita in the Union.

The Irish political and economic elites have been almost unanimous in their support of the integration project. The two main parties in Irish politics, Fianna Fáil and Fine Gael, have campaigned in favour of each successive Treaty revision (Gilland 2002). The main party on the left, the Labour Party, campaigned against accession, but moved to a pro-European stance after Ireland joined. Equally, the smaller Progressive Democrat party is pro-European. Hence, the mainstream parties that form governments in Irish politics have all adopted a pro-European line. The Green

Party has led the campaign for a no-vote in every referendum going back to the SEA in 1987, but after it joined a coalition government with Fianna Fáil and the Progressive Democrats in 2007, the party changed sides in the more recent referendum on the Lisbon Treaty and recommended a yes-vote.[41] The remaining Eurosceptic parties in Ireland are all to be found on the fringes of the political spectrum: Sinn Féin and the Workers Party and other small parties on the far left have all been consistently opposed to further European integration.

### 7.4.2. Irish referendums on European integration

The many Irish referendums on European matters have their roots in constitutional provisions. When ratification of an international treaty requires changes to the 1937 Irish Constitution, a referendum must be held to approve it (Mansergh 1999). A referendum was thus necessary before Ireland could join the EC in 1973. Both the governing party, Fianna Fáil, and the main opposition party Fine Gael, supported membership, as did the employers' and farmers' interest groups, while Labour and the trade unions opposed it. There were very clear economic arguments in favour of joining, given the fact that Ireland's largest trade partner, Britain, was joining, combined with the prospect of generous EC subsidies to Irish agriculture. A very large majority of 83 per cent of voters endorsed the Treaty, with a turnout of 71 per cent; the highest ever in an Irish referendum since the Constitution was approved (Sinnott 2002).

In 1986, the Irish government agreed to the SEA on the assumption that it would be ratified in the *Daíl*, the Irish Lower House, without a referendum.[42] Yet, this decision was challenged in the Supreme Court by anti-integration campaigner Raymond Crotty, and the Court ruled that a referendum was needed, since Title III of the Act contained a provision conceding sovereignty in the area of foreign policy.[43] The Court's decision created the precedence that all future Treaty revisions would require referendums in Ireland (Mansergh 1999). Hence, the government was forced to conduct a referendum in order to ratify the SEA, but as the *Taoiseach* (Irish Prime Minister) FitzGerald has noted, 'it wasn't a difficult campaign. It was about removing the barriers to trade, which were impeding us as the most exporting country in Europe. It was straightforward'.[44] All mainstream parties recommended a 'yes',[45] and the Act was passed by 70 per cent of voters with a turnout of 44 per cent. The Maastricht Treaty, which met substantial opposition in Denmark and France, also passed easily in Ireland. During the referendum campaign the *Taoiseach* Albert

Reynolds emphasized the IR£6 billion that Ireland would receive from the structural and cohesion funds if the voters said 'yes' to Maastricht[46] as well as economic benefits from the single currency. The referendum was passed by 69 per cent of Irish voters.

Compared with the Danish referendums, the Irish referendums on Europe have not been characterized by high intensity campaigns, until the recent votes on the Nice (2002) and Lisbon (2008) treaties. As examined in Chapter 4, partisan polarization is lower in Ireland, news coverage of referendums is limited, and there is generally little uncertainty about the outcome. Even by these standards, the fourth referendum on Europe, the ratification of the Amsterdam Treaty, was a very low-key affair that was largely over-shadowed by the ballot on the Good Friday Agreement held on the same day (Mansergh 1999). This referendum was also easily passed: 62 per cent voted in favour. This indicated a slow but steady decline in voter support in EU referendums, from 83 per cent in 1972 to 70 per cent in 1987 to 69 per cent in 1992 and finally, to 62, to per cent in 1998. However, because turnout had also declined, the actual growth in the no-camp is more modest than it appears[47] (Sinnott 2001, 2002).

Public support for the EU in Ireland has been among the highest in Europe since the late 1980s according to all indicators of public support. During the past decade, an average of 77 per cent of the Irish have expressed that membership of the EU is 'a good thing' compared with just 5 per cent that believed membership was a 'bad thing', as shown in Figure 7.6. However, given the low salience of the European issue and

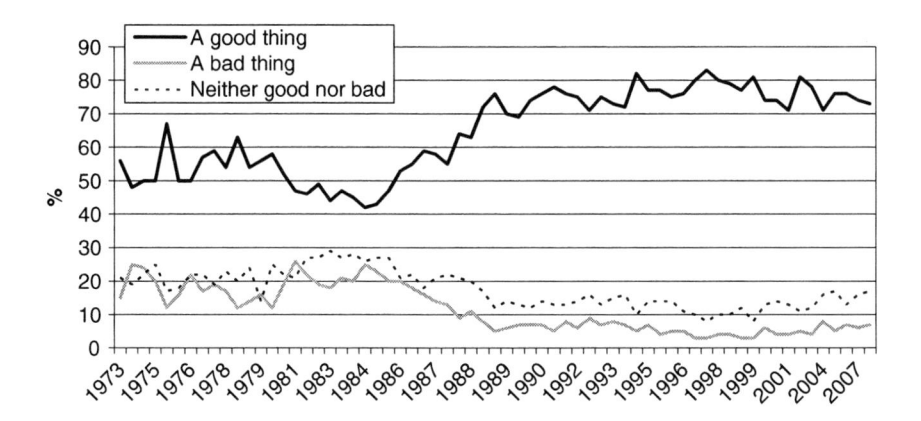

Figure 7.6. Irish attitudes towards EU membership
Source: Eurobarometer surveys 1973–2008.

the limited campaign activity in EU referendums in Ireland, we would expect EU attitudes to play a relatively limited role in deciding vote choices, as discussed in Chapter 2. As long as elites express a clear and unanimous pro-European message, the 'mainstream effect' is likely to induce a majority of voters to vote in favour of an EU ballot proposal (albeit with low turnout) as we saw in the first four Irish EU referendums. However, campaign factors may easily disturb this 'mainstream effect' in a low salience context if the message is less on target, since this may lead voters to base their choices on second-order considerations. It is therefore not entirely surprising that the Irish political establishment could not translate high levels of public support for EU membership into an acceptance of the Nice Treaty in 2001. As Labour's General Secretary, Mike Allen, has noted, 'nobody has really bothered in Ireland to make a coherent pro-European argument. In Nice, we were faced for the first time with having to catch up with 20 years of thinking about the European Union'.[48]

This chapter suggests that the dissemination of political information in the campaign played a vital role: the lack of campaigning by the yes-side, combined with an impassioned no-campaign, created uncertainty, even amongst traditionally pro-European voters, and reduced the utility of the ballot proposal. This, in turn, led to higher levels of abstention and no-voting. The next section considers this explanation in more detail.

## 7.5. Not so nice: the Irish referendum on the Nice Treaty

On paper, the yes-side was in a very strong position prior to the 2001 referendum on the ratification of the Nice Treaty. The Treaty had the support of Fianna Fáil and the Progressive Democrats in government as well as the main opposition parties, Fine Gael and the Labour Party. It was also supported by the Roman Catholic Church and by employer and trade union organizations (O'Mahony 2001). Against the Treaty were the small and peripheral parties, Sinn Féin and the Greens, as well as ideologically diverse groups, such as far left parties, pacifist groups, the Eurosceptic National Platform, and the 'No to Nice' campaign, led by conservative Catholics. But although the yes-side may have appeared much stronger on paper, they made very little effort to campaign and the no-side had the agenda-setting power during the campaign. The chief strategist of Fianna Fáil's campaign, Martin Mackin, explains the lack of campaigning by the government:

In the case of Fianna Fáil, we weren't sufficiently focused on it. We had a General Election coming. All our resources, our financial resources, human resources, intellectual resources were all focused on the election and preparing for that. And Nice was just something we had to do. We had to get it out of the way.[49]

Similarly, the Minister for Europe, Dick Roche, has admitted that the government was complacent because it was sure that it would be an easy win.[50] Moreover, the opposition parties sent very ambivalent signals about the Treaty,[51] and may not have been too keen to help the government with a large referendum victory so soon before a general election. Mike Allen has said that the opinion within the Labour party was that it was essentially 'the government's responsibility to get it through'.[52] As a consequence of this sense of complacency among established parties, there was very little campaigning in favour of the Treaty. But voters were exposed to a wide array of arguments against the Treaty from the no-side. The no-campaign emphasized that the Treaty meant loss of Irish neutrality and sovereignty and even highlighted concerns that it would force Ireland to adopt liberal European abortion laws. Moreover, the no-side argued that the Treaty diminished the influence of smaller member states, such as Ireland, within the Union. These arguments were expressed in powerful slogans including, 'You will lose: Power, Money and Influence' and 'No to Nice, No to NATO'.

Another important factor during the campaign was the restriction on public funding that had been agreed after the Supreme Court's McKenna judgement.[53] Following this judgement, the government was restrained from using public funds to advocate partisan positions in referendums, and this not only meant that the main parties had to spend their own funds to campaign, but also that the government had to set up the Referendum Commission, charged with presenting the arguments for and against in a balanced and impartial way.[54] The Referendum Commission sent a leaflet to every household in which the arguments for and against the Treaty were given equal prominence. The arguments in favour included that the Treaty was 'Good for Ireland, Good for Europe' (also the Labour Party's slogan), would facilitate enlargement, and would not be a threat to Irish neutrality. The arguments against included loss of sovereignty, loss of influence for small states and militarization of the EU, and a threat to Irish neutrality (Referendum Commission 2001). One of the leading anti-EU campaigners, Anthony Coughlan, has emphasized that the Referendum Commission played an important role during the campaign: 'it was probably one of the huge forces favouring the no-side the first time around in the sense that it provided public money equally to both sides'.[55]

Unfortunately, as there is very little polling data available from the referendum campaign, it is difficult to track changes in public opinion during the campaign. A poll from May indicated that 52 per cent of voters had decided to vote yes and just 21 per cent intended to vote no. A week before the vote, the no-side had increased its share of intended voters to 28 per cent and the yes-side had a reduced share of 45 per cent.[56] But in spite of the narrowing of the gap, these polling numbers still indicated an overwhelming victory for the yes-side. What happened during the campaign? The lacklustre and indifferent campaign from the yes-side, combined with the well-publicized arguments of the no-campaign, are likely to have caused a great deal of uncertainty among voters. As discussed in Chapter 2, a high level of uncertainty is likely to reduce the utility of the ballot proposal, thus inducing people to either stay at home or vote no (see Hypotheses 2.2 and 2.3). This appears to be what happened in the first referendum on the Nice Treaty, which resulted in a record-low turnout of 34.8 per cent and a majority of 53.9 per cent against the Treaty. This case study of the campaign thus suggests that this 'no' was as much a result of the uncertainty created by the lack of information during the campaign as it was a rejection of the substance of the Nice Treaty.

The post-referendum survey results support this argument. When asked why people chose to vote or abstain in the 2001 referendum, almost half of the no-voters and the abstainers justified their decision on the grounds of 'lack of information'. It is particularly interesting to note that lack of information is mentioned more often by no-voters in the 2001 referendum than substantive reasons, such as loss or sovereignty and neutrality, as Table 7.5 shows.

Another factor that may have contributed to the high level of abstention and no-voting is the fact that there seemed to be only limited consequences of a no-vote. Ireland was the first country to ratify the Treaty and the very low-intensity campaign by the government sent a signal to the voters that a yes-vote was not imperative for Ireland or for Europe. As the chairman of the anti-Nice Green Party, John Gormley, has explained: 'the stakes weren't high in the first Nice referendum, in a sense that people were given plenty of leeway. They could look at the arguments and decide: I don't understand this, I am going to vote No'.[57] Thus, due to the lack of information, most voters decided to stay at home, and of those who voted, many voted no on the basis of uncertainty about the proposed Treaty (Hayward 2003). While there is no indication that

**Table 7.5.** Reasons for vote choice in the Nice referendums

|  | Nice 2001 | Nice 2002 |
|---|---|---|
|  | % | % |
| **Vote Yes** |  |  |
| Generally a good idea, development of existing commitments | 44 | 53 |
| Enlargement a good thing | 22 | 29 |
| Influence of elites | 14 | 11 |
| **Vote No** |  |  |
| Lack of information | 39 | 14 |
| Loss of sovereignty | 16 | 8 |
| Neutrality issues | 12 | 17 |
| Bad idea in general | 7 | 25 |
| **Abstain** |  |  |
| Lack of understanding/information | 44 | 26 |
| Not interested/bothered | 20 | 32 |

*Sources*: Treaty of Nice Referendum 2001 and 2002, see Appendix 1.

dissatisfaction with the government contributed significantly to the Irish 'no',[58] the patterns of voting behaviour in this referendum nevertheless strongly resemble 'second-order' voting, given that the actual issue at stake—the Nice Treaty—appears to have played a very small role in voters' decision-making. Following the logic of the spatial model presented in Chapter 2 (Equation 2.1), we thus suggest that the value of $w_{ix}$ was very small (closer to zero than one) and consequently, a large proportion of voters relied on factors captured by the term $c_{ix}$, rather than relying on proximity consideration. Moreover, the utility of the proposal was reduced by the large uncertainty concerning the Treaty itself ($\sigma_{ix}^2$). The next section examines the second referendum on the Nice Treaty that followed the rejection of the ballot proposal.

## 7.6. A second vote on Nice

There was never much doubt that there would be a second referendum on the Nice Treaty. After the shock defeat in the first referendum, the *Taoiseach* Bertie Ahern told the other member states to continue with the ratification process of the Treaty. The Irish voters gave the coalition government a new mandate in a general election on 17 May 2002, and thereafter the government called for a second referendum on the Nice Treaty, scheduled for 19 October 2002. Unlike the Danish government, the Irish government did not negotiate any special exemptions or agreements with the EU. But in response to the concerns voiced over Ireland's neutrality in the first referendum, the government obtained a declaration at the Seville summit in June 2002 that clarified and confirmed Ireland's neutrality (Hayward 2003). Consequently, the ballot question was changed in the second referendum to include an amendment of the constitution specifying that a referendum was needed before Ireland can adopt any decision taken by the European Council to move to a common defence.[59] Although this was only a national agreement—and one that can be argued to be legally otiose since a move to join the defence pact most likely would have required a referendum anyway—it was a strategically clever way for the government to ensure that neutrality could not be used as an argument by the no-side in the second referendum. The no-campaign called this 'a political ploy'.[60]

However, it is unlikely that the neutrality amendment made the decisive difference to the outcome, given that it played a very limited role in the campaign and very few voters were aware of the amendment. More important was the fact that the yes-campaign led a much more intensive, passionate, and focused campaign than in the first referendum. The established parties had learned from their mistakes in the first referendum, and put all forces behind winning a second referendum. Fianna Fáil alone spent ten times as much in the second campaign, and in addition to the political parties, the major trade unions and IBEC, the business organizations, also ran vigorous and well-funded campaigns.[61] Importantly, a number of 'civil society' organizations were established on the yes-side, notably the Alliance for Europe, that brought together prominent figures from Irish civil society. Thereby, a 'No to Nice' could no longer be characterized as a 'No to the establishment'.

The government had also changed the rules governing the Referendum Commission prior to the second referendum. The Referendum Act 2001 removed the Commission's statutory function of presenting the arguments for and against referendum proposals and promoting debate on referendum proposals. Instead the Commission's role was limited to explaining the subject matter of referendum proposals and to encouraging the electorate to vote at the poll.[62] Thereby the government had effectively removed an important vehicle for the dissemination of the anti-Treaty argument. The no-side was also further weakened in the second campaign because it became increasingly clear that the different factions had very divergent objectives. The 'No to Nice' campaign, which had been one of the major forces during the first campaign, became a burden to the no-parties on the left—the Green Party and Sinn Féin—when it played the anti-immigration card and subsequently when it was exposed that its leader, Justin Barrett, allegedly had links with neo-fascist forces in Germany. According to the Green Party Chairman, 'bringing up immigration was a huge error. It damaged the campaign at an early stage of the campaign, because immediately you lose anyone of a liberal disposition'.[63]

Whereas the no-side appeared more split than in the first referendum, the yes-side ran a focused, energetic, and well-funded campaign and managed to dominate as agenda-setters throughout the campaign. Where the lethargic campaign leading up to the first referendum had signalled that little was at stake, this second campaign emphasized that the stakes were high: this was about jobs and growth and about Ireland's future.[64] As in the second Danish campaign on the Maastricht Treaty, the yes-side decided to put emphasis on the negative consequences of a 'no'. The campaign manager of the Alliance for Europe, Adrian Langan, has explained that the yes-side targeted many of the people who abstained in Nice One, by emphasizing the negative consequences of a second 'no':

We structured our campaign around the theme of *consequence*: the consequence of saying No. We said: There are real consequences. In Nice One people had not been told that there were consequences of voting No. We felt it was important to communicate that message. In particular to people who were likely to be pro-European, who stayed at home in the first referendum, we pointed out that staying at home is not a viable option. So there was an element of threat, but the threat was real.[65]

By emphasizing the consequences of a 'no' for Ireland's future, the yes-campaign strategically highlighted that the 'reversion point' was not the status quo, but rather a much more uncertain economic and political future for Europe. As discussed in Chapter 2, the yes-campaign may have adopted such a strategy to increase the uncertainty associated with the reversion point, thereby hoping to persuade more voters to accept the ballot proposal (Hypothesis 2.7).

The intensive campaign also served not only to inform people about the ballot and thus reduce uncertainty, but also activate to people's attitudes towards Europe. Given the high level of latent support for membership of the EU in Ireland, this was a successful strategy. A theme that became very important in the second referendum was that of enlargement. Combining the moral arguments of enlargement with the negative economic consequences of a 'no' was a part of the yes-side strategy, as Fianna Fáil's campaign manager, Martin Mackin, has explained:

## Europe in Question

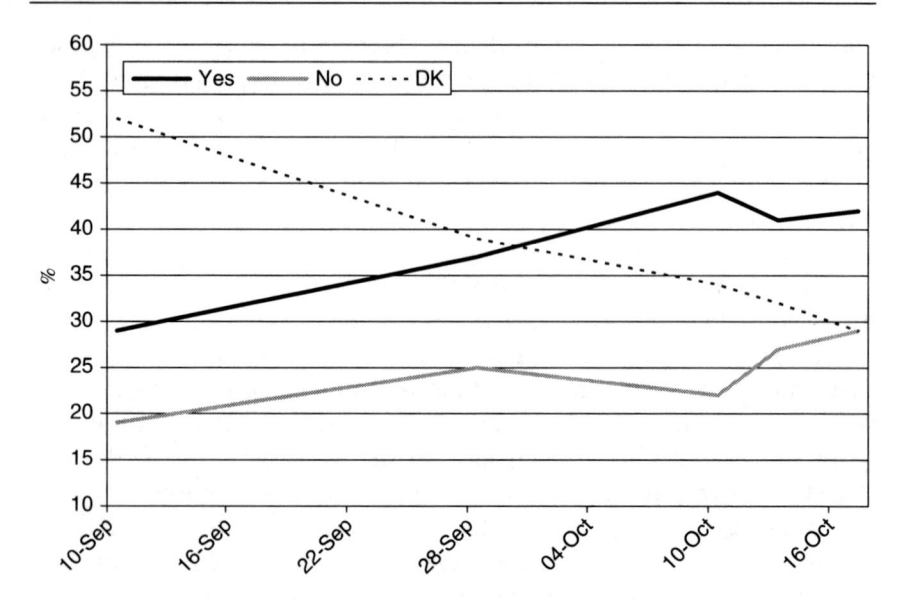

**Figure 7.7.** Vote intention during the 2002 Nice campaign
*Source*: IMBR and IMS polls.

In the last week of the campaign, we took a more altruistic approach, we talked about Poland and the Czech Republic. About enlargement. The moral argument. But we wanted to make sure that people felt their pockets were safe beforehand. So most of our arguments were about jobs, growth, opportunities for Ireland, new markets, more growth.[66]

As shown in Chapter 3, issue attitudes did become more important in the second Nice referendum, and a more in-depth study of the *type* of attitudes that mattered shows that it was mainly attitudes towards enlargement that influenced the greater likelihood of voting 'yes' in the second referendum (see Garry, Marsh and Sinnott 2005). Hence, the yes-campaign was clearly successful in setting the agenda and activating pro-European attitudes. Several polls tracked opinions during the campaign, and showed a clear increase in the share of voters intending to vote 'yes'. Figure 7.7 also shows that more than half of the voters were undecided before the campaign began (compared with less than 20 per cent before the Danish campaign in 1993), and hence there was great scope for the campaign to influence people's opinions.

When the Irish voted a second time on the Nice Treaty on 19 October, turnout had increased by 14 percentage points to 48.5 per cent and the yes-vote had increased by 17 percentage points to 62.9 per cent. Hence,

**Table 7.6.** Who switched in the 2002 Nice referendum?

| Mean values for each group of voters | Abstain | No–No | Switch to No | Switch to Yes | Abstain–Yes | Yes–Yes |
|---|---|---|---|---|---|---|
| Attitudes | | | | | | |
| EU attitude scale (1–21) | 9.1 | 6.7 | 7.9 | 9.6 | 10.6 | 11.7 |
| Enlargement (1–2) | 1.7 | 1.4 | 1.5 | 1.8 | 1.9 | 1.9 |
| Sorry if EU were scrapped (1–3) | 2.4 | 2.4 | 2.4 | 2.6 | 2.7 | 2.7 |
| Elite cues | | | | | | |
| Party endorsement (0–1) | 0.6 | 0.6 | 0.6 | 0.7 | 0.7 | 0.9 |
| Government satisfaction (0–2) | 0.5 | 0.3 | 0.5 | 0.5 | 0.7 | 0.9 |
| Knowledge | | | | | | |
| Political awareness (0–10) | 2.8 | 3.8 | 2.7 | 3.8 | 3.8 | 4.6 |
| Understanding of the Treaty (1–4) | 2.3 | 2.9 | 2.4 | 3.0 | 2.9 | 3.2 |
| Campaign exposure (0–30) | 13.5 | 15.8 | 15.2 | 16.4 | 16.8 | 17.8 |
| N | 608 | 133 | 65 | 110 | 150 | 262 |

*Source:* Treaty of Nice Referendum 2002, see Appendix 1.

just looking at the aggregate figures, one might suspect that the yes-majority was simply a product of the change in turnout: the yes-campaign had been successful in getting the pro-Europeans who abstained in the first referendum to vote yes the second time around. This is also a prominent explanation in the literature (see for example, Sinnott 2003*a*). Yet, while the increase in turnout clearly made an important difference, it does not tell the whole story.

### 7.6.1. Who switched in the 2002 referendum?

In order to explore the reasons behind the increase in the yes-vote in the second Nice referendum, we can compare the characteristics of voters who abstained, voters who stayed faithful to their yes- and no-positions, and citizens who decided to vote only in the second referendum or who changed their position between referendums (the 'switchers'). The first thing to note about the figures in Table 7.6 is that only a little over half of the 'swing' was caused by abstainers deciding to vote 'yes'. According to this post-referendum survey, 42 per cent of the swing was a result of no-voters shifting to a yes-vote in the second referendums. This indicates that the campaign did more than simply mobilize people; it also persuaded voters to adopt a different stance.

But why did a sizeable proportion of the electorate (8 per cent according to the survey) decide to change from a no- to a yes-vote? If wc look at the voters who changed their position to a 'yes', it is clear that they are more

**Europe in Question**

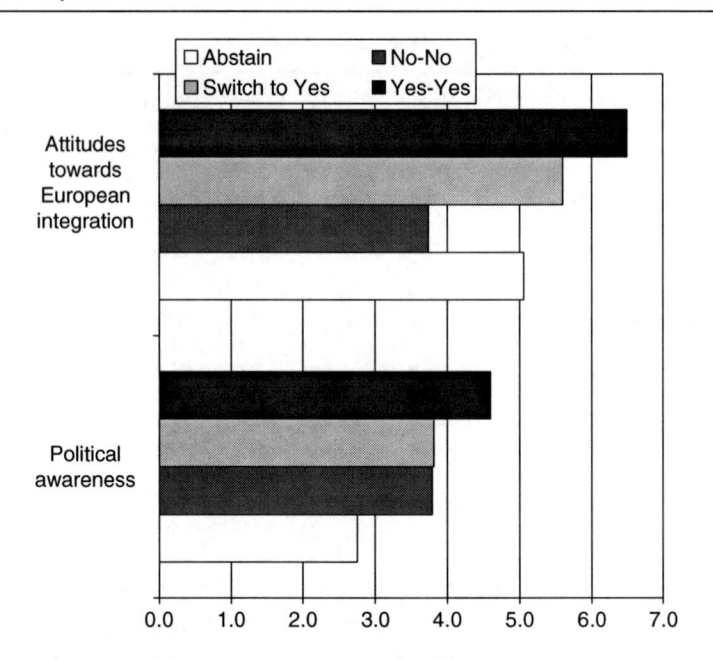

**Figure 7.8.** Comparing groups of Irish voters: attitudes and awareness

*Note*: In this figure, the EU attitude scale has been rescaled to a 10-point scale for the sake of presentation.

pro-European than the consistent no-voter. They are also more likely to prefer a pro-European party and to be satisfied with the government (especially the people who abstained in the first referendum). This suggests that attitudes, party cues, and government satisfaction could have played a role in inducing people to switch to 'yes'. Figure 7.8 shows that the voters who switched to 'yes' are in between the consistent yes- and no-voters on the EU attitude scale (although the differences between the groups were more pronounced in the Danish case). The main difference between the people who switched to 'yes' (from abstaining or from a no-vote) and the people who decided to stay at home in 2002 (which was still more than half of the eligible voters) is that the former group is more politically aware than the latter.

Looking at the characteristics of the group of people who switched to a yes-vote in 2002, we may ask ourselves why these people did not vote 'yes' the first time around. What changed between the two referendums? The answer to this question has already been alluded to in the above case study. Whereas there was very little campaigning in the first referendum, the second referendum was preceded by an intensive campaign that activated people's pro-European attitudes, gave effective party cues and increased the incentives to vote—and to vote 'yes'—on referendum day. A united elite has no 'mainstreaming' and persuasion effect if it fails to disseminate cues, as we saw in the first referendum on Nice. As described in Chapter 4, the campaign can act both as a motivator and as an informer. This was the case in the second referendum, where the yes-side managed to mobilize more people to say 'yes', and inform them in a way that enabled them to relate their own attitudes (for example, towards enlargement) to the ballot proposal. Table 7.5 shows that considerably fewer people mentioned 'lack of information' as a reason for abstaining or a no-vote in the second Nice referendum compared with the first. As Fianna Fáil's campaign strategist has noted:

The problem was not with the quality of the Treaty, but with communication of the outcome. In Nice One we didn't do that. In Nice Two we did it very well. The campaign made the difference. When that campaign started, the 17 per cent swing was not there.[67]

But the success of the second campaign was not only about a better communication of the ballot proposal. It was also about a different portrayal of the reversion point. Whereas the lax campaign in the first referendum suggested that a no-vote would make little difference (which was also one of the arguments promoted by the no-side), the yes-side adopted a new strategy in the second referendum that made it clear that a no-vote would have serious consequences both for Ireland and for the enlargement process. It is very likely that this also contributed to the increase in turnout as well as the increase in the share of yes-votes.

All in all, this case study of the Irish referendums on the Nice Treaty corroborates many of the arguments put forward in earlier chapters. First, the case study has shown that turnout and issue voting are generally lower when the salience of European integration is low and when the campaign provides little information or motivation. Second, it illustrates that an increase in campaign intensity can lead to a significant increase in levels of turnout and also potentially lead to more issue voting. Finally, these case studies show that when the elites do not make an effort to explain the consequences of a no-vote, voters are much more likely to reject the proposal.

## 7.7. Conclusion

> *The problem in a referendum is that you can ask the right question, but people answer other questions.*[68]
> —Dick Roche, Irish Minister of Europe.

Voters may interpret a question on the ratification of an EU Treaty in a multitude of different ways, as Dick Roche has observed in the above quote. One of the important lessons from these case studies of Danish and Irish referendums is the importance of the *framing* of the question during the referendum campaign. If the task of competent citizens in a referendum is to decide whether the policy described on the ballot is better or worse than the policy entailed by a rejection of the ballot, then the framing of these alternatives will make a significant difference to the answer provided.

The case study of the first Irish referendum on the Nice Treaty illustrates that when very little information is provided about the ballot, voters are much more likely to answer 'other questions' or not to answer at all. After the second more intensive campaign, where more information was provided, more people turned out to vote for the alternative that was most consistent with their attitudes. In contrast, there was plenty of information available in both of the Danish referendums on the Maastricht Treaty. But in the first referendum campaign, the question was framed as a choice between a move towards a European political union and status quo, and a majority of voters assessed that the latter option would be preferable. In the second referendum on Maastricht, the question was framed very differently: now it was a choice between limited political and economic integration and a possible second-rank status or exit from the European Community. This re-framing of the question is likely to have tipped the balance in favour of the yes-side.

As these case studies have shown, the framing of the question during the campaign is closely linked to both the quantity and the type of information provided in a referendum campaign. The *quantity* of information concerns the intensity of the campaign. When very little information is provided and elite cues are weak or divided, voters are more likely to be uncertain about the benefits of the ballot proposal, which will make them less likely to vote and more likely to reject the proposal. Lack of information also increases the likelihood of 'second-order' voting. The first referendum on the Nice Treaty provides a good example of what can happen when there is virtually no campaign effort on the part of the established political parties: voters stay at home, and those who turn out are more inclined to vote against the proposal because they are uncertain about the implications of voting yes.

But the framing of a question during a debate is not merely about *how much* information, but also *what type* of information. The type of information affects not only the uncertainty associated with each alternative, but also the 'position' of the choices. This is crucial since these case studies have shown that the people who switch sides between referendums tend to be the people who are located 'in between' the consistent yes- and no-voters on the EU attitude dimension. This suggests that by re-framing the 'position' of each of the alternatives, the campaign can persuade voters to change sides, as proposed by the theoretical model in Chapter 2. Naturally, the extent to which the yes-side or no-side have the agenda-setting powers during the campaign is very important, since it influences the prevailing interpretation of the ballot issue. For example, is the Nice Treaty about enlargement (yes-side) or about neutrality (no-side)? But agenda-setting powers are not only about how the proposal is interpreted. The framing of the reversion point is equally important. In the cases examined in this chapter, a large majority of citizens are in favour of continued membership of the EU. Hence, if the question is framed as a choice between the proposal and exit from the Union, most voters are likely to opt for the former. But importantly, such a 'threat' of exit from the Union must be credible, and therefore it matters whether the domestic (and international) political context makes the threat seem believable to the voters.

If campaign information matters, this in turn implies that the strategies of political elites are very important, since these elites provide the bulk of information. We have seen that the degree of success in a campaign depends on the extent to which the political elites can, on the one hand, present their favoured proposal as close to the 'bliss point' of voters and, on the other hand, create uncertainty about the consequences of the reversion point. But these case studies have also shown that the strategies employed by elites in referendums are not always solely determined by the objective of informing voters about the ballot proposals, but can also be influenced by domestic political considerations. The mainstream Irish political parties, for example, chose to spend very little effort or resources in the first campaign on the Nice Treaty because they wanted to save money for the upcoming general election, and the campaign by the Danish Social Democrats in 1992 was overshadowed by their internal leadership battle. In other cases, opposition parties may choose to make little effort to campaign despite being in favour of the proposal, because they are unwilling to hand an easy victory to the government,[69] and mainstream parties may avoid promoting a comprehensive debate on European integration to retain a stable equilibrium in party competition.

Hence, the extent of the problem of citizens 'answering other questions than the one posed to them' in referendums is partly dependent on whether the political elites have provided the necessary information and incentives for voters to enable them to answer the 'right question'. These case studies have corroborated the argument put forward in previous chapters of this book: the behaviour of voters in referendums is best understood by studying the information available to citizens and this, in turn, implies studying both the behaviour of political elites and the processing of information by the public. The next chapter examines how the campaign influenced attitudes and vote choices in the French and Dutch referendums on the Constitutional Treaty.

## Notes

1. Quotes from interviews with Dick Roche and Holger K. Nielsen. All Danish quotes are translated by the author.
2. The Accession bill was passed on 8 September 1972 with 141 members voting for and 34 members voting against Denmark's membership of the European Communities. Only the Socialist People's Party on the left was against membership.
3. Campaign slogans included: 'Vote Yes... for the sake of your salary'; 'Can you afford 20% devaluation?'; 'IMPORTANT: Don't be manipulated by extreme socialist and undemocratic forces. A No definitely means: stagnation, unemployment, and isolation. A Yes will secure the progress of democracy and continued economic growth in Denmark'; and finally, 'You want a happy family life. Yes. The Common Market creates a happy family life. Yes. Therefore, vote Yes to the Common Market. Vote Yes to the EC' (campaign ads reproduced in Skovmand 1977).
4. Danish governments have been reluctant to pursue further political integration in the EU. In the 1970s, Denmark was opposed to the idea of direct elections to the European Parliament at first, but eventually changed its stance. In the 1980s, Denmark was also reluctant to pursue further institutional reforms in the EEC (Laursen 1994). During the European Convention, the Danish delegates also opposed the more federal proposals.
5. Only Britain and Greece also voted no to the IGC.
6. Statement by the Social Democrats, quoted in Worre (1992: 95). The statement referred to the strengthening of the European Parliament's powers in the

SEA, which involved the cooperation procedure between Parliament and the Council that gave the Parliament real, if limited, legislative powers.
7. The possibility of a referendum was not presented until 14 January, when the Prime Minister announced in the daily radio news bulletin that the government considered calling a referendum if the Social Democrats voted against the SEA in Parliament. The final date for the referendum was not announced until 28 January—less than a month prior to the actual vote on 27 February 1986.
8. Headlines in the newspapers during the campaign were full of warnings about the dangers of a 'no', such as: '10 years with crisis and unemployment if Denmark says No' (*Jyllands-Posten*, 8 February 1986); 'Exit from the EU just as expensive as the Oil Crisis' (*Kristeligt Dagblad*, 8 February 1986); 'A No to the SEA costs 60,000 jobs' (*Jyllands-Posten*, 12 February).
9. The leadership of the small Christian People's Party (today the Christian Democratic Party) were in favour of recommending a yes-vote in 1992, yet the Party Congress decided in a very close vote to recommend a no-vote. In 1993, the Party recommended a yes-vote to the Edinburgh Agreement.
10. Interview with Niels Helveg Petersen. Helveg Petersen (member of the Social Liberal Party, *Radikale Venstre*) was the Danish Minister of Foreign Affairs from 1993 until 2000, when he resigned after the Danes rejected the Euro in a referendum. He was campaign director for the government's campaign leading up to the referendums on the Maastricht Treaty in 1993 and the Amsterdam Treaty in 1998.
11. Interview with Henrik Dam Kristensen. Dam Kristensen is Secretary General of the Danish Social Democrats and a former minister. He was campaign director of the government's campaign leading up to the referendum on the Euro in 2000.
12. Interview with Niels Helveg Petersen.
13. These were some of the arguments given by the Steen Gade and Gert Petersen (Socialist People's Party) against the Treaty in the Parliamentary debate. See transcripts in *Folketingstidende*, 17 March 1992.
14. Arguments posed by Annette Just (Progress Party) in the Parliamentary Debate on the Maastricht Treaty. See transcripts in *Folketingstidende*, 17 March 1992.
15. Interviews with Jens-Peter Bonde and Ole Krarup. Bonde is a Danish MEP for the June Movement and has previously been MEP for the People's Movement against the EU (*Folkebevægelsen mod EU*). He is one of the most prominent Eurosceptics in Europe. Krarup is a former Danish MEP for the People's Movement Against the EU.
16. Poul Nyrup Rasmussen was elected as leader in April 1992, 359 against 187 votes. The battle was more about personality than policy, but the party was nevertheless deeply divided.
17. For example, *Politiken* ran the following front-page story on 25 May, a week before the referendum: 'Social Democrats and Liberals are Fighting: They are

discussing who should take the responsibility for a Danish No. The Liberals are blaming the Social Democrats for not doing enough campaigning for the yes-side'.
18. Interview with Niels Helveg Petersen.
19. Table 7.4 presents data on vote choice by party affiliation. Only 35 per cent of social democratic voters voted in favour of the Maastricht Treaty in 1992.
20. A majority of social democrats (81%) followed the recommendation of their party and voted against the SEA in 1986, just like a majority, albeit small (55%), had followed the party-line in 1972 and voted in favour of accession (see Svensson 2002).
21. This finding can also be found in Siune et al (1992). They find that 'political union' is the most frequently mentioned theme in the media's coverage of the EU. In the newspapers, 18 per cent of all stories mention political union, while 37 per cent of television programmes are on this topic. In comparison, economic cooperation is only mentioned in 9 per cent of newspaper stories and 6 per cent of television programmes (Siune et al. 1992: 42–3).
22. Interview with Steen Gade. Gade is Member of the Danish Parliament for the Socialist People's Party *(Socialistisk Folkeparti)* and is the founder of the centre-left pro-European organisation New Europe *(Nyt Europa)*.
23. Socialist People's Party manifesto 1992 and interview with Jens Peter Bonde.
24. Interviews with Jens Peter Bonde, Ole Krarup, Holger K. Nielsen, Steen Gade, and Søren Espersen. Espersen is Member of Parliament for the Danish People's Party *(Dansk Folkeparti)*. He ran the party's campaigns leading up to the Amsterdam and the Euro referendums.
25. 'Denmark '92' later became the *June Movement,* which remains the strongest extra-parliamentary Eurosceptic group in Denmark.
26. Interview with Holger K. Nielsen.
27. *Politiken,* 'Nyrup: Danish Special Agreement with the EC. The Social Democrat leaders prepare for a no to the Union', 26 May 1992.
28. For an overview of the slogans used in the debates, see campaign ads reproduced in Skovmand (1977) and Bonde (1986).
29. Interview with Jens Peter Bonde.
30. Interview with Hans Engell. Engell is a former Danish politician and former Editor-in-Chief of the largest tabloid newspaper in Denmark, *Ekstrabladet*. He was the Minister of Defence from 1982 to 1987, Minister of Justice from 1989 to 1993 and leader of the Danish Conservative Party from 1993 to 1997.
31. At the meeting in Edinburgh, the European Council agreed to attach a 'Protocol' to the Maastricht Treaty with certain provisions relating specifically to Denmark, including opt-outs in the areas of citizenship, defence, justice and home affairs, and the EMU. These arrangements apply exclusively to Denmark and not to other existing or acceding Member States, and consequently, the Maastricht Treaty itself was not changed.
32. Interview with Niels Helveg Petersen.

33. The Socialist People's Party had written a memo before the referendum on 11 May 1992, which specified their position in the case of a no-vote (Socialistisk Folkeparti 1992). The demands in this memo were very similar to that of the National Compromise, and this compromise can therefore be seen as very closely aligned with the policy objectives of the party.
34. Interview with Steen Gade.
35. The ratification was adopted by 154 votes against 16 (Progress Party plus three members of the Socialist People's Party and one member of the Social Liberals), and there was thus a 5/6 majority in favour of the ratification. However, the bill specified that there would be a binding referendum.
36. The government resigned after the publication of the 'Tamil report' in January 1993. The main issue of the report was the Minister of Justice's handling of refugees from Sri Lanka (Siune, Svensson, and Tonsgaard 1994a). Some studies have claimed that the Tamil affair significantly affected the popularity of the government during the 1992 campaign (Schneider and Weitsman 1996: 596); yet, an analysis of the news coverage during 1992 and 1993 shows that this did not become an issue until *after* the first Maastricht referendum, and hence it would be a mistake to interpret the Danish 'no' in 1992 as a reaction to the Tamil affair.
37. Interview with Niels Helveg Petersen.
38. *Junibevægelsen* was formed on the 23 August 1992, a few months after the first Maastricht referendum, by the people within the Movement Against the EC, who believed that a broader Eurosceptic strategy against the Union but in favour of membership would be more successful.
39. Unfortunately, the survey does not contain a question explicitly about government satisfaction.
40. The Nice Treaty dealt mainly with the institutional adaptations required for the expansion of the Union to 25 Member States, which remained unresolved after the Treaty of Amsterdam. The Treaty of Nice was signed on 26 February 2001.
41. The Green Party held a special convention on 19 January 2008 to agree a position on the Lisbon Treaty. The result of the vote was 63 per cent in favour. The leadership of the Green Party thus failed to secure a two-thirds majority required to make support for the referendum official party policy, and individual members were thus free to be involved in the referendum debate on whatever side they chose. All Green Party members of the *Oireachtas* supported the Treaty.
42. Interview with Dr. Garret FitzGerald, *Taoiseach* from 1981 to 1987 for Fine Gael. During the 1972 accession referendum Dr FitzGerald was the leading spokesman for the very successful campaign in favour of joining the EEC. After accession he was appointed Foreign Minister, and pursued a strong pro-integrationist policy. Dr FitzGerald came out of retirement in the second Nice

referendum campaign in 2002 to campaign for a yes-vote as a part of the Alliance for Europe. He was one of the key figures in the campaign.
43. See *Crotty v. An Taoiseach* [1987] I.R. 713.
44. Interview with Dr. Garret FitzGerald.
45. Although it was a 'free vote' in the Labour Party. The Party had been opposed in 1972, but they had since adopted a more pro-European stance.
46. Interview with Brendan Halligan and transcripts from debates in Dáil Éireann. Halligan is chairman of the Irish Institute of European Affairs. He is former Member of the European Parliament, the *Seanad*, and the Dail, and he was General Secretary of the Irish Labour Party during the Irish accession referendum in 1972.
47. The percentage of the electorate no-vote was 12 per cent in 1972, 13 per cent in 1986, 18 per cent in 1992, 21 per cent in 1998, 18 per cent in 2001 and also 18 per cent in 2002.
48. Interview with Mike Allen, General Secretary of the Labour Party until 2008. Allen ran the Labour Party campaign in the two Nice referendums.
49. Interview with Martin Mackin, who was the General Secretary of Fianna Fáil, with responsibility for election strategy and campaign planning from 1998–2003. He was chief strategist for two Nice Treaty referendum campaigns.
50. Interview with Dick Roche, Irish Minister of State for European Affairs since 2002 and a member of *Dáil Eireann* for Fianna Fáil.
51. When the Treaty was negotiated, spokespeople for both Fine Gael and Labour were highly critical of the Nice Treaty. The Fine Gael leader called it 'one of the weakest negotiation outcomes achieved by an Irish government in the EU' and the Labour leader called it 'an appalling setback' (Gilland 2002: 528).
52. Interview with Mike Allen.
53. McKenna v. An Taoiseach (No. 2) [1995] I.R. 10.
54. The Commission was given the task of 'ensuring that the arguments of those in favour and those against the proposed amendment to the Constitution are put forward in a manner that is fair to all interests concerned'. See the Referendum Act 1998.
55. Interview with Anthony Coughlan, Secretary of the Irish Eurosceptic civil society organization, the National Platform. Professor Coughlan has been one of the most prominent Eurosceptics in Ireland for the past 40 years.
56. Market Research Bureau Ireland (MRBI) polls published on 19 May and 2 June 2001.
57. Interview with John Gormley, leader of the Green Party.
58. Unfortunately there was no question item on the government's performance in the post-referendum survey from 2001, so we cannot test the actual impact of this factor. However, the government was re-elected shortly after the Nice referendum, which suggests that this was not predominantly a vote against the government.

59. 'The State shall not adopt a decision taken by the European Council to establish a common defence pursuant to Article 1.2 of the Treaty referred to in subsection 7 of this section where that common defence would include the State'.
60. Interview with Anthony Coughlan.
61. According to Martin Mackin, Fianna Fáil spent 700,000 euro in the second Nice campaign, compared with 70,000 euro in the first campaign. In addition, Fine Gael spent 150,000 euro. Commentators estimate the assorted yes-side to have spent 1.7 million euro in the 2002 campaign, compared with 268,000 euro spent by the No-side (*Irish Independent* 21 October 2002; Hayward 2003). However, the no-side did not declare all of their spending, so the actual figures are most likely significantly higher.
62. See Referendum Act 2001 and Amendment of Referendum Act 1998.
63. Interview with John Gormley.
64. Ibid
65. Interview with Adrian Langan, Campaign Director for 'Alliance for Europe', a prominent civil society campaign group set up to ensure that the Nice Treaty would be passed in the second Nice referendum.
66. Interview with Martin Mackin.
67. Ibid
68. Interview with Dick Roche.
69. According to many of the Danish and Irish politicians interviewed, this was the case in several referendums, including the Danish Maastricht referendum in 1992, the Euro-referendum in 2000, and the Irish 2001 referendum on the Nice Treaty.

# 8

# Campaign Dynamics in the Referendums on the European Constitution

*The French expressed again on this occasion their anger and their exasperation toward a head of state, who not only failed to honour all his commitments, but also refused to hear the messages sent to him in previous elections.*

—François Hollande, president of the French
Socialist Party, May 2005

*By saying 'no', the French are calling on us to act quickly and vigorously to change the status quo. They are putting pressure on us to bring to an end the inertia and the nervousness..., to move the country forward as fast as possible.*

—Nicolas Sarkozy, president of the ruling party, the
Union for a Popular Movement, May 2005

The rejection of European Constitutional Treaty (ECT) by French and Dutch voters in the spring of 2005 in effect sounded the death knell for the European Constitution. Since all EU member states were required to ratify the Constitution, European leaders were forced to abandon the constitutional project and transform the treaty into the more modest Lisbon Treaty, which was subsequently rejected by Irish voters in June 2008. For the first time in the history of European integration, the people's verdict in a referendum brought an end to a treaty. In previous instances where voters rejected a treaty—in Denmark in 1992 and Ireland in 2001—subsequent referendums overturned the decision. But this time, it was the citizens of two of the founding member states who sent shockwaves through Europe. But why did the French and Dutch vote the way they did? This is the key question examined in this chapter.

Observers have offered different, and often contrasting, explanations of the referendum outcomes. The most prominent explanation follows the 'second-order' model, arguing that the no-votes were a protest against the national government rather than a rejection of the European project (see e.g. Dehousse 2006; Ivaldi 2006). This account was adopted by journalists, scholars, and politicians alike (see the quote from Hollande's speech above). After the vote, the *Financial Times* (2005) declared that, 'the French President's support was borrowed, not earned, and on Sunday many voters gleefully called in their loans'. It can be argued that it was convenient for both opposition leaders and European politicians to blame Jacques Chirac and the Dutch government for the outcome of the referendum, since that absolved the EU from any culpability. A contrasting, and potentially more troublesome, explanation suggests that the no-votes reflected concerns over European integration and that voting behaviour was characterized by 'issue voting'. Yet, it is unclear *which* issues played a prominent role: some have suggested that the ECT was rejected because European integration and enlargement are seen as a threat to national identity and sovereignty, others have suggested that this is because of an increase in levels of Euroscepticism across Europe and yet others have suggested that the no-votes were not a signal of voters wanting *less* Europe, but rather a *different* Europe (see Brouard and Tiberj 2006; Hainsworth 2006; Ivaldi 2006; Nijeboer 2006*b*; Sauger et al. 2007).

This chapter applies the theoretical and empirical insights presented in previous chapters to understand the vote choices of French and Dutch voters. First, it investigates the nature of the campaigns leading up to the two referendums in order to examine how much and in what way citizens' attitudes towards the European project were activated. We would expect that both the intensity and nature of the campaign affected individuals' vote choices. As shown in Chapter 4, more intense campaigns lead to more 'issue voting', whereas less intense campaigns bring about more 'second-order voting', since attitudes on specific issues are less accessible without campaign information. Moreover, we would expect the nature of the campaign to affect the *types* of issues and attitudes that matter to voters. Rather than assuming that campaigns simply prime generic feelings about the EU, we explore how the framing of the ballot question in campaigns influences which attitudes are relevant to the vote choice. This chapter therefore investigates the multidimensionality of attitudes towards Europe. Finally, we examine how attitudes and second-order factors influence vote choice in France and the Netherlands. Chapter 3 demonstrated that more politically aware voters rely more on their EU attitudes when deciding in referendums, and this chapter also explores which particular issues become more (or less) salient as voters are better informed.

In line with previous chapters, the analysis of the two referendums on the ECT shows that attitudes towards European integration mattered to voters, especially in the highly intense French campaign. The findings also suggest that the campaigns played an important role in framing certain issue attitudes, such as social issues in France and culture and identity concerns in the Netherlands. Hence, these no-votes reflected concerns over these specific aspects of European project rather than simply anti-EU sentiments and protest voting.

## 8.1. Campaigning on the constitution

The process establishing a Constitution for Europe followed from the Laeken declaration in December 2001, which proclaimed that 'the Union must be brought closer to its citizens'.[1] Paradoxically, the ratification of this constitutional project that was meant to bring the Union closer to the people clearly illustrated the gap between decisions taken by European politicians and citizens.

With the goal of creating a more democratic, transparent, and effective Union, the European Council meeting in Laeken established the so-called European Convention to produce a draft of a constitution for Europe. Under the stewardship of its President, Valéry Giscard d'Estaing, the European Convention brought together representatives from the European Parliament, national parliaments and governments, and the European Commission to formulate a constitution for the EU. The 'Draft Treaty establishing a Constitution for Europe' was published in July 2003. After protracted intergovernmental negotiations, the final text of the ECT was settled in June 2004 under the Irish Presidency. Ten member states announced that they would ratify the ECT by means of national referendums. This included not only the usual suspects of Denmark, France, and Ireland, but also Britain, the Czech Republic, Luxembourg, the Netherlands, Poland, Portugal, and Spain. The first referendum held in Spain in February 2005 was a quiet affair with an overwhelming elite consensus in favour of the treaty and high levels of diffuse support for European integration among Spanish citizens (Sorroza and Torreblanca 2005;

## Campaign Dynamics

Torreblanca 2005). Chapter 4 has shown that the Spanish referendum was one of the least intense referendums on European integration, characterized by limited media coverage and a relatively one-sided campaign in favour of the Constitution (see Figure 4.2). The outcome of the referendum was therefore unsurprising: a large yes-majority of 77 per cent and a low turnout of 42 per cent.[2] Chapters 3 and 4 also reveal that issue voting was very low in the Spanish referendum, whereas party endorsements played a prominent role (see Table 3.3 and Figure 4.4).

Following this low-key Spanish ratification of the Constitution, the ratification process was abruptly stalled by the no-votes in the French and Dutch referendums held within days of each other on 29 May and 1 June 2005 respectively.[3] In both countries, the ratification of the ECT was backed by the centre-right coalition government as well as the major centre-left opposition party. This elite consensus in the two founding member states was also initially reflected in high levels of public support for the European Constitution. In the autumn of 2004, 73 per cent of the Dutch and 70 per cent of the French said that they were in favour of a European Constitution.[4] Yet, despite these apparent similarities, the campaigns leading up to the two referendums were very different. Whereas the Dutch campaign only really began less than a month before the vote, the French campaign was drawn-out and very intense. The nature of the two campaign contexts is explored in further detail below.

### 8.1.1. *French and Dutch referendum campaigns*

To understand why the Dutch and the French voted no, we need to understand the dynamics of the campaigns. The comparison of the two campaigns in this chapter is based on a systematic content analysis of two national print media: *Le Monde* and *Le Figaro* in France, and *De Volkskrant* and *De Telegraaf* in the Netherlands. Every single referendum-related article in these newspapers has been coded in the 12 weeks leading up to the vote. This content analysis focuses on two main aspects of the campaign: the intensity of the campaign, measured as the average amount of daily coverage of the referendum, and the content of the campaign, measured by counting the issues addressed in each article.[5]

The first important difference between the two campaigns concerns the sheer volume of information: the intensity of the campaign. Chapter 4 measured the aggregate campaign intensity in terms of news coverage, partisan polarization, and closeness of the race. In Figure 8.1, we can

## Europe in Question

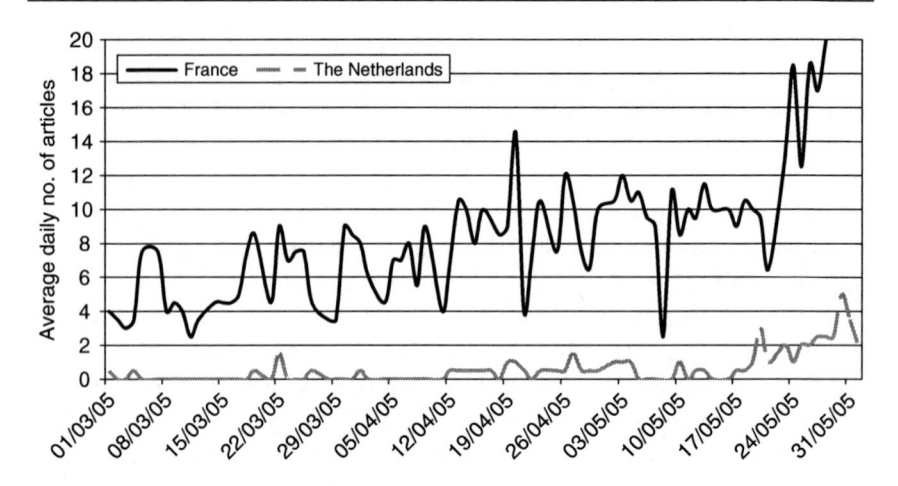

**Figure 8.1.** Intensity of campaign coverage
*Source: Le Monde, Le Figaro, De Volkskrant* and *De Telegraaf.*

see how the coverage of the referendum issue varied throughout the two campaigns.

Figure 8.1 clearly illustrates the higher intensity and longer duration of the French campaign compared to the Dutch. The French campaign began soon after the ECT was signed in June 2004, and it was therefore well underway on the 31 December 2004 when President Chirac confirmed he would call a referendum on the ECT. The polls suggested a solid majority of more than 60 per cent in favour of the ECT in the period leading up to the announcement. Yet, the campaign was not as smooth as Chirac and his government had hoped for. While the main newspapers and the mainstream parties—including the government parties, the leadership of the Socialist Party (PS) and the Green Party—recommended a yes-vote, there was substantial tension internally within these parties. The major opposition party, the PS, in particular, was deeply divided on this issue. In spite of an internal referendum held in December 2004 with 59 per cent in favour of the Constitution, a large faction of the PS campaigned for a no-vote (Hainsworth 2006; Ivaldi 2006; Sauger et al. 2007). The key dissident was the former French prime minister Laurent Fabius, who emerged as one of the leading voices of the no-side. The Green Party also advocated a yes-vote after an internal referendum produced an even narrower majority in favour (53 per cent against 42 per cent), yet there were many voices of dissent within the party.[6]

The parties on the left and right extremes of the political spectrum were all opposed to the Constitution. On the far left, the Communist Party (PCF), the Trotskyists, the anti-globalisation movement, and some trade unions campaigned on the no-side. On the far right, the National Front (FN), Philippe de Villiers' *Mouvement Pour La France*, the *Mouvement National Républicain*, Rally for France, and the hunting lobby as represented by *Chasse, Pêche, Nature et Traditions* were all opposed to the ECT. The no-side in France thus consisted of an odd mix of mainstream party dissidents and fringe organizations, similar to no-campaigns in most other EU referendums; it nonetheless managed to set the agenda on a number of issues (Brouard and Tiberj 2006; Hainsworth 2006; Ivaldi 2006; Marthaler 2005). The no-side linked the Constitution with the issues of immigration, accession of Turkey to the Union, and threat of European integration to French identity and sovereignty. Unlike the far-right campaign, the left-wing no-message was not anti-EU, but rather a condemnation of a particular kind of Europe—; a Bolkestein's Europe (named after the former EU-commissioner who proposed an increased liberalization of services), which threatened French workers and the social model. Fabius, in particular, stressed during the campaign that a no-vote was not a vote against Europe, but a vote for a more social Europe (Hainsworth 2006). Social and economic issues clearly dominated the no-campaign, both on the left and the right, with particular emphasis on the perceived neo-liberal, 'Anglo-Saxon' model allegedly promised by the Constitutional Treaty. The naysayers on the left criticized the EU's neo-liberal economic model that would leave French workers vulnerable to the free-market capitalism and globalization, and the naysayers on the right attacked the open borders and free-trade liberalism promoted by the Union. For example, Le Pen's FN denounced the 'extreme liberal and free-trade dogma of the European Constitution which would aggravate the economic and social catastrophe that is affecting the majority of French people' (quoted in Ivaldi 2006: 61).

Table 8.1 shows the main issues of the debate in both France and the Netherlands (as a proportion of overall referendum coverage). The key issues in the French campaign were the domestic economy and the effect of the EU on the economy, whereas concerns over enlargement, immigration, and identity received less attention in the media.[7] The campaign was also dominated by discontent with the government (both the president and the prime minister) and its policies. In the weeks leading up to polling day, the popularity of President Chirac and Prime Minsiter Raffarin reached its lowest point since 2002 at 39 and 21 per cent

**Table 8.1.** Issues in the campaign

| % of total referendum coverage | France | The Netherlands |
| --- | --- | --- |
| Government/Procedural issues | 24 | 30 |
| Foreign referendums | 12 | 29 |
| European Constitution | 11 | 18 |
| Domestic economy | 23 | 3 |
| Effect of EU on the economy/social model | 14 | 7 |
| EU enlargement | 9 | 6 |
| Immigration | 1 | 0 |
| National identity | 5 | 6 |

Sources: Le Monde, Le Figaro, De Volkskrant and De Telegraaf.

respectively (Ivaldi 2006: 49). Domestic themes thus played an important role, as the second-order model would predict, but in this campaign the troubles of the French economy and welfare state were linked to the liberal economic model promoted by the EU. The no-side thus managed to relate the fears over the pressures of globalization and the decline of the French social model directly to the issue of the Constitutional Treaty.

Unlike the French voters who have voted on aspects of European integration two times previously, the Dutch voters had their first say on the European project in the referendum on the Constitutional Treaty held only three days after the French no-vote. Previous to this, the Dutch had never held a national referendum, but the Dutch parliament—against the wishes of Prime Minister Balkenende—passed a bill that called for a consultative referendum on the European Constitution (Nijeboer 2005b).

The campaign in the Netherlands began much later than the French campaign and was less intense, as Figure 8.1 shows. The issue of European integration was not a highly salient issue in Dutch politics (Nijeboer 2005a, 2005b). There was a broad consensus in favour of the Constitution among the political establishment stretching from the parties constituting the centre-right governing coalition, consisting of the Christian Democrats (CDA), the Liberals (VVD), and the small Democrats '66 (D66), to the opposition centre-left Labour Party (PvdA), the Greens, the trade unions and business federations, and practically every newspaper in the country. This consensus in the Dutch parliament may have led to a certain level of complacency among pro-ECT parties that started their campaigning very late and without a coherent message to voters (Harmsen 2005; Nijeboer 2005b). The no-camp in comparison consisted of a mix of small parties: most importantly the Socialist Party (SP), but also populist right-wing groups such as List Pim Fortuyn, as well as the small orthodox–Calvinist *ChristenUnie*. Despite its size and ideological diversity, the no-campaign managed to set the agenda during most of the campaign, just as in France, and the government was forced to play catch-up (Harmsen 2005; Nijeboer 2005*a*, 2005*b*).

Much of the Dutch campaign focused on procedural issues, such as whether or not the government would respect a marginal no-vote. The CDA promised to respect a negative outcome, but demanded a minimum of 60 per cent of voters against, whereas the Liberals and the small Protestant parties were less forthcoming about how they would act in case of a no-vote (Nijeboer 2005*b*). As Table 8.1 shows, a great deal of attention was paid to the French referendum campaign (29 per cent of all coverage). In particular, the Dutch media closely followed the declining yes-vote in French opinion polls and discussed the possibility of a no-vote in both France and the Netherlands. However, in general, coverage of the referendum issue was far less intense and more sporadic than in neighbouring France. While the no-side dominated the agenda with a mix of arguments against the Constitution, the yes-side was largely on the defensive. On the far-right, the parties emphasized the threat that further European integration posed to national sovereignty and Dutch culture. The high-profile populist politician Geert Wilders, who had left the VVD in 2004 to form his own party, played a dominant role in the campaign. He vigorously opposed enlargement of the EU, particularly Turkish membership, and presented future expansion and the ECT as a potential threat to Dutch culture and sovereignty under the slogan 'The Netherlands must remain!' (Harmsen 2005; Aarts and van der Kolk 2006). The no-campaign on the left was led by the SP. In the same way as the far-left in France, it emphasized the dangers of a neo-liberal European Union (Harmsen 2005). Interestingly, however, the SP also focused on the dangers to Dutch liberal culture and Dutch identity. Hence, whereas the French campaign was dominated by economic and social issues, concerns over threats to sovereignty and culture were more focal in the Dutch campaign.

Despite these arguments pursued by the no-campaigns in both France and the Netherlands, the development in vote intention during the campaigns came as a surprise to most commentators. Figure 8.2 shows the percentage of voters intending a yes-vote (excluding undecided voters). In France, the majority in favour was around 60 per cent until late March, when the no-vote sharply increased. In the Netherlands, poll numbers were highly unstable until the campaign began in earnest about a month before the vote (partly due to the high number of undecided voters), and by then the intended yes-votes had plummeted to around 45 per cent.

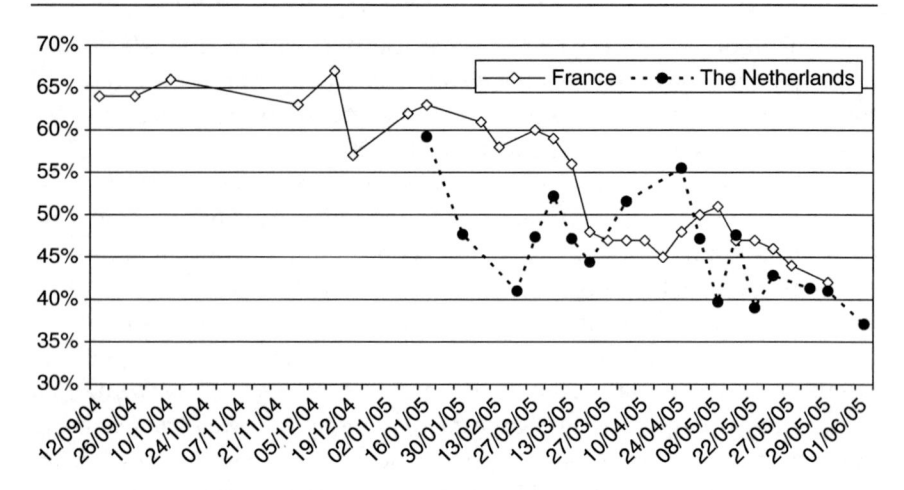

**Figure 8.2.** Vote intention in France and the Netherlands

*Note*: Percentage of respondents intending a yes-vote (excluding undecided respondents).
*Note*: Instituts BVA, CSA, IFOP, IPSOS, Louis Harris, SOFRES (France); De Hond, TNS-Nipo, Interview-NSS, Marketresponse, GfK Panel (the Netherlands).

Why did voters turn against the ECT during the course of the two campaigns? The most obvious answer is that the pro-ECT elites failed to persuade voters during the campaign. To examine the extent to which parties were able to convince their supporters of a yes-vote, we can look at the partisan divisions in voting behaviour. Tables 8.2 and 8.3 show the vote choice by party affiliation.[8]

We would expect that parties favouring the ECT would have a majority of supporters voting 'yes' in the referendums if voters take cues from their party. Tables 8.2 and 8.3 show that the governing centre-right parties in France and the Netherlands had some success at persuading

**Table 8.2.** Vote choices by party affiliation in France

|  | Seats in Parliament | Party position | Yes (%) | No (%) |
| --- | --- | --- | --- | --- |
| Union for a Popular Movement (UMP) | 357 | In favour | 76 | 24 |
| Socialist Party (PS) | 141 | In favour (*divided*) | 49 | 51 |
| Union for French Democracy (UDF) | 29 | In favour | 73 | 27 |
| Communist Party (PCF) | 21 | Against | 5 | 95 |
| Extreme left | 13 | Against | 32 | 68 |
| Greens | 3 | In favour (*divided*) | 38 | 62 |
| National Front (FN) | 0 | Against | 16 | 84 |
| No party | — | — | 33 | 67 |

**Table 8.3.** Vote choices by party affiliation in the Netherlands

|  | Seats in Parliament | Party position | Yes (%) | No (%) |
|---|---|---|---|---|
| CDA | 44 | In favour | 70 | 30 |
| PvdA | 42 | In favour | 50 | 50 |
| VVD | 28 | In favour | 63 | 37 |
| SP | 9 | Against | 8 | 92 |
| Greens (GroenLinks) | 8 | In favour | 66 | 34 |
| List Pim Fortuyn | 8 | Against | 8 | 92 |
| D66 | 6 | In favour | 82 | 18 |
| ChristenUnie | 3 | Against | 19 | 81 |
| Wilders | 1 | Against | 5 | 95 |
| No party | — | — | 32 | 68 |

their voters. In both countries, around two-thirds of government supporters voted in favour of the ECT. Party endorsements by the centre-right parties in government were fairly unambiguous in both France and the Netherlands, so it is perhaps not surprising that such a large proportion of their supporters followed the party line. More noticeable is the failure of the major centre-left opposition parties, *Parti Socialiste* and PvdA, in convincing their supporters to favour the treaty. In both cases, half of the centre-left voters rejected the treaty. In the Netherlands, the PvdA was conspicuous by its absence in the campaign, and in France, the open split in the Socialist Party meant that the party cues were ambiguous. A majority of French voters, whatever their party affiliation, could not identify the position of the Socialist Party on this issue (Sauger et al. 2007). The French Greens were also divided on the issue of the Constitution, and it is therefore unsurprising that a majority of their supporters voted 'no', whereas the Dutch Greens, who were more clearly in favour, persuaded a majority of their supporters. In contrast, in the 1992 French referendum on the Maastricht Treaty, when centre-left party cues were more unambiguous, four out of five PS voters and 57 per cent of Green party supporters had supported the treaty (Hainsworth 2006: 106). Hence, this evidence suggests that endorsements of parties that were openly split on the issue of Constitution did not work as effectively as for those parties with a more unequivocal position on the treaty. The consistency between party position and vote choice by supporters is by far the highest for parties on the far left (PCF, SP) and the far right (FN, List Pim Fortuyn, Wilders) in both countries.

The campaigns were not only about the dissemination of party endorsements, but also about information provision more generally. Given the intensity and polarization of the French campaign, we would expect this campaign, in particular, to activate issue preferences among citizens. To a lesser extent, we would also expect attitudes to matter to Dutch vote choices in conjunction with second-order factors, such as partisanship and feelings about the government. Chapter 4 showed that attitudes mattered more to voters in the high-intensity French campaign compared with the Dutch campaign (see Figure 4.4). But the intensity is not the only aspect of the campaign that may influence vote choices: The nature of the campaign messages can also frame the ballot issue in a certain way and bring specific issues to the forefront of voters' minds, while relegating others to the background. If the no-side, for example, was successful in dominating the campaign, we would expect that the themes promoted by this group of parties and organizations would play a greater role in the decision-making calculus of voters. To get an impression on the issues that were most important in the two campaigns, we can look at voters' answers to the open-ended question 'what are all the reasons why you voted [yes/no] at the referendum on the European Constitution' in the Flash Eurobarometer surveys conducted after the referendums (see Appendix 1).

Table 8.4 illustrates that 'diffuse support' for European integration was the most prominent reason for a yes-vote, according to respondents. Over half of French voters and a quarter of Dutch mentioned the importance of the 'European construction' as a reason for a yes-vote. Around a quarter of voters in both countries also mentioned that a yes-vote would strengthen their country in the Union or the Union as a whole. No-voters generally emphasized more concrete reasons for rejecting the ECT. In France, the concerns over the economic and social consequences of the Constitution were clearly the key reason for a no-vote: 57 per cent mentioned the negative consequences for employment and the French social model, and 37 per cent mentioned that the Constitution was too liberal. In contrast, the main reason mentioned by Dutch voters was the lack of information, whereas this was barely an issue among the French. This is perhaps not surprising given the differences in intensity of the two campaigns (see Figure 8.1). A quarter of Dutch no-voters also mentioned loss of national sovereignty and Dutch identity as a reason; a theme emphasized by the Dutch no-side. Second-order factors also appear to matter: 18 per cent of French voters and 21 per cent of Dutch admitted that their vote was a way of penalizing the government/President, or based on the recommendations of a particular party.

Broadly, the answers shown in Table 8.4 thus suggest that the campaigns—and in particular the no-vote campaigns—were successful in priming certain attitudes associated with the ballot question. In order

**Table 8.4.** Reasons for vote choice

|  | France (%) | The Netherlands (%) |
|---|---|---|
| **Reasons for Yes** | | |
| Important in order to pursue the European construction | 55 | 24 |
| Strengthens the role of country within the Union/in the world | 12 | 13 |
| Strengthens the EU over the United States | 11 | 10 |
| Strengthens the feeling of a European identity | 6 | 13 |
| Essential for the smooth running of the European institutions | 7 | 12 |
| First steps towards a political unification of Europe | 8 | 10 |
| Strengthens the economic and social situation | 8 | 10 |
| **Reasons for No** | | |
| Negative consequences for domestic employment/social model | 57 | 12 |
| Too complex/not enough information | 19 | 43 |
| Too liberal/not enough social Europe | 37 | 7 |
| Opposed to/influenced by government and other parties | 18 | 21 |
| Against further European integration | 9 | 24 |
| Loss of national sovereignty/identity | 5 | 21 |
| Opposed to enlargement | 9 | 9 |

*Note*: Open-ended questions and respondents were allowed to mention more than one reason.
*Sources*: Flash Eurobarometers 171 and 172, 2005.

to explore this in more detail, we can examine the dominant attitude dimensions among voters and analyse how these dimensions relate to vote choices.

## 8.2. Issue framing and attitudes

In previous chapters, we have treated EU attitudes as a simple unidimensional scale, ranging from Euroscepticism to support for the European project, as is the norm in the literature (see Gabel 1998*a*; McLaren 2002; Hooghe and Marks 2004). This simple scale allows us to compare the impact of attitudes on vote choice over time and across countries. Both theoretically and empirically, it has been shown to make sense to measure a unidimensional scale of diffuse support for European integration and membership of the EU. However, in a particular campaign certain aspects of integration attitudes might be more salient than others. As shown in Table 8.4, the campaign environments in France and the Netherlands primed particular aspects of the integration project. Using national survey data, we can further explore the multiple facets of public opinion in these two campaigns.

To analyse the attitudes and vote choices of French and Dutch voters, we use two national referendum surveys[9] that contain a wide range of attitude questions on different aspects of European and national politics. These survey items tap into different aspects of attitudes towards European integration, including concerns about identity loss, enlargement, the environment, economics, welfare, institutions and the pace of integration more generally. To investigate the structure of EU attitudes and identify specific dimensions, we use exploratory factor analysis (EFA). EFA enables us to assess whether the items tap into one or more underlying dimension as well as the degree to which particular items relate to the same dimension. For the analysis, we have chosen a range of interval or ordinal EU attitude items included in the referendum surveys. When exploring dimensionality using EFA, we are obviously constrained by the number and character of items included in the survey. Put differently, we will only be able to extract dimensions on the basis of the items included in the survey. Fortunately, both surveys contain more than twenty survey items relating to attitudes towards different aspects of European integration and the constitutional projects and all of the key issues identified in the campaign (economic issues, cultural and identity issues, enlargements etc.) were captured by questions in both surveys. Hence, this gives us some confidence in the significance of the dimensions extracted. In both the French and the Dutch case, the factor solution extracts four factors with standardized eigenvalues greater than 1. This suggests that attitudes towards European integration are multidimensional. The results of a constrained four-factor factor analysis with oblique rotation[10] for France are shown in Table 8.5.

To make sense of the results of EFA, we seek to interpret the meaning of the extracted factors on the basis of the relative factor loadings. Identifying the underlying meaning of each dimension is, of course, an inexact science, but by looking at the items that load highly on a particular factor we can get a good sense of what each dimension represents. The first factor in the French study reflects attitudes towards the ECT, but it is interesting to note that the item that loads highest on this dimension is the question on whether the Constitution guarantees the social rights of citizens (0.82), and concerns over potential loss of social protection also loads very highly (0.70). This suggests that concerns about social issues, such as threats to the French welfare model, are driving attitudes towards the Constitution in this dimension. Moreover, it is noteworthy that none of the generic 'attitudes towards the EU' questions load highly on this dimension. The second dimension taps into concerns about loss of national sovereignty and culture. The items on a weakened role for France in the world (0.81) and loss of identity and culture (0.70) load highest on this dimension.

**Table 8.5.** Factor analysis of attitude indicators in France

| Items | Factor 1<br>Social model and ECT | Factor 2<br>National sovereignty | Factor 3<br>Enlargement | Factor 4<br>Reversion point |
|---|---|---|---|---|
| The Constitution gives more power to the EP and the citizens | 0.75 | — | — | — |
| The Constitution is a threat to French secularism | — | — | — | — |
| The Constitution strengthens Europe's role in the world | 0.79 | — | — | — |
| A rejection of the Constitution would isolate France | 0.67 | — | — | — |
| The Constitution guarantees the social rights of citizens | 0.82 | — | — | — |
| Enlargement with Romania | — | — | 0.70 | — |
| Enlargement with Turkey | — | — | 0.83 | — |
| France pays for other countries | — | — | — | — |
| Loss of social protection in France | 0.70 | 0.56 | — | — |
| Loss of identity and culture | — | 0.70 | — | — |
| France will play a less important role in the world | — | 0.81 | — | — |
| Increase in the number of immigrants | — | 0.52 | 0.65 | — |
| Increase in unemployment | — | 0.59 | — | — |
| Leave the EU? | 0.62 | — | — | — |
| Are 25 member states too many? | — | — | 0.70 | — |
| Attachment to the European project | — | — | — | — |
| Has France benefited from European integration? | — | — | — | — |
| National sovereignty versus European integration? | — | — | — | — |
| A rejection of the Constitution would pave the way for another, less liberal, Europe | — | — | — | 0.87 |
| Eigenvalue | 5.71 | 1.61 | 1.31 | 1.05 |
| Proportion of variance explained | 30% | 8% | 7% | 6% |

Note: Principal factor analysis with oblique rotation. Only factor loadings above 0.5 are shown. N = 1009.
Source: French Referendum Study (2005).

The framing of cultural threat is also linked to immigration and social and economic issues. In this dimension, European integration appears as a threat to the sovereignty and culture of the nation itself. The third factor clearly represents enlargement concerns, as only questions on the size of EU and on enlargement with Turkey (0.83) and Romania (0.70) as well as concerns over immigration load highly (0.65). Interestingly, the last dimension is represented by a single question item on whether a rejection of the Constitution would pave the way for another, less liberal, EU. This dimension thus appears to represent the opinion on what will happen to the EU if the ECT is rejected by the French, thus capturing the perception of the 'reversion point' described in Chapter 2. Hence, we have labelled the four factors: social model and ECT, national sovereignty, enlargement, and reversion point.

The analysis of the Dutch survey data also results in a four-factor solution (see Table 8.6). In contrast to France, the more specific attitudes towards the ECT do not load highly on any of the factors. In the Netherlands, the first factor seems to represent a 'national sovereignty' dimension: concerns over loss of language (0.76) and culture and identity (0.76) as well as threats to employment (0.73) and farmers (0.73). The second dimension is more curious as it taps into 'postmaterialist' (or 'new politics') feelings towards the EU (see Inglehart 1971, 1977) about promotion of worldwide peace (0.80) and protection of the environment (0.65), and thus more diffuse reasons for supporting the EU. The third dimension clearly represents concerns about the Euro, while the last dimension taps into feelings about enlargement (in this survey, only questions on Turkey were included). We have thus labelled the four dimensions: national sovereignty, postmaterialism, euro, and enlargement.

It is not surprising that social issue concerns drive attitudes towards Europe in the French case, given the role such issues played in the campaign (37 per cent of all referendum coverage was concerned with economic policies, see Table 8.1). This also corresponds with the data from the Flash Eurobarometer survey presented in Table 8.4, where a majority of no-voters mentioned economic and social concerns as a key factor. In contrast, we find that concerns over threats to national identity and culture play a more prevalent role in Dutch attitudes. This also reflects the reasons mentioned by Dutch voters in the Flash Eurobarometer survey (21 per cent mentioned loss of national sovereignty/identity as a key reason), and suggests that the no-campaign's emphasis on the Dutch culture and sovereignty had an effect on public opinion. Moreover, with the debate surrounding the populist right-wing List Pim Fortuyn and Geert Wilders

Table 8.6. Factor analysis of attitude indicators in the Netherlands

| Items | Factor 1 National sovereignty | Factor 2 Postmaterialism | Factor 3 Euro | Factor 4 Enlargement |
|---|---|---|---|---|
| Democratic consequences of adopting ECT | — | — | — | — |
| Economic consequences of adopting ECT | — | — | — | — |
| Consequences for collaboration of adopting ECT | — | — | — | — |
| Consequences for social security system of adopting ECT | — | — | — | — |
| Consequences for the enlargement with Turkey | — | — | — | 0.81 |
| Transition from the guilder to the euro caused serious damage | — | — | 0.80 | — |
| The introduction of the euro is beneficial to the Dutch economy | — | — | 0.73 | — |
| Prices in the Netherlands have risen because of the euro | — | — | 0.90 | — |
| Euro introduction made foreign payments easier | — | — | — | — |
| Smaller member states will lose influence | 0.65 | — | — | — |
| Welfare will increase | — | 0.55 | — | — |
| Our language will be less used | 0.76 | — | — | — |
| Wealthier countries will be obligated to pay more | 0.54 | — | — | — |
| Environment will be better preserved | — | 0.65 | — | — |
| Social security will disappear | 0.57 | — | — | — |
| Our national identity and our national culture will disappear | 0.76 | — | — | — |
| Employment will move to other countries, where production is cheaper | 0.73 | — | — | — |
| Farmers in the Netherlands will have more trouble | 0.73 | — | — | — |
| Europe will try harder to achieve worldwide peace and stability | — | 0.80 | — | — |
| Opinion on European unification | — | — | — | — |
| Eigenvalue | 5.92 | 1.66 | 1.34 | 1.02 |
| Proportion of variance explained | 30% | 8% | 7% | 5% |

*Note:* Principal factor analysis with oblique rotation. Only factor loadings above 0.5 are shown. N = 1277.
*Source:* Dutch Referendum Study (2005).

and the murder of the controversial filmmaker Theo van Gogh by a Muslim radical in November 2004, the issues of Dutch identity and multiculturailism were already highly salient in the public sphere, and this may also have influenced people's perception of the ECT. More generally, we would expect that the Dutch campaign did less to activate attitudes (compared with France) given the low intensity of the campaign. Chapter 4 has already shown that generic attitudes towards the EU were indeed more important in the French compared to the Dutch vote, although they played an important role to voters in both referendums.

In the next section, we examine the extent to which these different attitude dimensions identified here influenced vote choices in the two referendums.

## 8.3. Explaining the no votes

To test the competing explanations of why the French and the Dutch voters rejected the Constitutional Treaty, we use the same national survey data as described above.[11] Our dependent variable is the vote choice in the referendums (yes is coded as 1; all non-voters were excluded from the analysis). Our key independent variables are the four attitudes dimensions (factor scores) derived from the factor analyses described in the previous section.[12] To examine the impact of second-order factors, we include two variables that tap into domestic politics. First, we include a variable of partisan identification, since we expect that voters are more likely to vote in favour of the ECT if they support a party that recommends a yes-vote. We include a dummy for each group of party supporters (with 'no party' as the reference category) to be able to examine the differential impact of party recommendations. Second, we include a variable that captures satisfaction with the executive (satisfaction with President Jacques Chirac in France and general government satisfaction in the Netherlands). Following the second-order election literature, we would expect that people are more likely to reject the ECT if they are dissatisfied with the performance of the national government. We also include a political awareness variable in the analysis, capturing respondents' awareness of and interest in the European Constitution. Finally, we include the same set of control variables as in the analyses presented in Chapter 3: age, gender, and income/class. We estimate two models: Model 1 estimates the direct effect of all variables, whereas Model 2 also includes an interaction between awareness and each of the four attitude dimensions to examine the

Table 8.7. Predicting vote choice in France

|  | Model 1 Logit (S.E.) | Model 2 Logit (S.E.) |
|---|---|---|
| EU attitudes | | |
| Social model and ECT | 2.88** (0.28) | 1.53** (0.55) |
| National sovereignty | 0.38* (0.18) | 1.01 (0.68) |
| Enlargement | 0.54** (0.19) | −0.14 (0.63) |
| Reversion point | 0.51** (0.17) | 0.17 (0.61) |
| Party (*No Party* as baseline) | | |
| Extreme left | 1.58 (1.07) | 1.95 (1.11) |
| PCF | −0.98 (1.13) | −1.08 (1.11) |
| PS | 0.24 (0.51) | 0.32 (0.51) |
| Greens | −0.40 (0.51) | −0.33 (0.60) |
| UDF | 0.51 (0.70) | 0.32 (0.51) |
| UMP | 0.63 (0.59) | 0.73 (0.72) |
| FN | −1.88* (0.90) | −1.82* (0.92) |
| Satisfaction with Chirac | 0.63** (0.20) | 0.61** (0.21) |
| Political awareness of ECT | −0.32 (0.21) | −1.99** (0.63) |
| Female | 0.76* (0.32) | 0.67* (0.32) |
| Age | 0.30* (0.14) | 0.36** (0.14) |
| Education | 0.24 (0.17) | 0.30 (0.18) |
| Income | 0.11 (0.10) | 0.10 (0.10) |
| Awareness * Social model | — | 0.09** (0.03) |
| Awareness * National sovereignty | — | −0.14* (0.22) |
| Awareness * Enlargement | — | 0.30 (0.21) |
| Awareness * Reversion point | — | 0.07 (0.20) |
| Constant | −3.69** (1.18) | −3.63** (1.20) |
| McFadden R Squared | 0.70 | 0.71 |
| Percentage correctly classified | 92% | 92% |
| N | 730 | 730 |

\* $p < .05$; \*\* $p < .01$.
Source: French Referendum Study (2005).

conditioning effect of awareness on the impact of different attitudes on vote choice. We expect that voters who are more politically aware will rely more on their issue attitudes (see Chapter 3). But, we do not necessarily expect that all attitude dimensions to be conditioned in a similar fashion. In general, we would expect that issues that have been prominent in the campaign will matter more to those voters who are more aware and therefore pay more attention to the campaign. In contrast, we do not expect that attitudes towards issues that were peripheral in the campaign will be mediated by awareness. In the French case, for example, we would therefore expect that social model concerns will matter more to the political aware voters, since economic and social issues were a salient topic in the campaign (see Table 8.1). As our dependent variables are binary, we estimate these models using logistic regression. The results for the French case are shown in Table 8.7.

As expected, the first model presented in Table 8.7 shows that each of the four attitude dimensions is significant, and particularly concerns over social issues have a very substantive impact on vote choices. Interestingly, the results show that voters' perception of the reversion point matters as much as attitudes towards enlargement and more than national sovereignty and identity concerns. This is also in line with the French Flash Eurobarometer survey (see Appendix 1) which shows that 83 per cent of no-voters believed that a no-victory would facilitate the renegotiation of the Constitution in order to achieve a more social text, while only 30 per cent of yes-voters shared this opinion. It is noteworthy that partisanship seems to make very little difference to French voters. Only FN voters were swayed by their party, when we control for attitudes. This corroborates our expectation that party cues matter less when the campaign environment is very intense. Conversely, satisfaction with Chirac does have a significant impact on vote choices, in accordance with the second-order national election explanation. Women are also less likely to vote 'no', as are younger voters. Overall, the fit of this model is excellent with a pseudo R squared of almost 0.70, and 92 per cent correctly predicted outcomes. Model 2 tests the conditioning impact of political awareness (see Hypothesis 2.6a). As hypothesized, we find that the first issue dimension—social model and ECT-specific attitudes—matters more to the more politically interested voters. In contrast, national sovereignty attitudes matter more to the less politically aware voters, whereas there is no mediating effect on awareness on the two remaining attitude dimensions. These findings suggest that issues that were more salient in the campaign matter more to voters who are more interested in politics.

Table 8.8 shows a similar model using the Dutch data. Again, Model 1 shows that all attitude factors are significant, except attitudes towards enlargement. However, in contrast to France, party attachment appears to play a significant role in the Netherlands. Supporters of the governing parties are significantly more likely to vote 'yes', whereas supporters of Wilders and the SP are more likely to vote 'no', even when controlling for attitudes. Note that there is no significant relationship between supporting the main opposition party, the PvdA, and vote choice. In the Netherlands, satisfaction with the government also increases the likelihood of a yes-vote. Again, we see that women and older people are more likely to vote 'yes'. In Model 2, we examine the mediating effect of political awareness on attitudes. As in France, the first attitude dimension matters more for politically aware voters. This is perhaps a little more surprising given that cultural concerns were not particularly salient in the media

Table 8.8. Predicting vote choice in the Netherlands

|  | Model 1 Logit (S.E.) | Model 2 Logit (S.E.) |
|---|---|---|
| EU attitudes | | |
| National sovereignty | 1.16** (0.12) | 0.51** (0.10) |
| Postmaterialism | 1.28** (0.12) | 1.63** (0.21) |
| Euro | 0.46** (0.12) | 1.29** (0.30) |
| Enlargement | 0.13 (0.09) | 0.11 (0.16) |
| Party (*No Party* as baseline) | | |
| CDA | 0.86** (0.30) | 0.82** (0.30) |
| PvdA | 0.38 (0.27) | 0.41 (0.27) |
| VVD | 0.99** (0.33) | 0.91** (0.33) |
| Greens | 0.68 (0.42) | 0.78 (0.41) |
| SP | −1.29** (0.48) | −1.37** (0.47) |
| Wilders | −1.55* (0.79) | −1.57* (0.47) |
| ChristenUnie | −0.66 (0.43) | −0.71 (0.42) |
| List Pim Fortuyn | −1.44 (1.26) | −1.04 (1.16) |
| D66 | 1.29* (0.62) | 1.20* (0.60) |
| Government satisfaction | 0.10* (0.05) | 0.11* (0.05) |
| Political awareness of ECT | 0.28 (0.17) | 1.24 (0.85) |
| Female | 0.37* (0.20) | 0.39* (0.20) |
| Age | 0.33** (0.07) | 0.31** (0.07) |
| Class | 0.12 (0.10) | 0.10 (0.10) |
| Awareness * National sovereignty | – | 0.11* (0.05) |
| Awareness * Postmaterialism | – | −0.15** (0.06) |
| Awareness * Euro | – | −0.20** (0.07) |
| Awareness * Enlargement | – | −0.06 (0.16) |
| Constant | −3.01** (0.57) | −4.35** (1.41) |
| Pseudo R Squared | 0.51 | 0.52 |
| Percentage correctly classified | 86 | 87 |
| N | 1120 | 1120 |

*$p < .05$; **$p < .01$.
Source: Dutch Referendum Study (2005).

coverage (see Table 8.1). However, the issue of identity and culture was emphasized by the no-campaign (Harmsen 2005; Arts and van der Kolk 2006) and moreover, multiculturalism was a salient issue on the political agenda, not least due to parties such as List Pim Fortuyn and Wilders. Model 2 also shows that the other issue dimensions, postmaterialism and the euro, mattered less to voters who are politically aware.

We are not only interested in the direction and the significance of these effects, but also in their relative magnitude. The coefficients in logit models (log odds) are difficult to interpret, let alone compare across models. To facilitate interpretation and comparison, we have calculated the marginal effects of each of the statistically significant variables. These have been calculated by increasing each of the variables by half a standard deviation from the mean (or in the case of binary variables, from 0 to 1), holding all the other variables at their mean, and calculating the change in the probability of a yes- or no-vote. The marginal effects are shown in Figures 8.3a (France) and 8.3b (the Netherlands).

Figure 8.3a illustrates that concerns over social threats and the Constitution are by far the most powerful predictor of vote choices in the French referendum. Half a standard deviation increase in concerns about social issues and the ECT increases the likelihood of a no-vote by 34 percentage points. In comparison, the other attitude dimensions only have a minor effect on vote choices with marginal effects of less than 10 per cent. Supporters of the FN have a 30 per cent higher likelihood of a no-vote, all other things being equal. Moreover, an increase in satisfaction with Chirac by half a standard deviation increases the probability of a yes-vote by only 6 percentage points.

In the Dutch case, the best predictor of vote choice is partisan preferences (see Figure 8.3b). Supporting CDA, VVD, or D66 increases the likelihood of a yes-vote by between 22 and 29 percentage points, while it is reduced by around 22 percentage points if the voter is a supporter of the SP or Wilders. In contrast, attitudes matter less in the Dutch case. The most important attitude dimensions are postmaterialism (diffuse support) and national sovereignty with marginal effects of around 15 per cent, all other things being equal. In the Netherlands, an increase in satisfaction with the government by half a standard deviation decreases the probability of a no-vote by 9 percentage points.

Given the high level of campaign intensity in the French case and the ambiguous messages sent by some parties (especially the Socialist Party), it is not surprising that party cues are of limited importance, while preferences play a large role. It is particularly interesting to note that attitudes relating to fears of a liberal market economy dominate vote decisions in France. Such concerns outweigh both second-order factors, such as government satisfaction and national sovereignty considerations. Party cues play a far more important role in the Dutch referendum, as we would expect, given the short, low-intensity campaign and the lower levels of dissent within the centre-left parties.

## 8.4. Conclusions

When referendum proposals are rejected, it is often very difficult for political leaders to translate a no-vote into a workable political solution. This became clear when the EU leaders tried to salvage the ECT after the no-votes in France and the Netherlands. Even when voters base their

## Campaign Dynamics

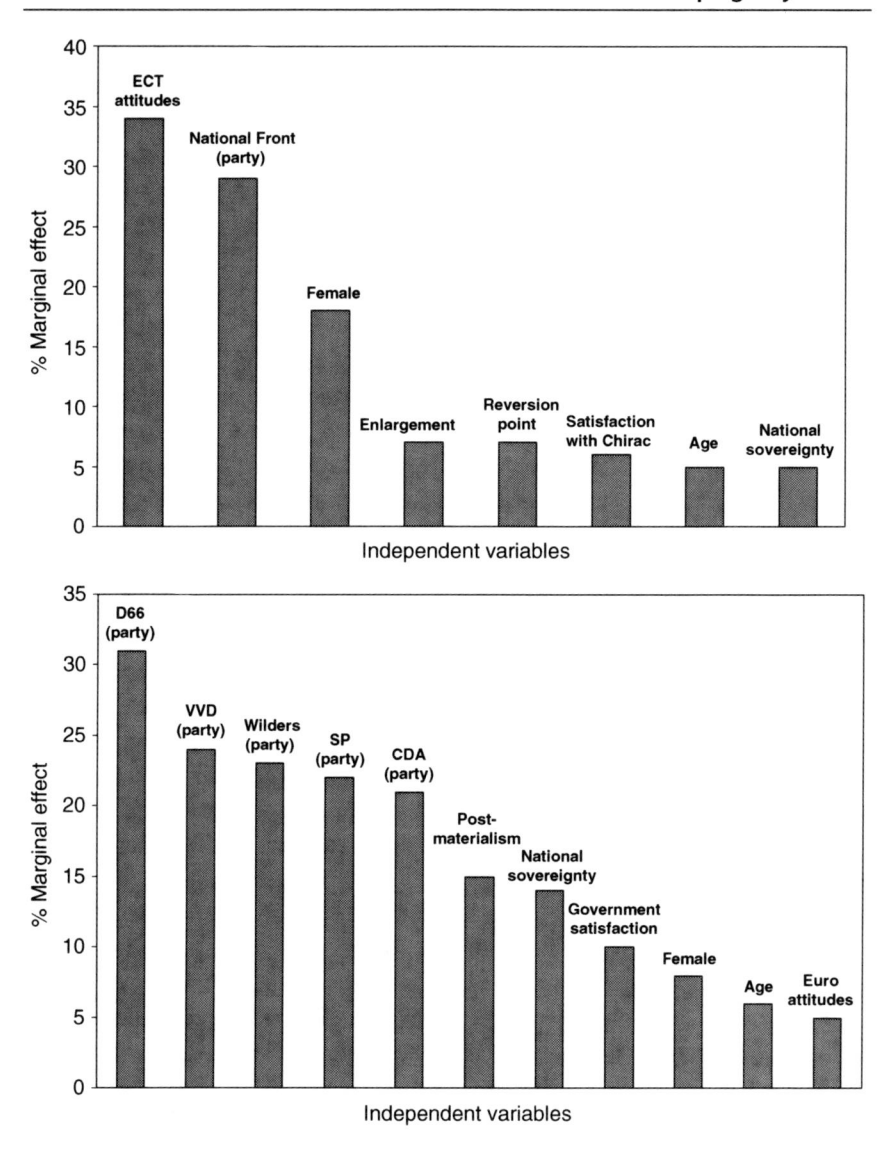

**Figure 8.3.** Marginal effects on vote choice in (*a*) France and (*b*) the Netherlands

*Note*: This figure indicates the marginal effect of half a standard deviation increase from the mean in each of the variables on the probability of a yes-vote (keeping all other variables at their mean). The first differences are based on model 1 in Tables 8.7 and 8.8.

225

vote choice on issue preferences, they will be responding to different elements of the treaty in question. A no-verdict can summarize a mix of considerations, but it cannot convey the considerations themselves. The aim of this chapter has been to disentangle the reasons why a majority of French and Dutch voters rejected the ECT in 2005, focusing specifically on the multifaceted nature of the considerations that determine vote choices.

The analysis of campaign coverage painted a picture of two distinctly different campaigns: the French campaign was long and impassioned, while the Dutch was short and relatively lacklustre in comparison. The campaign issues also differed: the French campaign focused on economic and social issues both in France and in the EU, and while the Dutch campaign was more preoccupied with procedural issues, the French campaign highlighted issues of national sovereignty and culture. Some of these differences in the campaigns were also reflected in people's attitudes towards Europe and the ECT. A factor analysis revealed that the dominant dimension in French EU attitudes was not diffuse support for European integration or fears over cultural threats, but rather concerns over the liberal market economy and loss of the French social model. Conversely, in the Netherlands, traditional concerns over loss of a national cultural identity and cost of membership were more prevalent. These analyses thus provide a more nuanced picture of the sort of attitudes that matters to people in referendums. While the issue attitudes are correlated and can be analysed as a single dimension, as we seen in previous chapters, we achieve a more detailed understanding of why voters choose to reject or approve of a treaty by examining the multidimensionality of attitudes.

The analysis of voting behaviour has shown that these attitude dimensions were important determinants of vote choices. In France, concerns over threats to the social model were the driving force behind vote choices, whereas, to a lesser degree in the Netherlands, postmaterialist attitudes and fear about cultural threats played a role. Given the differences in campaign intensity (discussed more fully in Chapter 4) we would expect attitudes on the ECT to play a larger role among French than Dutch voters. We also found that more politically aware citizens tend to rely more on their attitudes on issues that were salient in the campaign. These findings thus lend further support to the theoretical framework presented in Chapter 2: both the supply of and demand for information influence the extent to which voters rely on their issue-specific attitudes, as opposed to feelings about domestic politics. While satisfaction with the government is not insignificant, the results suggest that attitudes towards the European project matter more. Yet, these European attitudes have also become intertwined with traditional domestic concerns. In France, concerns over the liberal Europe and the Services Directive were linked with dissatisfaction with the policies of the incumbent centre-right government. Hence, while the European dimension has traditionally been seen as orthogonal to the domestic Left-Right dimension (see Hix 1999), these referendums are good examples of how both Left-Right contestation and 'new politics' can affect attitudes towards aspects of the integration project (see Hooghe et al. 2002). Our findings suggest that many French voters saw the referendum not as an opportunity to express their diffuse support for the European project, but rather to communicate how they wanted the European project to evolve. In the Netherlands, the no-votes seem to have been influenced by concerns, such as multiculturalism and loss of national identity, which the populist right had made salient.

Paradoxically, these no-votes may thus indicate an increasing Europeanization of national politics: to a number of citizens, the issue of European integration is no longer disconnected from traditional Left-Right and liberal—authoritarian political cleavages. Yet, nor is the European issue firmly fixed within the existing policy space; and depending on which aspects of the issue are emphasized, the position of voters may change accordingly. This opens up the possibility that the national debates on Europe will become less about whether European integration is desirable as such, and more about what kind of Europe people want. It also indicates that the battle for the future of European integration will increasingly be fought on many fronts. These findings also have wider implications for the role of direct democracy in EU politics. Is it good for democracy in Europe to allow voters a say over treaty ratification? Or does it only provide ambiguous answers to complex questions, which are better handled by elected politicians? These questions are addressed in greater detail in the final chapter.

## Notes

1. The Laeken Declaration adopted by the European Council, 15 December 2001.
2. Turnout in the 2004 parliamentary election in Spain was, by comparison, 77 per cent.

3. Despite the decision by the European Council to put the ratification process on hold, Luxembourg decided to go ahead with its referendum on the Constitutional Treaty on 10 July 2005. The Treaty was backed by a united political establishment and was approved by 56.5 per cent of voters in the referendum with a turnout of 89 per cent valid voters (voting is compulsory in Luxembourg).
4. See Eurobarometer 62. Fieldwork was carried out in the autumn of 2004.
5. Intercoder reliability was assessed on a sub-sample of articles and was above 0.85 for each of the key indicators (using Percent Agreement calculation).
6. When a joint session of both chambers (*le Congrès*) voted to allow a law that would adopt the ECT on 28 February 2005 only 155 out of 246 Socialist MPs voted in favour (3 voted no, 88 abstained). The Green parliamentary party was also split: four MPs voted yes and three voted no.
7. The study of Piar and Gerstlé (2005) draws similar conclusions about the patterns of the French campaigns using other media sources (two main TV news programmes). See also Gerstlé (2006).
8. The party preference of voters was determined on the basis of a question of which party they felt closest to (in France) and hypothetical vote choice (in the Netherlands).
9. The Dutch Referendum Study (2005) and the French Referendum Study (2005). See Appendix 1.
10. I use oblique rotations rather than orthogonal solutions, since it is unreasonable to assume that the different dimensions of attitudes towards European integration and the Constitution would be entirely orthogonal. If the latent variables are correlated, as we assume, then an oblique rotation will produce a better estimate of the true factors and a better structure than an orthogonal rotation. In both cases, the higher correlations between the factors is below 0.5, and therefore they do not present a major problem of multicolinearity when inserted in the regression analysis. In both France and the Netherlands, factors 1, 2, and 3 are all correlated at around 0.4, whereas factor 4 (Reversion Point in France and Enlargement in the Netherlands) is not significantly correlated with the other factors.
11. Both studies are two-wave panel studies. The second wave of the French study was conducted just before the French vote. It would have been preferable to use a post-referendum study, but this was the only study with sufficient question items to conduct the analysis. I have cross-validated the findings from the vote choice model using the Flash Eurobarometer post-referendum study in France and the key findings are the same.
12. Note that if we use the factor scores in the regression analysis instead of using summated rating scales of the same items (additive indices of items with the factor loadings above 0.5), the results are almost identical.

I also performed a factor analysis with orthogonal rotation and saved the factor scores, and the main results were the same. This strongly suggests that the results are not an artefact of any one particular statistical approach.

# Part IV

# Conclusions and Implications

# 9
# Lessons and Future Challenges

*What government is the best? That which teaches us to govern ourselves.*[1]
—Goethe

*If people are not capable of reasoned political choices, then effective self-governance is an illusion.*[2]
—Lupia and McCubbins

No institution in modern democracies brings us closer to the ideal of 'self-governance' by the mass public than referendums. Yet, as Lupia and McCubbins emphasize in the above quote, referendums can only bring about effective self-governance if citizens are capable of making reasoned political choices. As European integration has become the most frequently voted upon issue in referendums across nations, the study of direct democracy in the EU raises many important empirical and normative questions for Europe and beyond. How do people decide in referendums? To what extent do political elites influence citizens' behaviour? Do voters consider the issue on the ballot, or do they simply use referendums as an opportunity to express their dissatisfaction with political elites? Or put differently: Are voters sufficiently competent to decide directly on issues of European integration?

This book has shown that citizens do think about the broader issues of European integration when they go to the ballot box in EU referendums. Generally voters seek to weigh up the benefits associated with accepting of the ballot (e.g. the benefits of membership of an effective EU) against the potential costs (e.g. further integration in policy areas that encroach on national sovereignty). Or conversely, they try to choose between the perils of accepting a proposal that may take away powers from the nation state and the danger that rejecting the proposal could sideline their country in the EU. Voters aim to choose the option that is most aligned with their own preferences on European integration and their beliefs about the consequences of either outcome, relying on information from a variety of sources. Most importantly, the findings have shown that the way in which voters approach referendums on European integration crucially depends on the informational environment of each referendum campaign as well as individual characteristics.

At the heart of the argument presented in this book is the notion that the supply and processing of political information affect the political behaviour of citizens in referendums. The campaign environment determines the information presented to individual citizens and, in turn, shapes the way in which people decide. It has been shown that intense campaigns, which provide more information and debate about the ballot, mobilize people to turn out and vote. Moreover, voters are more likely to engage with the issue at stake and rely on their attitudes towards Europe when the campaign is intense. Information provision is not only about the quantity of information but also about the nature of information provided. The book has shown that political elites have considerable scope to frame the issues at stake in the referendum. Despite a broad consensus on European integration among mainstream parties, citizens are almost always presented with competing messages in referendum campaigns. The challenge for the government and other pro-ballot groups is to persuade voters that the ballot proposal is closely aligned with their preferences, whereas a no-vote would have grave consequences for the country. Such campaign strategies are more effective if both the messenger (e.g., the government) and the message are perceived by voters to be credible and trustworthy.

Yet, opinion formation and vote choices depend not only on the information provided by elites, but also on how this information is received. Citizens do not respond in the same manner to the political environment. Some voters pay very little attention to politics, regardless of the intensity of the campaign, and if they turn out to vote in a referendum they are likely to base their voter choices on a multitude of different factors. Other voters pay a great deal more attention to political events. Such 'political sophisticates' are likely to perform a more careful cost-benefit analysis of the proposal based on their preferences on European integration and the information provided by trusted elites. These voters thus rely more on their attitudes towards the EU and are also more likely to resist endorsements from political parties if these are incompatible with their underlying preferences. The book has thus shown that voters, particularly the politically interested, decide on ballot proposals in ways that correspond to their underlying preferences. The book also shows that the campaign environment can influence the factors that become decisive to the outcome.

In this concluding chapter, these findings on voting behaviour in European integration referendums are related to broader issues. First, the chapter considers the implications for our understanding of voting behaviour more generally. Thereafter, it discusses how these findings may help us to address the normative question of whether direct democracy is a desirable mechanism for taking decisions on European integration. Finally, it evaluates the recent proposals for reforming and extending the use of direct democracy in the EU in light of these findings.

## 9.1. Implications for our understanding of direct democracy

The book started by examining how voters make choices in referendums on European integration. Unlike most work on direct democracy that seeks to assess the fundamental desirability of direct democracy, this book has attempted to examine how voters behave when making decisions in referendums. But although the primary aim has not been to make a normative assessment of direct democracy, the examination of voting behaviour nevertheless has important implications for any evaluation of direct democracy. This is because the notion of 'voter competence' is necessarily at the heart of any assessment of the merits of direct democracy. One of the most persistent objections against the use of direct democracy—in Europe and elsewhere—is that referendums are undesirable because citizens vote against their own interest. As Lupia and Matsusaka (2004: 467) note: 'Many people believe that ordinary citizens are incompetent because they base their political choices on limited factual foundations'. This raises the question of whether citizens are able to make reasonable competent decisions in a direct democracy. To address this question, we must first establish what we mean by competence. Thereafter, we can evaluate the evidence for and against voter competence presented in this book and consider the factors that are conducive to voter competence.

### 9.1.1. *Conceptualizing voter competence*

What is 'voter competence' in the context of direct democracy? Competence refers to the ability to perform some task. To evaluate voter competence, we must therefore start by identifying the task that voters are asked to undertake (Kuklinski and Quirk 2001; Lupia n.d.). In a referendum, the task of voters is to choose between two policy alternatives, the ballot proposition and the reversion point (the outcome if the proposal is rejected). How do we assess whether voters have the ability to choose 'correctly'? Following the simple model of voter competence developed in Chapter 6, it can be argued that the criterion we use to evaluate the performance is crucially determined by the objective of the task (the referendum). Since the purpose of holding referendums on aspects of European integration, at least from a normative perspective, is the public legitimation or veto of an EU-related proposal, the referendum outcome is meant to convey information about citizens' preferences on the ballot proposal to which political representatives can respond. In the case of a yes-vote to a treaty, for example, voters send the signal to national representatives that they approve of the new treaty, whereas a no-vote indicates that voters disapprove of the proposal, and this forces politicians to renegotiate or entirely abandon the treaty. But an adequate response from elected representatives to a referendum outcome also requires that vote choices actually reflect preferences relating to the ballot proposal. If vote choices are almost entirely unrelated to voters' preferences towards the treaty—either because voters have insufficient information to relate their preferences to the proposal or because they simply choose to vote on the basis of other issues—then it makes little sense for national governments to perceive a yes-vote as a legitimization of the treaty or indeed a no-vote as a valid rejection of the treaty. Hence, to achieve the politically desirable outcome of legitimizing a treaty change, it is vital that voters decide on the question posed to them. The criterion by which the performance is to be evaluated is therefore the link between the question asked (the ballot proposal) and the answer provided by the individual (the vote choice). Or put differently: the degree of *issue-voting* can be used as a criterion for evaluating voter competence in referendums. A competent vote in referendums can thus be defined as one that is based on preferences specific to the issue on the ballot, and that would be the same if full information were available (see also Chapter 6).

To be competent, voters need not be fully informed about the proposal, but they do require some information to relate their own preferences to the question on the ballot. We know that ordinary citizens know relatively little about politics in general, and even less about European politics. But just as voters can rely on 'informational shortcuts', such as party labels in elections to decide which candidates are most likely to serve their interests, the referendum campaign also provides voters with various information shortcuts or 'heuristics' that allow citizens to infer their own position on a ballot issue without detailed information about the proposal itself. However, elite cues will not necessarily provide citizens with the information required to allow them to vote 'competently', that is, supply them with sufficient information to relate their own preferences to the ballot proposal. The next question is, therefore: How well do voters perform in referendums given the criteria of competence elaborated here?

### 9.1.2. How do voters choose?

If the key indicator of voter competence in referendums is the extent to which vote choices are based on issue preferences, the evidence presented in this book suggests that European voters are fairly competent. Scholars, politicians, and commentators alike have argued that referendums on European integration are primarily plebiscites on the performance of national governments. Yet, the analyses presented in Chapter 3 and 4 demonstrate that attitudes towards European integration matter more than any other factor in deciding vote choices in referendums. That is not to say that feelings about the government are insignificant. Voters are generally more likely to vote against the ballot proposals if they are unhappy with the performance of the government of the day. Moreover, voters listen to the recommendations of the parties they trust and tend to vote accordingly. However, the evidence presented in this book suggests that referendum outcomes in EU referendums are not primarily about punishing the government. Nor do voters blindly follow the advice of their preferred politicians. Citizens do take cues from parties and rely on information provided in the campaign, but their responses to this information are conditioned by their underlying attitudes towards the integration project.

The experimental evidence presented in Chapter 5 has shown that issue frames and elite endorsements can sway public opinion. We found that frames which emphasize the consequences of a yes- or a no-vote in the referendum influence citizens' vote intentions. Moreover, government endorsements make citizens who are positively disposed towards the government more likely to support a ballot proposal. Overall, these survey experiments suggest that while public opinion is swayed by elite frames, such information also provides them with firmer opinions on the proposal and these opinions are broadly in line with pre-existing attitudes and loyalties. Equally, the findings from the analysis of the Norwegian membership referendum in Chapter 6 illustrate that most voters are capable of using party endorsements of ballots as proxies in referendums. These results thus highlight that information should not be understood narrowly as factual knowledge about the ballot issue, since elite cues can guide voter decisions. However, the results also show that simply being exposed to the cues of political parties has no 'competence-enhancing' effect on behaviour, unless voters have a basic knowledge of party positions. In other words, elite cues are no substitute for voters actually knowing something about politics.

Before we can address the question of whether direct democracy is a 'good thing' both in general and in the context of European integration, we must first examine which conditions are conducive to competent behaviour. While the objective of this book has been to present general patterns of behaviour that can be generalized across voters and across countries, a key aim has also been to show how behaviour depends on the characteristics of the individual and the campaign context. One of the important implications of this study for our understanding of vote choices more generally has been to highlight which kind of campaigns can aid voter competence, and how voters differ in their approach to referendums.

### 9.1.3. *The heterogeneous electorate*

Few citizens possess detailed information about the intricacies of European integration and treaty reforms, and no one is ever fully informed about the consequences and the relative merits of the choices in referendums. As Lupia (2006: 231) points out, 'for most large-scale elections there are two kinds of people: those who realize that they do not know all the relevant facts, and those who are deluded enough to think that they do. We cannot know everything about most of the political phenomena we encounter'. What matters more is under which conditions voters can make effective choices about what information to rely on. Some voters pay more attention to and are more knowledgeable about political events, and this also affects the way in which they approach referendums. But while the variation in individuals' level of political awareness is

## Lessons and Future Challenges

well-documented, most studies of vote choice in referendums treat the electorate as homogeneous in terms of how they approach the ballot choice. This book has illustrated how voting behaviour is conditioned by the political awareness of the individual (Zaller 1992). Voters who are more politically aware (Chapter 3) and more exposed to campaign information (Chapter 4) rely more on their attitudes towards the EU when deciding on a yes- or no-vote and are more likely to reject the cues if they are incompatible with their attitudes. The survey experiments presented in Chapter 5 reveal that those who pay more attention to politics are also more responsive to elite frames, but their response is conditioned by underlying preferences. Hence, these findings highlight that while poorly informed voters may be capable of approximating the behaviour of 'fully informed' voters by using shortcuts, the way in which they arrive at their decisions is not necessarily identical.

### 9.1.4. Conditions conducive to voter competence

Another important implication of this study of EU referendums is that vote choices can only be understood by analysing the context in which these choices are made. The most obvious context in an election or a referendum is the campaign itself. This book has focused on two general aspects of this campaign environment: the intensity of the campaign and the framing of the choice set.

The analyses have shown that high intensity campaigns generally provide more information to voters and act as both an informer and a mobilizer of citizens: in intense campaigns, more people turn out to vote and issue voting is more common than in less intense campaigns (Chapter 4). Voters exposed to issue frames are also more likely to express an opinion on the ballot question (Chapter 5). Of course, there may be such a thing as too much information, which may bring about confusion, or deceptive information which is potentially misleading. However, in the cases explored in this book, it has been found that more intense campaigning and debate will generally increase levels of participation and engagement and enable voters to make more sophisticated choices. Although intense campaigns will involve contradictory statements and opinions, the fact that citizens receive messages from different sources makes them more capable of evaluating the credibility of the information and making choices aligned with their underlying preferences. For example, Chapter 7 has shown that in the high intensity campaign leading up to the Danish Maastricht referendum in 1992, the issue of European integration was very salient and issue preferences became the deciding factor for most voters. In contrast, the almost non-existant campaign preceding the 2001 Irish referendum on the Nice Treaty resulted in low turnout and limited issue voting. In both cases the ballot proposal was rejected, yet for very different reasons. When Irish voters were provided with more information on the Nice Treaty in the 2002 referendum, they voted in favour by a large majority. Equally, a small number of Danish voters changed their position in a second referendum on the Maastricht Treaty after Denmark had been granted several exemptions from the most integrationist aspects of the Treaty. In the first case, more information mobilized voters and activated issue attitudes, and in the second case changes in the alternatives presented to voters led to a positive outcome.

This brings us to the second aspect of the campaign environment, namely the framing of the choice set. Intensity only tells us something about how much information is available to citizens, but of course it is equally important what kind of information is provided. Political elites provide information through *endorsements* (speaking out in favour or against the proposal) and by *framing* the choice set. This book has shown that endorsements provide incredibly important cues for voters in referendums and that most people rely heavily on the recommendations by their preferred parties. Most referendum campaigns are two-sided, and hence voters will tend to side with the party or group that they normally support. In referendums, however, party endorsements rarely provide unambiguous cues. In ballots on European integration, most mainstream parties tend to favour the proposal, whereas the no-side often consists of a disparate mix of small left- and right-wing parties and non-partisan groupings. When relatively simply proxies such as party identification are applied to complex issues, people must possess sufficient knowledge to apply the proxy effectively. In elections, this is often the case, since party competition is structured around familiar dimensions. But when that is not the case, relying on a simple proxy is more hazardous. As the analysis of the Norwegian referendum in Chapter 6 has illustrated, people need some minimal knowledge about party positions on the EU in order to use party endorsements effectively. Hence, while elite cues such as party endorsements can allow people with limited information to vote competently, but it does not imply that some knowledge is entirely optional or that ignorance is desirable.

Political elites can also influence voters by framing the choice set in a certain way. As emphasized throughout this book, a referendum is not simply about voting for or against the ballot proposal. It is a choice between the ballot proposal and the outcome that would occur if the ballot is rejected, *the reversion point*. The way in which voters evaluate the reversion point may be as important as their evaluation of the ballot proposal itself. This implies that referendums are more similar to elections than scholars often assume. In elections voters also choose between two or more parties (or candidates) and the vote choice depends not only on the qualities of the party they decide to vote for, but also on the qualities of the party they choose not to vote for. For example, it is not unheard of that voters choose to re-elect a poorly performing incumbent government primarily because they are more uncertain about the viability of the opposition. Equally, voters may vote in favour of a ballot primarily because the consequences of a no-vote appear to be worse. This also has implications for voter competence. Clearly, voters are able to make more informed choices when they have credible information not only about the ballot proposal, but also about the reversion point. In the context of EU referendums (especially treaty ratification referendums), it is often relatively unclear what will happen if a country rejects the ballot. As Chapters 7 and 8 have shown, this uncertainty about the location of the reversion point has important implications for vote choices and is not generally conducive to producing outcomes that elites can interpret and act upon.

In sum, the analyses in this book have shown that referendum campaigns that generate interest among voters and provide credible information about the consequences of a yes- and a no-vote will result in more competent vote choices. These are conclusions that are not specific to referendums on European integration. While the book has focused specifically on this type of referendum, it has covered a broad set of ballot questions and countries, and the inferences concerning the heterogeneity of the electorate and the importance of the context are likely to apply to other referendums as well, whether they are sub-national or national. Many of the same inferences can also be extended to elections: the degree of issue voting in elections is expected to depend on the campaign context and the political interest of individuals. But the crucial difference is that in elections voters evaluate issues to decide on a party or a candidate, whereas in referendums the voters' choice ultimately concerns the issue. Direct democracy is thus more explicitly concerned with issues and policy outcomes than elections to representative institutions, where campaigns and vote choices increasingly focus on non-issue-related factors, such as the personal quality of candidates and party leaders (Clarke et al. 2004).

In that sense, referendums correspond more closely to the traditional democratic ideal of the well-informed citizens who deliberate and decide on the basis of policy issues (Bowler and Donovan 1998).

But this still leaves the question: *Are referendums on European integration a good thing?*

## 9.2. More direct democracy for Europe?

Often direct democracy is presented as a challenge to representative democracy, but more accurately, referendums can be seen as a device used in representative democracies with the objective to legitimize significant policy proposals and induce the elected (and non-elected) representatives to govern with due regard to the prevailing sentiments of citizens. There is a growing trend of using direct democracy as a means of legitimizing aspects of the European integration project. In the decade between 1998 and 2008, twenty-four referendums were held on aspects of European integration (see Table 1.1). Referendums constitute a very direct way of giving citizens a say on the otherwise largely elite-driven European project, and this could potentially enhance citizens' engagement in and support for the future of European integration, but may also—as we have seen in the past—allow citizens to undercut their elected representatives.

Ideally referendums provide citizens with the opportunity to endorse or veto important policy proposals such as constitutional reforms. This not only bestows legitimacy upon these proposals, if they are approved, but also encourages politicians to make agreements in line with public preferences for fear that their proposals will otherwise be rejected in referendums. In the context of European integration, proponents of extending the use of direct democracy also envision that direct democracy may produce other indirect benefits, such as increased interest in and support for the integration process, thus alleviating the democratic deficit of the Union and contributing to the formation of a European *demos* (Abromeit 1998; Hug 2002; European Convention 2003a; Feld and Kirschgässner 2003).

These potential benefits of a direct democratic process are, however, highly conditional on the nature and the context of the specific referendum. As discussed at length above, a certain level of voter competence is required to ensure that there is a direct link between voter preferences and referendum outcomes. But even in referendums where most voters are sufficiently informed and motivated to decide on a ballot proposal on

Lessons and Future Challenges

the basis of their preferences towards the proposal, a negative outcome may present a dilemma for political elites. This is further complicated by the fact that all EU referendums are decided nationally, yet their outcomes have implications for the EU as a whole. The constitutional crisis in the EU brought about by the no-votes in France, the Netherlands, and Ireland aptly illustrates some of the potential problems generated by the use of direct democracy in Europe, and makes the normative questions raised in the introduction of this book more relevant than ever: Are national referendums on European integration an appropriate method of decision-making and increasing citizen involvement in the EU?

### 9.2.1. The constitutional deadlock

The no-votes in the ECT and Lisbon referendums serve to highlight two key concerns about the role of direct democracy in the process of European integration: the translation of the people's choice into a political solution and the use of national referendums in a system of multi-level government. First, 'effective self-governance' requires not only reasoned political choices, but also that these choices are translated into policy outcomes. In EU referendums, it is often very difficult for political leaders to translate a ballot rejection into a workable political solution. Even when voters base their vote choice on issue preferences, no-voters will react to different elements of the treaty in question and often their objections will not relate directly to the treaty itself, but to aspects of European integration more generally. As shown in Chapter 8, the French no-vote to the Constitutional Treaty was for some voters a no-vote to the 'neo-liberal' model in Europe and for others a no-vote to the surrender of national sovereignty. Politicians can only respond appropriately to the expression of voter preferences if these expressions relate to the question posed and, given that European integration spans over many aspects of people's lives, a yes- or a no-vote to a general question on European integration can be very difficult to translate into a concrete solution. While the no-votes, particularly in France, were based on genuine public concerns about the direction of European integration, they did not necessarily represent a wholesale rejection of the constitutional project or indeed the EU. Hence, European elites faced different options. They could continue the ratification process, but after the French and Dutch no-votes it seemed unlikely that the ECT would be passed by more Eurosceptic electorates. Moreover, it was unthinkable to move forward with the constitutional project without France, so a French solution was necessary regardless of

243

the ratification in other countries. At the other extreme, the EU could have entirely abandoned the constitutional project. Yet the Constitutional Treaty represented the result of years of careful negotiation and compromise and contained reforms that were, in the eyes of many, necessary in order for the EU to operate effectively as a Union of 25 (and 27). Moreover, the Constitutional Treaty had been ratified in 17 member states (two referendums and 15 parliamentary ratifications) and many European leaders were unhappy that French and Dutch voters should be allowed to dictate the end of the constitutional project. Hence, the compromise position was a redrafting of the ECT as the Reform Treaty (Lisbon Treaty), which removed the symbolism of a constitution and some of the more controversial reforms, yet retained the key institutional initiatives.[3] This redrafting was in itself an attempt by elites to gauge which elements of the ECT had brought about the negative public response. Moreover, it was an attempt to avoid the necessity of holding national referendums on the new treaty, since the parliamentary route of ratification was more likely to ensure the implementation of the treaty. In spite of these efforts, the only referendum held on the Lisbon Treaty led to a no-vote and thus sent European leaders back to the drawing board.

The multi-level nature of the EU brings about an additional complication with the use of direct democracy. Whilst decisions are taken by intergovernmental and supranational institutions at the European level, EU referendums are conducted at the national level. Individual national electorates are asked to decide on a treaty that is a political compromise made by several national governments. This raises the question of whether it is fair that a small majority of voters in one or more countries can determine the future of the European project for all European nations. As noted by members of the European Convention: 'in a Union of twenty-five, one country can block the European treaty. Not only can this be seen as unfair and undemocratic, it must also be recognized that the present position puts undue pressure on certain member states which have a constitutional obligation to hold a referendum' (European Convention 2003a: 3, see also Auer 2005).

These concerns lead to questions regarding the future conduct of referendums in the EU. How can the outcomes of referendums be translated into political outcomes? Should referendums on EU treaties be conducted at the national or European level? One possible solution to the problems that have been highlighted by the constitutional deadlock is to hold simultaneous Europe-wide referendums on treaty ratification in all member states.

## 9.2.2. Europe-wide referendums

The proposal of a Europe-wide referendum on EU treaties is far from novel. In 1949, before the emergence of the European Community, Charles de Gaulle declared that 'I think that the organisation of Europe has to proceed from Europe itself. I consider that the start shall be given by a referendum of all free Europeans' (de Gaulle 1970: 309). One of the most prominent European federalists, Altiero Spinelli, also advocated the creation of a European Constitution, which should be ratified by European citizens in a referendum (Spinelli 1964, 1989). Equally, several scholars writing on European democracy have proposed the idea of Europe-wide referendums on European treaty reforms (Abromeit 1998; Auer 1997; Epiney 1997; Esposito 2002; Feld and Kirschgässner 2003; Frey 1996; Habermas 2006; Nentwich 1998). These works have evaluated referendums in Europe from the perspective of normative political theory. More recently, such ideas have also been translated into concrete policy proposals. In the European Convention, a group of members representing a wide range of party groups and member states proposed a 'Referendum on the European Constitution' (European Convention 2003a). The proposal advocated that the draft European Constitution should be approved not only by national parliaments and the European Parliament, but also by the citizens of Europe in a binding referendum. These referendums should be held simultaneously on the same day in all member states. Ultimately, this proposal was not successful and the rest, as they say, is history.[4] But what are the merits of this proposal, and other suggestions for Europe-wide referendums, in light of the findings of this book?

A Europe-wide referendum potentially has several advantages over national EU referendums as it could bring about high intensity campaigns, clarify the reversion point, and diminish the chances of institutional deadlock. It may also encourage European politicians to be more responsive to voter preferences and may even foster a European *demos*. Conversely, such a proposal also raises the tricky question about the nature of a European citizenry and the dangers of majoritarianism in segmented polities.

First, we turn to the issue of the informational environment in such campaigns. If a Europe-wide referendum is held on a weighty issue such as a European Constitution, this is likely to generate high-intensity debates across Europe, and thus mobilize voters and provide them with information to vote competently on the basis of the merits of the ballot proposal. The mere fact that the referendum is now a European rather than a national event may also induce voters to focus on European issues rather than domestic ones. Sceptics may argue that European Parliament elections, which are held the same week across Europe, continue to be 'second-order national election[s]' without a genuine European debate (Franklin and van der Eijk 1996; Marsh 1998; van der Eijk and van der Brug 2007). However, the crucial difference would be that the vote choice in a European referendum would be clearly associated with a specific outcome, whereas a vote in a European Parliament election has only a tentative connection to actual policy outcomes (Føllesdal and Hix 2006; Hix 2005). Much therefore depends on the specification of the reversion point in a Europe-wide referendum. In other words, what happens if a country rejects the proposal? The answer to this question depends partly on the majority rule employed in the referendum. If the requirement is a majority in all individual member states, as suggested by Abromeit (1998), then the reversion point would be much the same as in national referendums: since the EU cannot move forward without the consent of all member states, it would be unclear whether a referendum would lead to the abandonment of the proposal, a renegotiation, or a second referendum. Moreover, such a stringent majority requirement would make policy changes very difficult and would only enhance the possibility of institutional deadlock in the Union (Auer 2005; Hug 2002). More commonly, advocates of a Europe-wide referendum propose a 'double' majority of voters and member states (Frey 1995; Epiney 1997; Feld and Kirschgässner 2003).[5] This is also echoed in the Convention's proposal for a European referendum:

As Europe consists of citizens and member states, the fairest and most democratic means of consulting the people would be by a referendum based on a dual majority, i.e. a majority of citizens and a majority of states would be necessary to secure ratification. If in any member state the proposed constitution is rejected in the referendum, the state in question can (...) use one of the following options. It could (...) hold a second referendum. It could try to regulate its relationship to the new 'constitutional' European Union by a bilateral treaty; or it could choose to leave the European Union (European Convention 2003a: 4).

There are several advantages to this type of dual majority requirement in comparison to a more stringent proposal of majority in all member countries. First, it makes the consequences of a negative vote in individual member states very explicit. A failure to ratify the treaty would relegate the countries in question to a 'lower tier' of cooperation within the Union (given that a majority of member states vote in favour of the reforms). Indeed, one proposal from the Convention was to create a form of 'associate membership' of the Union in order to allow a recalcitrant member state who failed to ratify the ECT in a referendum to form a looser association with the Union (European Convention 2003b). Such explicit consequences may encourage national governments to fight an intensive campaign and would also make the location of the reversion point clear to voters. This may also prevent the deadlock situation created by a failure to ratify a treaty in a few member states. Furthermore, the anticipation of such a referendum may induce national and European elites to be more responsive to public opinion during the reform process itself and encourage them to inform the public about the implications of the proposed reforms.

The introduction of a Europe-wide referendum is also thought to have a number of indirect advantages (Auer 1997; Abromeit 1998; Esposito 2002; Feld and Kirschgässner 2003). One of the key shortcomings of an EU democracy is the lack of a European *demos*, interpreted as a shared European political conscience of the citizens. As a Europe-wide referendum would help to promote a debate on political issues at a European level and increase the salience of issue of European integration in the national political sphere, it may aid the formation of a European *demos* and foster a common policy understanding and identity. In the words of Habermas: 'this convergence [to a democratically constituted EU] depends on the catalytic effect of a constitution. This would have to begin with a single European referendum, arousing a Europe-wide constitutional debate, which would in itself represent a unique opportunity for transnational communication, and which would have the potential for a self-fulfilling prophecy' (Habermas 2006: 35). The hopes of an EU-wide referendum bringing about a European *demos* should not be exaggerated, however. Elements of direct democracy might be helpful to the process of constituting a European public sphere, but are neither necessary nor sufficient for a European *demos* to emerge.

Moreover, the proposal of Europe-wide referendums raises the question of whether it possible to think of a European referendum without the recognition of a European people? The EU is a hybrid organization, neither a purely international organization nor a federal state with a single people. It is widely recognized that the EU consists of 27 *demoi* rather than a single European *demos* with a collective identity. In the absence of clearly constituted *demos*, majoritarian decisions are often seen as unworkable, since minorities are unlikely to accept majority decisions. Of course, (qualified) majority decisions are already commonly used in the decision-making processes of the EU. Yet, treaty changes have so far firmly belonged to the domain of intergovernmental policy-making with national vetoes. A Europe-wide referendum, such as the one proposed by members of the European Convention, would not force any nation to accept a treaty against its will. However, it would take away the ability of individual nations to veto the institutional reforms of the EU. This may be unacceptable to certain member states. It is, for example, difficult to imagine that member states would move forward with a European Constitution with France as an 'associate member'. Moreover, such referendums could lead to a two-speed EU and might thus potentially bring about the disintegration of the EU if a number of national electorates voted against the reform proposal.

In conclusion, a Europe-wide referendum offers many potential benefits by facilitating a genuine European debate and competent voting and by reducing the chances of institutional deadlock. However, it also raises the question of whether European citizens and their representatives are as yet ready to take important decisions at the European-level by majority and accept the consequences.

## 9.3. Conclusion

Much of the debate about whether referendums on European integration are good or bad ultimately depends on our understanding of the way in which citizens decide in referendums. If referendum outcomes are plebiscites on the national governments, reflecting the will of ill-informed dissatisfied voters, they are less desirable as a mechanism of decision-making on European integration than if outcomes indicate choices made by knowledgeable voters on the basis of their attitudes towards the issue at stake. At the heart of the idea of direct democracy is an expectation that competent voters make decisions on the basis of preferences relevant to the issues concerned. Otherwise it is impossible to translate the voice of the people into policy outcomes.

This book has contributed to the discussion of the merits of referendum democracy in Europe by demonstrating that issue voting is prevalent in referendums on European integration, in particular when voters are provided with sufficient information and clear recommendations from political elites. These findings imply that a large proportion of voters have the capability of voting competently and responsibly on European issues, given that adequate information is made available. Further, this suggests that voter competence may be enhanced when political parties instigate serious and open debates on the issue of European integration and when the campaigns offer extensive information on the issue. It has further demonstrated that detailed factual information is not necessary for voters to act in a reasoned manner, since party political cues can act as substitutes. These findings are important as they help us understand which types of informational environments can impede or promote competent voting in EU referendums.

Referendums are often criticized for presenting citizens with choices that are too complex and thereby generating outcomes that have little or no connection with the ballot proposal. Yet the findings of this book have shown that voters are smarter than they are often given credit for. They may not be fully informed about European politics, but they do consider the issues at stake before they go to the ballot box, and they make use of the information provided by parties and the campaign environment. Direct democracy may not always produce the outcomes that are desired by politicians. However, voters are far more competent than commonly perceived.

## Notes

1. *'Welche Regierung die beste sei? Diejenige die uns lehrt uns selbst zu regieren'* (Ger.), Sprüche in Prosa, III, 225.
2. Lupia and McCubbins (1998: 12–13).
3. The ECT created a 'constitutional treaty' for the EU in a single document, whereas the Lisbon Treaty is merely an amending treaty in line with previous treaties. The Lisbon Treaty also drops all references to the symbols of the EU—the flag, the anthem and the motto—which were contained in the ECT. Yet the Lisbon Treaty preserves many of the revisions and developments to EU treaty law, including making the Charter of Fundamental Rights binding (although the Charter is not an integral part of the Lisbon Treaty, as was proposed in the ECT, and the Lisbon Treaty contains a Protocol with national exceptions for the United Kingdom and Poland); partial abolition of the pillar structure; clearer division of competencies between the Union and the member states; decision-making by qualified majority as the main principle in the Council; the election of a President of the European Council for a term of two and a half years; the introduction of a High Representative of the Union for Foreign Affairs and Security Policy (the ECT introduced a 'Union Minister of Foreign Affairs', but with the exception of the title being changed, this invention remains unchanged in the Lisbon Treaty).

4. Whereas the proposal to hold a Europe-wide referendum did not make it into the final treaty, both the ECT and the Lisbon Treaty contain a provision for citizens' initiatives. According to this provision of direct democracy 'one million citizens who are nationals of a significant number of member states' can call upon the European Commission to submit a proposal on a matter that falls within its area of competence. The Commission would not have to follow this request, but considerable public pressure could be expected in such a case (see Article I-47.4 of the ECT and Article 11.4 of the Lisbon Treaty).
5. This requirement of two types of majorities is almost identical to the one employed in Switzerland for constitutional changes (Hug 2002).

APPENDIX 1

# List of Data Sources

The analyses presented in this book are based on data from the sources referenced below. The responsibility for the analyses and interpretations presented in this book rests solely with the author.

### Surveys (in chronological order)

*Standard Eurobarometer Surveys*, various. Carried out for the European Commission. Essex: UK Data Archive.

*Folkeavstemningen om EF – 1972*. Survey data were made available by the Norwegian Social Science Data Service (NSD). The dataset is owned by Statistisk Sentralbyrå Seksjon for intervjuundersøkelser (SSB).

*EF-undersøgelsen 1972 (før-efter)*. Principal Investigators: Jørgen Elklit, Peter Hansen, Nikolaj Petersen and Ole Tonsgaard. DDA-194, 2nd edition by Claus Lewinsky and Karsten Boye Rasmussen. Odense: Danish Data Archive 1982.

*Observa prøvevalg 1972*. Principal Investigator: Observa, DDA-0909, 1st edition by Henning Lauritsen, Jens Wagner, Kirsten Pagh and Karsten Boye Rasmussen. Odense: Danish Data Archive 1994.

*Stortingsvalget – 1973*. Oslo: Norsk Samfunnsvitenskapelig datatjeneste (NSD).

*Euro-barometer 6*. November 1976. Principal Investigators: Jacques-René Rabier and Ronald Inglehart. Ann Arbor: ICPSR.

*Folkeafstemningen om EF-pakken, 27. februar 1986*. Principal Investigators: Ole Borre, Hans Jørgen Nielsen, Steen Sauerberg and Torben Worre. DDA-1192, 1st edition by Ralph Bjørn Eriksen and Per Nielsen. Odense: Danish Data Archive 1986.

*Folkeafstemningen om Maastrichtaftalen, 1992*. Principal Investigators: Karen Siune, Ole Tonsgaard, and Palle Svensson. DDA-1743 1st edition by Brigitte Jensen and Søren Hviid Pedersen. Odense, Danish Data Archive 1999.

*Maastricht Treaty, 1992*. Referendum survey carried out by IMS, Dublin.

*Folkeafstemningen om Edinbrughaftalen, 18. maj 1993*. Principal Investigators: Karen Siune, Ole Tonsgaard, and Palle Svensson. DDA-1783 1st edition by Jette Strand and Birgitte G. Jensen. Odense, Danish Data Archive 2000.

## Appendix 1

*EU-avstemningen 1994*. Survey data were made available by the Norwegian Social Science Data Service (NSD). The dataset is owned by Statistisk Sentralbyrå Seksjon for intervjuundersøkelser (SSB).

*Telefoninterviews efter EU-folkeafstemningen 28. maj 1998*. Principal Investigator: Jørgen Goul Andersen. DDA-6118, 1st edition by Jette Strand Madsen and Birgitte Grønlund Jensen. Odense, Danish Data Archive 2000.

*Amsterdam Treaty and Good Friday Agreement*. Exit poll carried out by Landsdowne and RTE, 1998.

*Euro-afstemningen 2000*. DDA-4013 1st edition. Odense: Danish Data Archive 2003.

*The Mannheim Eurobarometer Trend File, 1970–1999* (2001) Principal Investigator: Hermann Schmitt, ZUMA and MZES, ZA study 3521. Essex: UK Data Archive.

*2001 British Election Study (BES) rolling campaign panel survey* (RCPS), conducted by British Gallup. Principal Investigators: Harold D. Clarke, David Sanders, Marianne C. Stewart and Paul Whiteley. Essex: UK Data Archive.

*Treaty of Nice Referendum 2001*. Public Opinion Survey carried out for the European Commission Representation in Ireland by Irish Marketing Surveys, Limited, in association with EOS Gallup Europe. Principal Investigator: Richard Sinnott.

*Treaty of Nice Referendum 2002*. Public Opinion Survey carried out for the European Commission Representation in Ireland by Irish Marketing Surveys, Limited, in association with EOS Gallup Europe. Principal Investigator: Richard Sinnott.

Panel Study of Nice Referendums 2001 & 2002. *Two-wave panel study of 233 citizens in the Dublin region*. Principal Investigators: Michael Marsh and Richard Sinnott.

*The European Constitution: Post-referendum survey in Spain*. Flash Eurobarometer 168, March 2005. Conducted by EOS Gallup Europe and requested and coordinated by the European Commission.

*French Referendum Survey 2005*. Two-wave pre-referendum panel study. Conducted by TNS-Sofres. Principal Investigator: Sylvain Brouard, CEVIPOF, Sciences Po Paris.

*The European Constitution: Post-referendum survey in France*. Flash Eurobarometer 171, June 2005. Conducted by TNS Sofres/EOS Gallup Europe and requested and coordinated by the European Commission.

*The European Constitution: Post-referendum survey in The Netherlands*. Flash Eurobarometer 172, June 2005. Conducted by TNS Sofres/EOS Gallup Europe and requested and coordinated by the European Commission.

*The Dutch Referendum Study 2005*. Pre-and post-referendum panel study. Conducted by GfK Benelux. Principal Investigators: Kees Aarts and Henk van der Kolk, University of Twente.

*The European Constitution: Post-referendum survey in Luxembourg*. Flash Eurobarometer 174, July 2005. Conducted by TNS Sofres/EOS Gallup Europe and requested and coordinated by the European Commission.

# Appendix 1

*Lisbon Treaty Referendum Experiment*, 2008. Conducted by YouGov, January 2008. Principal Investigator: Sara B. Hobolt.

*Post Lisbon Treaty Referendum Opinion Poll*, June 2008. Conducted by Red C Opinion Poll for the *Sunday Business Post*. Principal Investigator: Michael Marsh.

## Newspapers

Denmark: *Berlingske Tidende, Politiken*

The Netherlands: *De Telegraaf, De Volkskrant*

France: *Le Monde, Le Figaro*

Ireland: *Irish Independent, Irish Times*

Luxembourg: *Luxemburger Wort*

Norway: *Aftenposten, Dagbladet*

Spain: *El Mundo, El Pais*

## Expert surveys

Leonard Ray, expert survey data on party positions about European Integration, 1984, 1988, 1992, 1996 (described in Ray 1999).

Leonard Ray, Expert Survey of Norwegian Party Positions, 1998 (described in Ray and Narud 2000).

Gary Marks and Marco Steenbergen (1999) *Party Expert Dataset*. Available from: http://www.unc.edu/~gwmarks/data.htm

Chapel Hill Party Dataset 2002. Principal Investigators: Liesbet Hooghe, Gary Marks, Marco Steenbergen and Milada Vachudova. Available from: http://www.unc.edu/~gwmarks/data.htm

# APPENDIX 2
# Descriptive Statistics

**Table 2.1A.** Descriptive statistics

|  | N | Mean | SD | Min | Max |
|---|---|---|---|---|---|
| *Dependent variables* | | | | | |
| Vote | 23,433 | 0.56 | 0.50 | 0 | 1 |
| Turnout | 30,721 | 0.77 | 0.42 | 0 | 1 |
| Ballot-specific knowledge | 18,826 | 2.47 | 0.93 | 1 | 4 |
| *Independent variables* | | | | | |
| EU attitudes | 31,200 | 11.46 | 4.85 | 0 | 21 |
| Party recommendation | 31,200 | 3.21 | 1.05 | 1 | 4 |
| Government satisfaction | 31,200 | 2.55 | 0.56 | 1 | 4 |
| Political awareness | 31,200 | 6.26 | 3.30 | 0 | 13 |
| Social class | 31,200 | 2.87 | 1.24 | 1 | 5 |
| City | 31,200 | 0.31 | 0.46 | 0 | 1 |
| Gender | 31,200 | 0.53 | 0.50 | 0 | 1 |
| Age | 31,200 | 3.17 | 1.34 | 1 | 5 |
| Education | 31,200 | 2.40 | 1.10 | 1 | 4 |
| Campaign exposure | 31,200 | 5.62 | 3.01 | 0 | 13 |

*Note:* Descriptive statistics for variables included in models in Chapters 3 and 4. Details on individual surveys can be found in Appendix 1.

# Bibliography

Aardal, Bernt (1995). Ideologi på tvers?, in A.T. Jenssen and H. Valen (eds.) *Brussels midt imot*. Oslo: Ad Notam Gyldendal, 165–84.
—— and Henry Valen (1997). The Storting Elections of 1989 and 1993: Norwegian Politics in Perspective, in K. Strøm and L. Svåsand (eds.) *Challenge to Political Parties: The Case of Norway*. Ann Arbor, MI: University of Michigan Press, 61–76.
—— Anders Todal Jenssen, Henrik Oscarsson, Risto Sänkiaho, and Erika Säynässalo (1998). Can Ideology Explain the EU Vote?, in A.T. Jenssen, P. Pesonen and M. Gilljam (eds.) *To Join or Not to Join*. Oslo, Scandinavian University Press, 235–65.
Aarts, Kees and Henk van der Kolk (2006). Understanding the Dutch 'No': The Euro, the East and the Elite. *PS: Political Science & Politics* 39(2): 243–6.
Abramowitz, Alan I. (1988). An Improved Model for Predicting Presidential Election Outcomes. *PS: Political Science and Politics* 21(4): 843–7.
Abromeit, Heidrun (1998). *Democracy in Europe: Legitimising Politics in a Non-state Polity*. New York: Berghahn.
Aldrich, John H. (1993). Rational Choice and Turnout. *American Journal of Political Science* 37(1): 246–78.
Alvarez, Michael R. (1997). *Information and Elections*. Ann Arbor, MI: The University of Michigan Press.
—— and John Brehm (2002). *Hard Choices, Easy Answers*. Princeton, NJ: Princeton University Press.
Ansolabehere, Stephen and Shanto Iyengar (1996). *Going Native: How Political Advertisements Shrink and Polarize the Electorate*. New York: Free Press.
Arrow, Kenneth (1974). *The Limits of Organization*. New York: Norton.
Auer, Andreas (1997). Le référendum européen: définitions, repères historiques et jalons d'études, in A. Auer and J.-F. Flauss (eds.) *Le référendum européen*. Brussels: Bruylant, 23–47.
—— (2005). Adoption, Ratification and Entry Into Force. *European Constitutional Law Review* 1: 131–5.
Aylott, Nicholas (2002). Let's Discuss This Later. Party Reponses to Euro-Division in Scandinavia. *Party Politics* 8(4): 441–61.
Banks, Jeffrey S. (1990). Monopoly Agenda Control and Asymmetric Information. *Quarterly Journal of Economics* 105(2): 445–64.

# Bibliography

Banks, Jeffery S. (1993). Two-Sided Uncertainty in the Monopoly Agenda Setter Model. *Journal of Public Economics* 50(3): 429–44.

Bartels, Larry M. (1986). Issue Voting Under Uncertainty: An Empirical Test. *American Journal of Political Science* 30(4): 709–28.

—— (1988). *Presidential Primaries and the Dynamics of Public Choice*. Princeton, NJ: Princeton University Press.

—— (1996). Uninformed Votes: Information Effects in Presidential Elections. *American Journal of Political Science* 40(1): 194–230.

Becker, Theodore L. and Richard A. Couto (1996). *Teaching Democracy by Being Democratic*. Abingdon: Greenwood Publishing Group.

Berelson, Bernard, Paul F. Lazarfeld, and William N. McPhee (1954). *Voting: A Study of Opinion Formation in a Presidential Campaign*. Chicago, IL: University of Chicago Press.

Berinsky, Adam and Jeffrey Lewis (2007). An Estimate of Risk Aversion in the U.S. Electorate. *Quarterly Journal of Political Science* 2(2): 139–54.

Bonde, Jens-Peter (1986). *En vejledende folkeafstemning*. Insert in *Notat* 393, May 1986.

Bowler, Shaun and Todd Donovan (1998). *Demanding Choices. Opinion, Voting, and Direct Democracy*. Ann Arbor, MI: The University of Michigan Press.

Brady, Henry E. and Paul M. Sniderman (1985). Attitude Attribution: A Group Basis for Political Reasoning. *American Political Science Review* 79(4): 1061–78.

Brouard, Sylvain and Vincent Tiberj (2006). The French Referendum: The Not So Simple Act of Saying Nay. *PS: Political Science & Politics* 39(2): 261–8.

Buch, Roger and Kasper M. Hansen (2002). The Danes and Europe: From EC 1972 to Euro 2000 – Elections, Referendums and Attitudes. *Scandinavian Political Studies* 25(1): 1–26.

Butler, David and Austin Ranney (eds.) (1978). *Referendums. A Comparative Study of Practice and Theory*. Washington, DC: AEI studies.

—— —— (eds.) (1994). *Referendums Around the World. The Growing Use of Direct Democracy*. Washington, DC: The AEI Press.

—— and Donald Stokes (1969). *Political Change in Britain* (1st edition). London, Macmillan.

—— —— (1974). *Political Change in Britain* (2nd edition). London: Macmillan.

Bützer, Michael and Lionel Marquis (2002). Public opinion formation in Swiss federal referendums, in D.M. Farrell and R. Schmitt-Beck (eds.) *Do Political Campaigns Matter? Campaign Effects in Elections and Referendums*. London: Routledge, 163–82.

Campbell, Angus, Philip E. Converse, Warren E. Miller, and Donald E. Stokes (1960). *The American Voter*. New York: Wiley.

Carmines, Edward G. and James A. Stimson (1986). On the Structure and Sequence of Issue Evolution. *American Political Science Review* 80(3): 901–20.

—— —— (1989). *Issue Evolution. Race and the Transformation of American Politics*. Princeton, NJ: Princeton University Press.

# Bibliography

Christin, Thomas, Simon Hug, and Pascal Sciarini (2002). Interests and Information in Referendum Voting: An Analysis of Swiss Voters. *European Journal of Political Research* 41(6): 759–76.

Chong, Dennis and James N. Druckman (2007a). Framing Theory. *Annual Review of Political Science* 10: 103–26.

—— (2007b). Framing Public Opinion in Competitive Democracies. *American Political Science Review* 101(4): 637–55.

Clarke, Harold D., David Sanders, Marianne C. Stewart, and Paul Whiteley (2004). *Political Choice in Britain*. Oxford: Oxford University Press.

—— (2005). Government Performance and Referendum Voting: Experiments with the Euro. Unpublished Manuscript.

Converse, Philip E. (1964). The Nature of Belief Systems in Mass Publics, in D. Apter (ed.) *Ideology and Discontent*. New York: Free Press.

—— (1975). Public Opinion And Voting Behavior, in F. Greenstein and N. Polsby (eds.) *Handbook of Political Science* (Vol. 4). Reading, MA: Addison-Wesley.

—— (2000). Assessing the Capacity of Mass Electorates. *Annual Review of Political Science* 3: 331–53.

Cox, Gary and Michael Munger (1989). Closeness, Expenditures and Turnout in the 1982 U.S. House Elections. *American Political Science Review* 83(1): 217–31.

Crewe, Ivor, Bo Sarlvik, and James Alt (1977). Partisan Dealignment in Britain, 1964–74. *British Journal of Political Science* 7(1): 129–90.

Cronin, Thomas E. (1989). *Direct Democracy: The Politics Of Initiative, Referendum, And Recall*. Cambridge, MA: Harvard University Press.

Davis, Otto A., Melvin J. Hinich, and Peter Ordeshook (1970). An Expository Development of a Mathematical Model of the Electoral Process. *American Political Science Review* 64(2): 426–48.

Dee, Thomas S. (2003). Are There Civic Returns to Education?. NBER Working Papers 9588, National Bureau of Economic Research.

Delli Carpini, Michael and Scott Keeper (1991). Stability and Change in the United States Public's Knowledge of Politics. *Public Opinion Quarterly* 55(4): 583–612.

—— (1996). *What Americans Know About Politics and Why it Matters*. New Haven, CT: Yale University Press.

de Gaulle, Charles (1970). *Discours et messages, Vol. 2: Dans l'attente. Février 1946-Avril 1958*. Paris: Plon.

de Vreese, Claes H. (2004). Primed by the Euro: The Impact of a Referendum Campaign on Public Opinion and Evaluations of Government and Political Leaders. *Scandinavian Political Studies* 27(1): 45–65.

—— (ed.) (2007). *Dynamics of Referendums Campaigns. An International Perspective*. Basingstoke: Palgrave.

—— and Hajo G. Boomgaarden (2003). Valenced News Frames and Public Support for the EU: Linking Content Analysis and Experimental Data. *Communications* 3(4): 361–81.

## Bibliography

de Vreese, Claes H. and Holli A. Semetko (2002). Public Perception of Polls and Support for Restrictions on the Publication of Polls: Denmark's 2000 Euro Referendum. *International Journal of Public Opinion Research* 14(4): 367–90.

——— (2004). *Political Campaigning in Referendums: Framing the Referendum Issue.* London: Routledge.

de Vries, Catherine (2007). Sleeping Giant: Fact or Fairytale?: How European Integration Affects National Elections. *European Union Politics* 8(3): 363–85.

DeVellis, Robert F. (1991). *Scale Development. Theory and Applications.* London: Sage Publications.

Downs, Anthony (1957). *An Economic Theory of Democracy.* New York: Harper-Collins.

Druckman, James N. (2001a). The Implications of Framing Effects for Citizen Competence. *Political Behavior* 22(3): 225–55.

——(2001b). On the Limits of Framing Effects: Who Can Frame? *The Journal of Politics* 63(4): 1041–66.

——and Kjersten R. Nelson (2003). Framing and Deliberation: How Citizens' Conversations Limit Elite Influence. *American Journal of Political Science* 47(4): 729–45.

Enelow, James and Melvin J. Hinich (1981). A New Approach to Voter Uncertainty in the Downsian Spatial Model. *American Journal of Political Science* 25(3): 483–93.

——— (1984). *The Spatial Theory of Voting.* Cambridge: Cambridge University Press.

Epiney, Astrid (1997). Le référendum européen, in A. Auer and J.-F. Flauss (eds.) *Le référendum européen.* Bruxelles: Bruylant, 287–315.

Esposito, Frédéric (2002). The European Referendum: A Tool to Legitimate the European Integration Process?, in S. S. Nagel (ed.) *Policymaking and Democracy: A Multinational Anthology.* Lanham, MD: Lexington, 15–38.

European Commission (2005). The Commission's Contribution to the Period of Reflection and Beyond: Plan-D for Democracy, Dialogue and Debate. COM(2005) 494.

European Convention (2003a). Referendum on the European Constitution. Contribution Submitted by Several Members, Alternate Members and Observers of the European Convention. CONV 658/03, Brussels 31 March 2003.

——(2003b) How to Bring the Constitution into Force. Contribution submitted by Andrew Duff, member of the Convention. CONV 764/03, Brussels 28 May 2003.

Evans, Geoffrey (1998). Euroscepticism and Conservative Electoral Support: How an Asset Became a Liability. *British Journal of Political Science* 28(4): 573–90.

——(1999). Europe: A New Electoral Cleavage?, in G. Evans and P. Norris (eds.) *Critical Elections: British Parties and Voters in Long-Term Perspective.* London: Sage, 207–22.

——(2000). The Continued Significance of Class Voting. *Annual Review of Political Science* 3: 401–17

# Bibliography

—— (2002). European Integration, Party Politics and Voting in the 2001 Election. *British Elections and Parties Review* 12: 95–110

Farrell, David M. and Rüdiger Schmitt-Beck (eds.) (2002). *Do Political Campaigns Matter? Campaign Effects in Elections and Referendums*. London: Routledge.

Feld, Lars P. and Gerhard Kirschgässner (2003). The Role of Direct Democracy in the European Union. CESifo Working Paper No. 1083.

Ferejohn, John A. and James H. Kuklinski (eds.) (1990). *Information and Democratic Processes*. Urbana, IL: University of Illinois Press.

*Financial Times Europe* (2005). From Sunday's Non to Economic Reform, 31 May 2005.

Folketinget (1992). Danmark i Europa [Det nationale kompromis], 27 October 1992, Copenhagen.

Føllesdal, Andreas and Simon Hix (2006). Why There Is a Democratic Deficit in the EU: A Response to Majone and Moravcsik. *Journal of Common Market Studies* 44(3): 533–62.

Franklin, Charles H. (1991). Eschewing Obfuscation? Campaigns and the Perception of US Senate Incumbents. *American Political Science Review* 85(4): 1193–214.

Franklin, Mark (2001). How Structural Factors Cause Turnout Variations at European Parliament Elections. *European Union Politics* 2(3): 309–28.

—— (2002). Learning from the Danish Case: A Comment on Palle Svensson's Critique of the Franklin Thesis. *European Journal of Political Research* 41: 751–7.

—— (2004). *Voter Turnout and the Dynamics of Electoral Competition in Established Democracies Since 1945*. Cambridge: Cambridge University Press.

—— Cees van der Eijk, and Michael Marsh (1995). Referendum Outcomes and Trust in Government: Public Support for Europe in the Wake of Maastricht. *West European Politics* 18(3): 101–17.

—— Michael Marsh, and Lauren McLaren (1994). Uncorking the Bottle: Popular Opposition to European Unification in the Wake of Maastricht. *Journal of Common Market Studies* 32(4): 455–72.

—— —— and Christopher Wlezien (1994). Attitudes toward Europe and Referendum Votes: A Response to Siune and Svensson. *Electoral Studies* 13(2): 117–21.

—— —— (1997). The Responsive Public: Issue Salience, Policy Changes, and Preferences for European Unification. *Journal of Theoretical Politics* 9: 347–63.

Frey, Bruno S. (1995). A Directly Democratic and Federal Europe. *Constitutional Political Economy* 7(4): 267–79.

Furedi, Frank (2005). To Say or Imply that the Public is Too Stupid to Grasp the High-Minded and Sophisticated Ideals of the Advocates of the EU is to Express a Profound Sense of Contempt Towards Ordinary People. *New Statesman*, 13 June 2005.

Gabel, Matthew J. (1998*a*). *Interest and Integration. Market Liberalization, Public Opinion and European Union*. Ann Arbor, MI: The University of Michigan Press.

—— (1998*b*). Public Support for European Integration: An Empirical Test of Five Theories. *The Journal of Politics* 60(2): 333–54.

## Bibliography

Gaines, Brian J., James H. Kusklinski, and Paul J. Quirk (2007). The Logic of the Survey Experiment Reexamined. *Political Analysis* 15(1): 1–20.

Gallagher, Michaek and Pier Vincenzo Uleri (eds.) (1996). *The Referendum Experience in Europe*. Basingstoke: Macmillan.

Gamson, William A. and Andre Modigliani (1987). The Changing Culture of Affirmative Action, in R.D. Braungart (ed.) *Research in Political Sociology*, Vol. 3. Greenwich: JAI, 133–77.

Garry, John, Michael Marsh, and Richard Sinnott (2005). 'Second Order' Versus 'Issue Voting' Effects in EU Referendums: Evidence from the Irish Nice Treaty Referendums. *European Union Politics* 6(2): 201–21.

Gelman, Andrew and Gary King (1993). Why Are American Presidential Election Polls so Variable When Voters Are so Predictable? *British Journal of Political Science* 23(4): 49–51.

Gerber, Alan and Donald Green (2000). The Effects of Canvassing, Telephone Calls and Direct Mail on Voter Turnout: A Field Experiment. *American Political Science Review* 94(3): 653–63.

Gerstlé, Jacques (2006). The Impact of Television on French Referendum Campaign in 2005. *Notre Europe* Studies and Research No 53.

Gilland, Karin (2002). Ireland's (First) Referendum on the Treaty of Nice. *Journal of Common Market Studies* 40(3): 527–35.

Habermas, Jürgen (2006). Why Europe Needs a Constitution, in R. Rogowski and C. Turner (eds.) *The Shape of the New Europe*. Cambridge: Cambridge University Press.

Haider-Markel, Donald P. and Mark R. Joslyn (2001). Gun policy, opinion, tragedy and blame attribution: the conditional influence of issue frames. *The Journal of Politics* 63(2): 520–43.

Hainsworth, Paul (2006). France Says No: The 29 May 2005 Referendum on the European Constitution. *Parliamentary Affairs* 59(1): 98–117.

Harmsen, Robert (2005). The Dutch Referendum on the Ratification of the European Constitutional Treaty. EPERN Referendum Briefing Paper No 13.

Hayward, Katy (2003). 'If at First You Don't Succeed...': the Second Referendum on the Treaty of Nice, 2002. *Irish Political Studies* 18(1): 120–32.

Hillygus, D. Sunshine (2005). Campaign Effects and the Dynamics of Turnout Intention in Election 2000. *The Journal of Politics* 67(1): 50–68.

Hix, Simon (1999). Dimension and Alignments in European Union Politics: Cognitive Constraints and Partisan Responses. *European Journal of Political Research* 35(1): 69–125.

——(2005). *The Political System of the European Union*, 2nd edition. London: Palgrave.

Hobolt, Sara B. (2005). When Europe Matters: The Impact of Political Information on Voting Behaviour in EU Referendums. *Journal of Elections, Public Opinion and Parties* 15(1): 85–109.

—— (2006). How Parties Affect Vote Choice in European Integration Referendums. *Party Politics* 12(5): 623–47.

—— (2007*a*). Taking Cues on Europe? Voter Competence and Party Endorsements in Referendums on European Integration. *European Journal of Political Research* 46(2): 151–82.

—— (2007*b*). Campaign Information and Voting Behaviour in C.H. de Vreese (ed.) *Dynamics of Referendum Campaigns. An International Perspective.* Basingstoke: Palgrave.

—— Jae-Jae Spoon, and James Tilley (2009). A Vote Against Europe? Explaining Defection at the 1999 and 2004 European Parliament Elections. *British Journal of Political Science* 39(1):93–115.

Hooghe, Liesbet (2003). Europe Divided? Elites vs. Public Opinion on European Integration. *European Union Politics* 4(3): 281–304.

—— and Gary Marks (2004). Does Identity or Economic Rationality Drive Public Opinion on European Integration? *PS: Political Science and Politics* 37(3): 415–20.

—— —— and Carole J. Wilson (2002). Does Left/Right Structure Party Positions on European Integration?, *Comparative Political Studies* 35(8): 965–89.

Hug, Simon (1997). Integration through Referendums. *Aussenwirtschaft* 52(1–2): 287–310.

—— (2002). *Voices of Europe: Citizens, Referendums and European Integration.* Boulder, CO: Rowman & Littlefield Publishers.

—— and Thomas König (2002). In View of Ratification. Governmental Preferences, and Domestic Constraints at the Amsterdam Intergovernmental Conference. *International Organization* 56(2): 447–76.

—— and Pascal Sciarini (2000). Referendums on European Integration. Do Institutions Matter in the Voter's Decision? *Comparative Political Studies* 33(1): 3–36.

Inglehart, Ronald (1970*a*). Cognitive Mobilization and European Identity. *Comparative Politics* 3(1): 45–70.

—— (1970*b*). Public Opinion and Regional Integration. *International Organization* 24(4): 764–95.

—— (1971). The Silent Revolution in Europe: Intergenerational Change in Post-Industrial Societies. *American Political Science Review* 65(4): 991–1017.

—— (1977). *The Silent Revolution: Changing Values and Political Styles Among Western Publics.* Princeton, NJ: Princeton University Press.

—— (1990). *Culture Shift in Advanced Industrial Society.* Princeton, NJ: Princeton University Press.

Irwin, Galen (1995). Second-Order or Third-Rate: Issues in the Campaign for the Elections for the European Parliament 1994. *Electoral Studies* 14(2): 183–98.

Iyengar, Shanto (1987). Television News and Citizens' Explanations of National Affairs. *American Political Science Review* 81(3): 815–32.

—— and Donald R. Kinder (1987). *News That Matters: Television and American Opinion.* Chicago, IL: University of Chicago Press.

# Bibliography

Iyengar, Shanto and Adam F. Simon (2000). New Perspectives and Evidence on Political Communication and Campaign Effects. *Annual Review of Political Psychology* 51: 149–69.

——Donald R. Kinder, Jon Krosnick, and Mark D. Peters (1984). The Evening News and Presidential Evaluations. *Journal of Personality and Social Psychology* 46(4): 778–87.

Ivaldi, Gilles (2006). Beyond France's 2005 Referendum on the European Constitutional Treaty: Second-Order Model, Anti-Establishment Attitudes and the End of the Alternative European Utopia. *West European Politics* 29(1): 47–69.

Jaccard, James (2001). *Interaction Effects in Logistic Regression*. Thousand Oaks, CA: Sage.

Jacoby, William G. (2000). Issue Framing and Public Opinion on Government Spending. *American Journal of Political Science* 44(4): 750–67.

Kahn, Kim Fridkin (1995). Characteristics of Press Coverage in Senate and Gubernatorial Campaigns: Information Available to Voters. *Legislative Studies Quarterly* 20(1): 23–36.

——and Patrick J. Kenney (1997). A Model of Candidate Evaluations in Senate Elections: The Impact of Campaign Intensity. *The Journal of Politics* 59(4): 1173–205.

Kahneman, Daniel and Amos Tversky (1979). Prospect Theory: An Analysis of Decisions Under Risk. *Econometrica* 47, 263–91.

————(1984). Choices, Values, and Frames. *American Psychologist* 39: 341–50.

Kaltenthaler, Karl C. and Christopher J. Anderson (2001). Europeans and Their Money: Explaining Public Support for the Common European Currency. *European Journal of Political Research* 40(2): 139–70.

Kaufmann, Bruno and M. Dane Waters (eds.) (2004). *Direct Democracy in Europe. A Comprehensive Reference Guide to the Initiative and Referendum Process in Europe*. Durham, NC: Carolina Academic Press.

Key, Valdimer O. Jr. (1966). *The Responsible Electorate: Rationality in Presidential Voting, 1936–1960*. Cambridge, MA: The Belknap Press of Harvard University Press.

Kinder, Donald R. (1986). Presidential Character Revisited, in Richard Lau and David Sears (eds.) *Political Cognition*, Hillsdale, NJ: Lawrence Erlbaum, 233–56.

——and Lynn M. Sanders (1990). Mimicking the Political Debate with Survey Questions: The Case of White Opinion on Affirmative Action for Blacks. *Social Cognition* 8(1): 73–103.

————(1996). *Divided by Color: Radical Politics and Democratic Ideals*. Chicago, IL: Chicago University Press.

Kirk, Lisbeth (2007). Treaty Made Unreadable to Avoid Referendums, says Amato, *EUObserver.com*, 16 July 2007.

Kriesi, Hanspeter (2005). *Direct Democratic Choice. The Swiss Experience*. Lanham, MD: Lexington.

―― Ruud Koopmans, Jan Willem Duyvendak, and Marco Giugni (1995). *New Social Movements in Western Europe*. Minneapolis/London: University of Minnesota Press/UCL Press.

Krosnick, Jon A. (1988*a*). Attitude Importance and Attitude Change. *Journal of Experimental Social Psychology* 24(3): 240–55.

―― (1988*b*). The Role of Attitude Importance in Social Evaluation: A Study of Policy Preferences, Presidential Candidate Evaluation, and Voting Behavior. *Journal of Personality and Social Psychology* 55(2): 196–210.

Kuklinski, James H. and Paul J. Quirk (2001). Conceptual Foundations of Citizenship Competence. *Political Behaviour* 23(3): 285–311.

―― ―― Jennifer Jerit, and Robert F. Rich (2001).The Political Environment and Citizen Competence. *American Journal of Political Science* 45(2): 410–24.

Laitin, David D. (2002). Comparative Politics: The State of the Subdiscipline, in I. Katznelson and H.V. Milner (eds.) *Political Science: The State of the Discipline*. New York: Norton.

Lassen, David Dreyer (2005). The Effect of Information on Voter Turnout: Evidence from a Natural Experiment. *American Journal of Political Science* 49(1): 103–18.

Lau, Richard R. and David P. Redlawsk (1997). Voting Correctly. *American Political Science Review* 91(3): 585–98.

Laursen, Finn (1994). Denmark and the Ratification of the Maastricht Treaty, in F. Laursen and S. Vanhoonacker (eds.) *The Ratification of the Maastricht Treaty*, Dordrecht: M. Nijhoff, 61–86.

Lavine, Howard, Eugene Borgida, John L. Sullivan, and Cynthia J. Thomsen (1996). The Relationship of National and Personal Issue Salience to Attitude Accessibility on Foreign and Domestic Policy Issues. *Political Psychology* 17(2): 293–316.

Lawler, Peter (1997). Scandinavian Exceptionalism and European Union. *Journal of Common Market Studies* 35(4): 565–94.

Lazarsfeld, Paul F., Bernard Berelson, and Hazel Gaudet (1944). *The People's Choice: How the Voter Makes up His Mind in a Presidential Campaign*. New York: Duell, Sloan and Pearce.

LeDuc, Lawrence (2002). Opinion Change and Voting Behaviour in Referendums. *European Journal of Political Research* 41(6): 711–32.

―― (2003). *The Politics of Direct Democracy: Referendums in Global Perspective*. Toronto: Broadview Press.

Lijphart, Arend (1997). Unequal Participation: Democracy's Unresolved Dilemma. *American Political Science Review* 91(1): 1–14.

Lindberg, Leon N. and Stuart A. Scheingold (1970). *Europe's Would-be Polity. Patterns of Change in the European Community*. Englewood Cliffs, NJ: Prentice Hall.

Lipset, Seymour Martin and Stein Rokkan (1967). Cleavage Structures, Party Systems and Voter Alignments: An Introduction, in S. M. Lipset and S. Rokkan (eds.) *Party Systems and Voter Alignments: Crossnational Perspectives*. New York: Free Press.

## Bibliography

Lodge, Milton, Marco R. Steenbergen, and Shawn Brau (1995). The Responsive Voter: Campaign Information and the Dynamics of Candidate Evaluation. *American Political Science Review* 89(2): 309–26.

Lupia, Arthur (1992). Busy Voters, Agenda Control, and the Power of Information. *American Political Science Review* 86(2): 390–403.

—— (1994). Shortcuts Versus Encyclopedias: Information and Voting Behavior in California Insurance Reform Elections. *American Political Science Review* 88(1): 63–76.

—— (2001). Dumber than Chimps? An Assessment of Direct Democracy of Voters, in L.J. Sabato, H.R. Ernst, and B.A. Larson (eds.) Dangerous Democracy? The Battle over Ballot Initiatives in America. New York: Rowman & Littlefield Publishers.

—— (2006). How Elitism Undermines the Study of Voter Competence. *Critical Review* 18(1): 217–32.

—— (n.d.) Questioning Our Competence: Tasks, Institutions, and the Limited Practical Relevance of Common Political Knowledge Measures. Unpublished manuscript.

—— and Richard Johnston (2001). Are Voters to Blame? Voter Competence and Elite Maneuvers in Referendums, in M. Mendelsohn and A. Parkin (eds.) *Referendum Democracy. Citizens, Elites and Deliberation in Referendum Campaigns*. Basingstoke: Palgrave.

—— and John G. Matsusaka (2004). Direct Democracy: New Approaches to Old Questions. *Annual Review of Political Science* 7: 463–83.

—— and Mathew D. McCubbins (1998). *The Democratic Dilemma. Can Citizens Learn What They Need to Know?* Cambridge: Cambridge University Press.

———— and Samuel L. Popkin (2000). Beyond Rationality: Reason and the Study of Politics, in A. Lupia, M. D. McCubbins, and S. L. Popkin (eds.) *Elements of Reason: Cognition, Choice and the Bounds of Rationality*. Cambridge: Cambridge University Press.

Luskin, Robert C. (1987). Measuring Political Sophistication. *American Journal of Political Science* 31(4): 856–99.

—— (1990). Explaining Political Sophistication. *Political Behavior* 12(4): 331–61.

McCombs, Maxwell and Donald Shaw (1972). The Agenda-Setting Function of Mass Media. *Public Opinion Quarterly* 36(2): 176–87.

McGuinness, Damien (2005). Going Dutch on the European Constitution, *Der Spiegel*, 27 May 2005.

McIver, John P. and Edward G. Carmines (1981). *Unidimensional Scaling*. Thousand Oaks, CA: Sage.

McKelvey, Richard and Peter C. Ordeshook (1986). Information, Electoral Equilibria and the Democratic Ideal. *The Journal of Politics* 48(4): 909–37.

McLaren, Lauren M. (2002). Public Support for the European Union: Cost/Benefit Analysis or Perceived Cultural Threat? *The Journal of Politics* 64: 551–66.

# Bibliography

——(2004). Opposition to European Integration and Fear of Loss of National Identity: Debunking a Basic Assumption Regarding Hostility to the Integration Project. *European Journal of Political Research* 43: 895–911.

——(2006). *Identity, Interests and Attitudes to European Integration*. Basingstoke: Palgrave Macmillan.

Madison, James (1787). The Federalist No. 10. The Utility of the Union as a Safeguard Against Domestic Faction and Insurrection. *Daily Advertiser*, November 22, 1787.

Magleby, David B. (1984). *Direct Legislation: Voting On Ballot Propositions In The United States*. Baltimore, MD: Johns Hopkins University Press.

Mair, Peter (2000). The Limited Impact of Europe on National Party Systems. *West European Politics* 23(4): 27–61.

Mansergh, Lucy (1999). Two Referendums and the Referendum Commission: The 1998 Experience. *Irish Political Studies* 14(1): 123–31.

Marks, Gary and Marco Steenbergen (eds.) (2004). *European Integration and Political Conflict*. Cambridge: Cambridge University Press.

——Carole J. Wilson, and Leonard Ray (2002). National Political Parties and European Integration. *American Journal of Political Science* 46(3): 585–94.

Marsh, Michael (1998). Testing the Second-Order Election Model after Four European Elections. *British Journal of Political Science* 28(4): 591–607.

——and Mark N. Franklin (1996). The Foundations: Unanswered Questions from the Study of European Elections, 1979–1994, in C. van der Eijk and M.N. Franklin (eds.) *Choosing Europe?* Ann Arbor, MI: University of Michigan Press, 11–32.

Marthaler, Sally (2005). The French Referendum on Ratification of the EU Constitutional Treaty, 29 May 2005. *Representation* 41(3): 228–36.

Matsusaka, John G. (1995). Explaining Voter Turnout Patterns: An Information Theory. *Public Choice* 84(1–2): 91–117.

——(2003). Direct Democracy, in C.K. Rowley and F. Schneider (eds.) *Encyclopaedia of Public Choice*. Kluwer Academic Publishers.

Mendelsohn, Matthew and Fred Cutler (2000). The Effect of Referendums on Democratic Citizens: Information, Politicisation, Efficacy and Tolerance. *British Journal of Political Science* 30: 685–701.

——and Andrew Parkin (eds.) (2001). *Referendums Democracy. Citizens, Elites and Deliberation in Referendum Campaigns*. Basingstoke: Palgrave.

Merrill III, Samuel, and Bernard Grofman (1999). *A Unified Theory of Voting*. Cambridge: Cambridge University Press.

Midtbø, Tor and Kjell Hines (1998). The Referendum-Election Nexus: An Aggregate Analysis of Norwegian Voting Behaviour. *Electoral Studies* 17(1): 77–94.

Mill, John Stuart (1970 [1888]). Two Methods of Comparison, in E. Amitai and F.L. Du bow (eds.) *Comparative Perspectives: Theories and Methods*. Boston, MA: Little Brown, 205–10.

Nelson, Thomas E. and Donald R. Kinder (1996). Issue Frames and Group-Centrism in American Public Opinion. *The Journal of Politics* 58(4): 1055–78.

Nelson, Thomas E. and Zoe M. Oxley (1999). Issue Framing Effects and Belief Importance and Opinion. *The Journal of Politics* 61(4): 1040–67.

────── and Rosalee A. Clawson (1997). Toward a Psychology of Framing Effects. *Political Behavior* 19(3): 221–45.

Nentwich, Michael (1998). Opportunity Structures for Citizens' Participation. The Case of the European Union, in A. Weale and M. Nentwich (eds.), *Political Theory and the European Union, London*. London: Routledge, 125–40.

Niedermayer, Oskar and Richard Sinnott (eds.) (1995). *Public Opinion and Internationalized Governance*. Oxford: Oxford University Press.

Nielsen, Hans Jørgen (1993). *EF på Valg*. Copenhagen: Columbus.

Nijeboer, Arjen (2005*a*). The First Dutch Referendum. A Pre-Ballot Assessment, *Notre Europe* Policy Paper no. 14.

────── (2005*b*). People's Vengeances. The Dutch Referendum. *European Constitutional Law Review* 1: 393–405.

Norris, Pippa (1997). Second-Order Elections Revisited. *European Journal of Political Research* 31: 109–24.

O'Mahony, Jane (2001). Not So Nice: The Treaty of Nice, The International Criminal Court, the Abolition of the Death Penalty – the 2001 Referendum Experience. *Irish Political Studies* 16(1): 201–13.

Partin, Randall (2001). Campaign Intensity and Voter Information. A Look at Gubernatorial Contests. *American Politics Research* 29(2): 115–40.

Petersen, Nikolaj (1996). Denmark and the European Union 1985–96. A Two-Level Analysis. *Cooperation and Conflict* 31(2): 185–201.

Piar, Christophe and Jacques Gerstlé (2005). Le cadrage du référendum sur la Constitution européenne: la dynamique d'une campagne à rebondissements, in A. Laurent and N. Sauger (eds.) *Le référendum de ratification du Traité constitutionnel européen: comprendre le non français*, Cahier du CEVIPOF 42.

Popkin, Samuel L. (1991). *The Reasoning Voter. Communication and Persuasion in Presidential Campaigns*. Chicago, IL: The University of Chicago Press.

Qvortrup, Mads (2005). *A Comparative Study of Referendums. Government by the People*. 2nd edition. Manchester: Manchester University Press.

Rahn, Wendy M., John H. Aldrich, Eugene Borgida, and John L. Sullivan (1990). A Social-Cognitive Model of Candidate Appraisal, in J. A. Ferejohn and J. H. Kuklinski, (eds.) *Information and Democratic Processes*. Urbana/Chicago, IL: University of Illinois.

Raudenbush, Stephen W. and Anthony S. Bryk (2002). *Hierarchical Linear Models: Applications and Data Analysis Methods*, 2nd edition. Newbury Park, CA: Sage.

Ray, Leonard (1999). Measuring Party Positions on European Integration: Results from an Expert Survey. *European Journal of Political Research* 36(2): 283–306.

────── and Hanne Marthe Narud (2000). Mapping the Norwegian Political Space: Results from an Expert Survey. *Party Politics* 6(2): 225–39.

Referendum Commission (2001). *Arguments For & Against The Treaty of Nice*. Dublin: The Referendum Commission.

Reif, Karlheinz (1984). National Electoral Cycles and European Elections 1979 and 1984. *Electoral Studies* 3(3): 244–55.

—— and Ronald Inglehart (eds.) (1991). *Eurobarometer. The Dynamics of Public Opinion*. Basingstoke: Macmillan.

—— and Hermann Schmitt (1980). Nine Second-Order National Elections. *European Journal of Political Research* 8(1): 3–44.

Riker, William H. (1982). *Liberalism Against Populism. A Confrontation Between the Theory of Democracy and the Theory of Social Choice*. San Francisco, CA: W.H. Freeman and Co.

Romer, Thomas and Howard Rosenthal (1979). Bureaucrats Versus Voters: On the Political Economy of Resource Allocation by Direct Democracy. *Quarterly Journal of Economics* 93(4): 563–87.

—— —— (1978). Political Resource Allocation, Controlled Agendas, and the Status Quo. *Public Choice* 33(4): 27–44.

Rosenstone, Steven J. (1983). *Forecasting Presidential Elections*. New Haven, CT: Yale University Press.

—— and John Mark Hansen (1993). *Mobilization, Participation, and Democracy in America*. New York: Macmillan.

Saglie, Jo (2000). Values, Perceptions and European Integration: The Case of the Norwegian 1994 Referendum. *European Union Politics* 1(2): 227–49.

Sauger, Nicolas, Sylvain Brouard, and Emiliano Grossman (2007). *Les Français contre l'Europe? Les sens du référendum du 29 mai 2005*. Paris: Presses de Sciences-Po.

Schmitt-Beck, Rüdiger and David M. Farrell (2002). Do Political Campaigns Matter? Yes, But It Depends, in D.M. Farrell and R. Schmitt-Beck (eds.) *Do Political Campaigns Matter? Campaign Effects in Elections and Referendums*. London: Routledge.

Schneider, Gerald and Lars-Erik Cederman (1994). The Change of Tide in Political Cooperation: A Limited Information Model of European Integration, *International Organization* 48(4): 633–62.

—— and Patricia Weitsman (1996). The Punishment Trap: Integration Referendums as Popularity Contests. *Comparative Political Studies* 28(4): 582–607.

Schuck, Andreas R. T. and Claes H. de Vreese (2006). Between Risk and Opportunity. News Framing and Its Effects on Public Support for EU Enlargement. *European Journal of Communication* 21(1): 5–32.

—— —— (2008). The Dutch No to the EU Constitution: Assessing the Role of EU Skepticism and the Campaign. *Journal of Elections, Public Opinion & Parties* 18(1): 101–28.

Sciarini, Pascal, Nicholas Bornstein, and Bruno Lanz (2007). The Determinants on Environmental Issues: A Two-Level Analysis, in C.H. de Vreese, (ed.) *Dynamics of Referendums Campaigns. An International Perspective*. Basingstoke: Palgrave, 234–66.

## Bibliography

Scott, Dermot (1994). *Ireland's Contribution to the European Union.* Dublin: Institute for European Affairs.

Setälä, Maija (1999). *Referendums and Democratic Government.* New York: St. Martin's Press.

Shaw, Daron R. (1999). The Effect of TV Ads and Candidate Appearances on Statewide Presidential Votes, 1988–96. *American Political Science Review* 93(2): 345–61.

Shepsle, Kenneth A. (1972). The Strategy of Ambiguity: Uncertainty and Electoral Competition. *American Political Science Review* 66: 555–68.

Sinnott, Richard (2001). Attitudes and Behaviour of the Irish Electorate in the Referendum on the Treaty of Nice. URL: http://www.ucd.ie/dempart/workingpapers/nice1.pdf

—— (2002). Cleavages, Parties and Referendums: Relationships Between Representative and Direct Democracy in the Republic of Ireland. *European Journal of Political Research* 41: 811–26.

—— (2003a). Ireland: Turnout Decides. Presentation to the Conference on European Public Opinion, Brussels, September 18, 2003.

—— (2003b). Attitudes and Behaviour of the Irish Electorate in the Second Referendum on the Treaty of Nice. URL: http://www.ucd.ie/dempart/workingpapers/nice2.pdf

Siune, Karen and Palle Svensson (1993). The Danes and the Maastricht Treaty: The Danish EC Referendum of June 1992. *Electoral Studies* 12: 99–111.

—— —— and Ole Tonsgaard (1992). *Det blev et nej.* Aarhus: Politica.

—— —— —— (1994a). The EU: The Danes Said 'No' in 1992, but 'Yes' in 1993: How and Why?, *Electoral Studies* 13(2): 107–16.

—— —— —— (1994b). *fra et nej til et ja.* Aarhus: Politica.

Skovmand, Sven (1977). *64 Sider af Danmarks Historien.* Copenhagen: Det ny Notat.

Slothuus, Rune (2008). More Than Weighting Cognitive Importance: A Dual-Process Model of Issue Framing Effects. *Political Psychology* 29(1): 1–27.

Sniderman, Paul M. (2000). Taking Sides: A Fixed Choice Theory of Political Reasoning, in A. Lupia, M.D. McCubbins, and S.L. Popkin (eds.) *Elements of Reason: Cognition, Choice, and the Bounds of Rationality.* Cambridge: Cambridge University Press, 67–75.

—— Richard A. Brody, and Philip Tetlock (1991). *Reasoning and Choice: Explorations in Political Psychology.* Cambridge: Cambridge University Press.

—— James M. Glaser and Robert Griffin (1990). Information and Electoral Choice, in J.A. Ferejohn and J.H. Kuklinski (eds.) *Information and Democratic Processes.* Urbana, IL: University of Illinois Press, 117–35.

Snijders, Tom A. B. and Roel J. Boskers (1999). *Multilevel Analysis. An Introduction to Basic and Advanced Multilevel Modeling.* London: Sage.

Socialistisk Folkeparti (1992). Forhandlingsudspil fra SF i tilfælde af et nej ved folkeafsteminingen om EF-union, 11 May 1992.

## Bibliography

Sorroza, Alicia and Jose I. Torreblanca (2005). Ratification Monitor: Update Spain. Real Instituto Elcano.
Spinelli, Altiero (1989). *Una strategia per gli Stati Uniti d'Europa*. Bologna: Il Mulino.
Steenbergen, Marco and David Scott (2004). Contesting Europe? The Salience of European Integration as a Party Issue, in G. Marks and M. Steenbergen (eds.) *European Integration and Political Conflict*. Cambridge: Cambridge University Press.
Suksi, Markku (1993). *Bringing in the People. A Comparison of Constitutional Forms and Practices of the Referendum*. Dordrecht: Martinus Nijhoff Publishers.
Sulfaro, Valerie A. (1996). The Role of Ideology and Political Sophistication in the Structure Foreign Policy Attitudes. *American Politics Quarterly* 24(3): 303–37.
Sulkin, Tracy (2001). Explaining Campaign Intensity. *American Politics Research* 29(6): 608–24.
Stimson, James A. (2004). *Tides of Consent*. Cambridge: Cambridge University Press.
Svensson, Palle (1994). The Danish Yes to Maastricht and Edinburgh. The EC Referendum of May 1993. *Scandinavian Political Studies* 17(1): 69–82.
—— (2002). Five Danish Referendums on the European Community and European Union: A Critical Assessment of the Franklin Thesis. *European Journal of Political Research* 41: 733–50.
—— (2003). *Folkets Røst, Demokrati og Folkeafstemninger i Danmark og andre europæiske lande*. Aarhus: Aarhus Universitetsforlag.
Szczerbiak, Aleks and Paul Taggart (eds.) (2004). *Choosing Union: The 2003 EU Accession Referendums: Special Issue of West European Politics*, September 2004.
Tomz, Michael, Jason Wittenberg, and Gary King (2003). CLARIFY: Software for Interpreting and Presenting Statistical Results. Version 2.1. Stanford University, University of Wisconsin and Harvard University. Available at http://gking.harvard.edu/
Torreblanca, Jose I. (2005). Spain's Referendum on the European Constitution: A Double Disappointment. Real Instituto Elcano, ARI Paper No. 57/2005.
Uleri, Pier Vincenzo (1996). Introduction, in Michael Gallagher and Pier Vincenzo Uleri (eds.) *The Referendum Experience in Europe*. London: Macmillan Press.
van der Brug, Wouter and Cees van der Eijk (eds.) (2007). *European Elections and Domestic Politics: Lessons from the Past and Scenarios for the Future*. Notre Dame: University of Notre Dame Press.
van der Eijk, Cees and Mark Franklin (2004). Potential for Contestation on European Matters at National Elections in Europe, in G. Marks and M. Steenbergen (eds.) *European Integration and Political Conflict*. Cambridge: Cambridge University Press.
—— —— (eds.) (1996). *Choosing Europe? The European Electorate and National Politics in the Face of Union*. Ann Arbor, MI: The University of Michigan Press.
Wattenberg, Martin P. (1998). *The Decline of American Political Parties, 1952–1996*. Cambridge, MA: Harvard University Press.

# Bibliography

Westlye, Mark C. (1991). *Senate Elections and Campaign Intensity*. Baltimore, MD: Johns Hopkins University Press.

Widfeldt, Anders (2004). Elite Collusion and Public Defiance: Sweden's Euro Referendum in 2003. *West European Politics* 27(3): 503–18.

Wolfinger, Raymond E. and Steven J. Rosenstone (1980). *Who Votes?* New Haven, CT: Yale University Press.

Worre, Torben (1992). Folkeafstemningen om den europæiske unionstraktat, 2. juni 1992, in B. Nüchel Thomsen (ed.) *The Odd Man Out? Danmark og den europæiske integration 1948–1992*, Odense: Odense Universitetsforlag.

Worre, Torben (1995). First No, Then Yes: The Danish Referendums on the Maastricht Treaty 1992 and 1993. *Journal of Common Market Studies* 33(2): 235–58.

Zaller, John R. (1992). *The Nature and Origins of Mass Opinion*. Cambridge: Cambridge University Press.

# Index

abstention, *see* turnout
accession, *see* enlargement; membership referendums
age 66, 74, 76–8, 100–3, 225
agenda-setting 11, 12, 14, 46, 86, 144, 169, 186, 191–2, 197, 209, 211
Ahern, Bertie 189
Allen, Mike 186–7, 202
Alvarez, Michael 48–9, 51, 87
Amato, Giuliano 15
ambivalence, *see* voter uncertainty
Amsterdam Treaty 9, 19, 72–3, 94–5, 185
Antonsen, Charlotte 138, 159
attitudes
 dimensionality of 43–4, 56, 68–70, 82, 145, 149–51, 215–27
 towards European integration 3–5, 25–30, 54, 66–9, 71–80, 104–6, 165–6, 179, 185–6, 194, 215–20, 237
Austria 9, 11, 27–8
awareness, *see* political awareness

Banks, Jeffrey S. 45, 46
Barroso, José Manuel 23
Bartels, Larry M. 87, 139
Bonde, Jens-Peter 172, 199
Bowler, Shaun 22, 40, 49, 136–7
Britain 5, 9, 11, 13, 27, 28, 118–30, 183, 184, 198, 206
Bulgaria 12, 27, 28

campaign 4, 17, 35–6, 52–3, 84–108, 115, 168–77, 186–93, 207–15, 239–41
 effects 86–92
 exposure 91, 98–104, 109, 178, 193, 239
 intensity 40, 42, 52–3, 87, 90–8, 104–7, 172, 191, 195, 207–8, 224, 239–40
 issues 169–73, 181, 187, 191–2, 196, 198, 205, 207, 209–10, 226
 spending 40, 88, 90, 92–3, 172, 190, 203
Campbell, Angus 6, 32, 33
Central and Eastern Europe 5, 9

Chirac, Jacques 41, 205, 208, 209, 220–2, 224–5
Chong, Dennis 112, 116, 130
Christian democratic parties 145–7, 183–4, 186, 199, 210
Christin, Thomas 40, 88
class 33, 71–4, 76–8, 82, 86, 100–2, 103–5, 223
cleavages, *see* policy dimensions
closeness of the race 91, 93, 95, 168
Commission, *see* European Commission
common market 60,163–6, 169, 198
communist parties, *see* far left parties
competence, *see* voter competence
competitiveness 88, 90, 92–3, 115
 *see also* party competition
compulsory voting 96, 228
 *see also* turnout
consequences of a no-vote 12–13, 114, 129, 164, 168–70, 180, 188, 191, 195, 241
 *see also* reversion point
conservative parties 125–9, 145–7, 148–9, 181, 183–4, 186
constitutional courts 22, 184, 187
constitutional provisions for referendums 10–12, 159, 166, 184, 190, 244
Constitutional Treaty 3, 8, 9, 12–15, 23, 41, 74, 94–5, 105–107, 204–27, 243–50
Convention on the Future of Europe 15, 198, 206, 244, 245–8
Converse, Phillip E. 32, 38
Coughlan, Anthony 187, 202
Council, *see* European Council
credibility 30, 58, 97, 130, 131, 144, 174, 239
Crotty, Raymond 184, 202
cues 17, 23, 24, 31, 35–40, 53–8, 70, 80, 88, 90, 113–17, 126, 130, 136, 144–58, 178, 180, 193, 195, 196, 212–3, 222, 237–8, 240, 249
 *see also* elite endorsements; heuristics; party endorsements

271

# Index

Cyprus 9, 11, 28
Czech Republic 9, 28, 192, 206

Dam Kristensen, Henrik 167, 199
de Gaulle, Charles 245
de Vreese, Claes H. 84, 88, 114
deception 36–7, 55, 89–90, 144
democracy
  direct democracy 3, 5–7, 235, 241–9
  representative democracy 5–6, 242
democratic deficit 14, 25, 106, 145, 170, 242
*demos* 242, 245, 247
Denmark 9, 11–14, 27, 28, 72, 84, 94–5, 105, 138, 161–82, 204, 206, 240
Donovan, Todd 22, 40, 49, 136–7
Downs, Anthony 30, 32, 34–6, 38, 61, 99
Druckman, James N. 112–16, 117, 130, 131, 140, 144

Eastern Europe, *see* Central and Eastern Europe
Economic and Monetary Union 119, 166, 170, 200
  *see also* Maastricht Treaty; single currency
economic integration, *see* European integration
Edinburgh Agreement 9, 174–6, 179–81, 200
education 25, 61, 82, 99–101, 103–5, 109
elections 6, 23, 29–30, 34, 55, 88–9, 99, 136, 141, 158, 167, 237, 238–41
  American 6, 40, 49, 87, 99, 136, 139
  European 27, 30, 138, 141, 145, 158, 198, 246
elite
  consensus 14, 163–4, 183–4, 206, 207, 210
  divisions 14, 88, 90, 169, 190
  endorsements 17, 31, 36, 40, 55, 110, 113, 115–7, 119–26, 136, 237, 240
  strategies 10, 13–14, 57– 9, 89, 90, 113, 165–8, 197–8, 234
  *see also* cues; party
Ellemann-Jensen, Uffe 161, 168, 169
endorsements, *see* elite endorsements; political parties
Engell, Hans 174, 200
enlargement 9, 11, 13, 182, 183, 187, 189, 191–3, 195, 205, 209–11, 215, 217–25
enlightenment 36–7, 39, 89
Euro referendum 9, 13, 84, 94–5, 98, 105, 118–25, 205
  *see also* single currency

Eurobarometer surveys 26, 28, 67, 68, 137, 165, 185, 214, 218, 222
Europe-wide referendum 244–8
European Commission 8, 23, 106, 137–8, 206, 250
European Constitution, *see* Constitutional Treaty
European Convention, *see* Convention on the Future of Europe
European Council 8, 22, 163, 200, 249
European Economic Area 9, 12
European Free Trade Agreement (EFTA) 9, 12
European integration 3, 5, 7–16, 242–9
  economic integration 21, 135, 169–70, 200
  political integration 44, 135, 163–4, 166, 167, 169–71, 174, 178, 196, 198, 200, 215
  *see also* attitudes towards European integration
European Parliament 8, 13, 14, 25–8, 138, 141, 164, 166, 206, 245
  elections 27, 30, 138, 141, 145, 158, 198, 246
Euroscepticism 14, 19, 145, 165–6, 205, 215
  Eurosceptic movements 108, 163, 168, 171, 176, 186, 187, 190, 199, 200, 201, 202, 209
  Eurosceptic parties 145–7, 148–9, 184, 186, 208–9, 210
  *see also* attitudes towards European integration
experiments 18, 87, 103, 111, 117–30, 144, 237–8

far left parties 145–6, 148, 149, 167, 184, 186, 209, 211, 212–3, 221
far right parties 145–6, 148, 167, 175, 176, 209, 210, 211, 213, 218, 227
Farrell, David 87
Finland 9, 11, 22, 28
FitzGerald, Garret 184, 201, 202
frames
  competing frames 115, 130, 234, 239
  consequences frames 111, 114, 118, 121
  equivalency frames 117, 119, 121, 122, 123, 125, 130
  issue frames 115, 117, 122, 123, 128–9, 130, 215, 237, 239
  valence frames 114
framing effects 20, 110–31, 144, 196, 215, 240–1

272

# Index

France 3, 8, 9, 12, 14, 28, 41, 74, 94–5, 98, 105–7, 184, 204–27, 243–4, 248
Franklin, Mark N. 29–30, 31,141, 145, 158, 177, 180, 182

Gade, Steen 170, 175, 200
Garry, John 30, 141, 142
gender 71, 74, 76–8, 100–1, 103, 222, 225
Germany 28
Giscard d'Estaing, Valéry 206
Good Friday Agreement 94, 185
Gormley, John 188, 202
government
   performance 24, 50, 76, 105, 125–6
   responsiveness 5–6, 7, 158, 242, 245, 247
   satisfaction 29–30, 56, 72–8, 79, 104–5, 117, 126, 173, 177, 193–4, 220, 222–5, 237
   *see also* party
Great Britain, *see* Britain
Greece 11, 27, 28, 198
green parties 183–4, 188, 190–1, 201, 208, 213, 228
Greenland 22

Habermas, Jürgen 245, 247
Helveg Petersen, Niels 165, 169, 174, 176, 199
heuristics 35–9, 54–5, 67, 116, 138–9, 142–4, 237, 239
   *see also* cues; elite endorsements
Hollande, François 204
Hooghe, Liesbet 26, 27, 145–6
Hug, Simon 10, 22, 29, 31, 40, 88

identity
   European 215, 246–7
   national 5, 9, 15, 27, 172–3, 205–6, 209–11, 214–20, 222–3, 226–7
ideology 32, 36, 145–7
   ideological proximity 29–30, 34–5, 36, 42–58, 66–7, 75–80, 136, 140–2, 144–51, 172–3, 180–1
   left-right 34, 56, 145–7, 149–51, 227
   *see also* attitudes; policy dimensions
income 66, 99, 100, 220
information
   processing 4, 16–7, 24, 31, 35, 37–9, 40, 53–6, 59, 143, 153, 234–7
   supply 4, 16–17, 24, 31, 40, 57–9, 88–92, 99, 162, 234–7
   shortcuts, *see* heuristics
   *see also* campaign intensity; knowledge; political awareness

Inglehart, Ronald 25, 27, 218
initiatives 5, 22, 250
institutional deadlock 243–8
interest groups 37, 38, 108, 144, 159, 161, 163, 167–8, 184, 186, 190, 209, 210
   *see also* Eurosceptic movements
intergovernmental conference (IGC) 22, 163–4, 198, 209
   *see also* treaty negotiations
Ireland 3, 8, 9, 11, 12, 13, 15, 22, 27–8, 73, 94–5, 161–2, 182–97, 204, 206, 243
issue
   evolution 90
   salience 24, 31, 42–3, 50–8, 84–5, 90, 92–3, 97, 104, 112–4, 130 148, 182, 185–6, 195, 247
   voting 24, 29–30, 47, 53–7, 92, 97–8, 104–7, 140–2, 155, 157, 172, 195, 205, 236, 239–41
Italy 9, 22, 28
Iyengar, Shanto 32, 86

Johnston, Richard 37, 40

Kahn, Kim Fridkin 87, 92, 93
Kenney, Patrick J. 87, 92, 93
Key, V.O. 84
Kinder, Donald R. 110
knowledge 6, 20, 32, 34, 35–41, 43, 47–50, 52–7, 70, 79, 82, 100, 103–4, 116, 136–9, 150–7, 179–80, 188–9, 193–4, 214–5, 221–4, 238–40
   *see also* political awareness
Kuklinski, James H. 87, 107, 118, 139–40, 143

Labour parties, *see* social democratic parties
Laeken Declaration 14–15, 22, 206
Lau, Richard R. 55, 115, 144–5
leaders, *see* elite
LeDuc, Lawrence 60, 88
left-right, *see* ideology; policy dimensions
legitimacy 141–2, 158, 236, 241–3
Liechtenstein 22
Lisbon Treaty 3, 8, 9, 10, 13, 15, 23–4, 94–5, 120–2, 125–9, 184, 204, 243–44, 249, 250
Lupia, Arthur 36, 37, 38, 39, 40, 89, 140, 233, 235, 238
Luxembourg 9, 12, 28, 74, 94–6, 206

Maastricht Treaty 7, 9, 95–5, 161–92, 196, 213, 240
McCreevy, Charlie 24

273

# Index

McCubbins, Mathew D. 36, 37, 38, 39, 89, 233
McKelvey, Richard D. 36
Mackin, Martin 186–7, 191–2, 195, 202, 203
Madison, James 6
mainstream effect 57, 186, 195
 *see also* Zaller, John R.
Malta 9, 12, 28
Marks, Gary 145
Marsh, Michael 29–30, 141, 142, 177, 180
Matsusaka, John G. 6, 103, 235
media coverage 36, 84, 88, 90–1, 92–5, 98–100, 144, 163, 169, 199, 207–9, 211
 *see also* newspapers
membership referendums 9, 11–12, 45, 72–4, 94–5, 105, 147–57, 163, 184
Michigan model 33
mobilization 87–8, 97–9, 234, 239, 245
monetary union, *see* Economic and Monetary Union

National Compromise (Denmark) 174, 175, 201
 *see also* Edinburgh Agreement
national identity, *see* identity, national
national sovereignty 141–2, 145, 166, 172–3, 174, 184, 187–9, 209–10, 214–5, 216–26, 243
Nelson, Thomas E. 110, 112
Netherlands, the 9, 13, 14, 28, 74, 94–5, 106, 204–27, 243
neutrality 22, 187–90, 197
news coverage, *see* media coverage
newspapers 84, 93–5, 161, 162, 183, 207, 208
 *see also* media coverage
Nice Treaty 8, 9, 10, 84, 94–5, 161–2, 182–97, 201, 240
Nielsen, Holger K. 161, 171, 175
Norway 9, 11, 14, 73–4, 94–6, 105, 147–58
Nyrup Rasmussen, Poul 169, 171, 175, 199

opinion formation 4, 54, 57–8, 88, 110, 116, 118, 234
opinion polls 35–6, 93, 95, 161, 165, 168, 172, 173, 176, 188, 192, 208, 211
opt-outs 174, 200, 240, 249
 *see also* Edinburgh Agreement
Ordeshook, Peter C. 36

parliaments 10, 15, 93, 138, 148, 163–4, 166, 167, 169, 174, 175, 184, 206, 210, 212–3, 245
 *see also* European Parliament

participation 90, 98, 100, 103, 107, 239
 *see also* turnout
partisanship 33, 35–6, 54–5, 56, 58, 70, 77–9, 86, 111, 116–7, 123–9, 145–6, 173, 177, 214, 222–4, 240
party
 competition 90, 148, 198, 240
 endorsements 23, 24, 36, 54, 70–1, 76–8, 80, 88, 113–18, 130, 138, 144–58, 207, 212, 213, 220, 237, 240
 identification, *see* partisanship
 intra-party divisions 14, 164, 169, 197, 201, 208, 224, 228
 polarization 19, 87, 90, 93–5, 108, 213
 positions 43–50, 145–7, 148–58, 180, 238, 240
 strategies 10, 57–9, 87, 90, 113, 163–6, 167–8, 183, 197, 234
 *see also* elite; Christian democratic parties; conservative parties; Eurosceptic parties; far left parties; far right parties; green parties; social democratic parties
persuasion 36–7, 39, 86, 89, 113, 195
 *see also* elite strategies
Poland 9, 28, 192, 206, 249
polarization, *see* party polarization
policy dimensions
 European integration 43–4, 56, 58, 81–2, 145–7, 149–51, 159, 167–8, 227
 left-right 56, 145–51, 159, 167–8, 227
 *see also* ideology
political awareness 16–7, 24, 37–9, 40–57, 70, 76–80, 82, 116–17, 123–30, 153, 157, 178–9, 193–4, 220–4, 238–9
political parties *see* party
Popkin, Samuel L. 35
populism 23, 148, 210, 211, 218–9, 227
postmaterialism 25, 27, 35, 74, 218–9, 223–5
proximity model 30, 34, 42–9

Quirk, Paul J. 118, 139–40, 143, 236

rational choice 33–4, 140
Receive-Accept-Sample model 38–9, 40
 *see also* Zaller, John R.
recommendations, *see* elite endorsements; party endorsements
Redlawsk, David P. 55, 115, 144–5
referendum
 binding/non-binding 9–10, 14, 31, 166, 201, 210, 245

274

required/non-required 9–10, 12, 31, 166, 190
*see also* direct democracy; membership referendums; individual treaties; single issue referendums
Referendum Commission (Ireland) 187, 190, 202
Reform Treaty, *see* Lisbon Treaty
reversion point 42–6, 47, 49, 52, 55–7, 57–9, 89, 113–22, 129–30, 142, 152, 170–1, 179–82, 191, 195, 217–8, 221–2, 225, 236, 241, 245–7
Reynolds, Albert 184–5
risk aversion 48–9, 61
Roche, Dick 161, 187, 196, 202
Romania 9, 12, 28, 217–18
Rome Treaty 21, 164

saliency, *see* issue salience
Sarkozy, Nicolas 204
Schlüter, Poul 162–3, 170, 171
Schmitt-Beck, Rüdiger 87
Sciarini, Pascal 40, 88
second-order election model 29–30, 42, 45, 56, 66–7, 70–1, 140–2, 177–8, 182, 189, 196, 205, 210, 214, 220, 246
single *see also* currency 9, 22, 84, 88, 118–20, 121–9 166, 170, 174, 185, 218–9, 223
*see also* Euro referendum
Single European Act (SEA) 9, 10, 22, 72, 95, 162, 164, 165, 167, 184, 199
single issue referendums 9, 13, 45, 67
*see also* Euro referendum
Sinnott, Richard 30, 141, 142, 185, 193
Slovakia 9, 28
Sniderman, Paul M. 35–6, 37, 53, 116, 144
social democratic parties 11, 41, 56, 120, 123–9, 145–7, 148–9, 161, 164, 167, 169, 170, 174, 175, 181, 183, 184, 186, 187, 197, 204, 208, 210, 212–3
social model 209–10, 214–22, 225
socialist parties, *see* social democratic parties
Spain 9, 11, 28, 74, 94–5, 98, 206, 227
spatial model of vote choice 42–57, 179–80, 189
Spinelli, Altiero 245

Sulkin, Tracy 92
survey experiments, *see* experiments
Svensson, Palle 29–30, 166, 177, 180
Sweden 9, 11, 14, 27, 28
Switzerland 9, 12, 14, 22

timing of referendums 11, 12, 13, 144
treaty
negotiations 12, 14, 15, 164, 174, 206, 244
ratification 7, 9, 10–12, 14, 15, 18, 112, 196, 206–7, 243–8
*see also* individual treaties
Treaty establishing a Constitution for Europe, *see* Constitutional Treaty
Treaty of Amsterdam, *see* Amsterdam Treaty
Treaty of Lisbon, *see* Lisbon Treaty
Treaty of Nice, *see* Nice Treaty
Treaty of Rome, *see* Rome Treaty
Treaty on European Union, *see* Maastricht Treaty
turnout 9, 13, 29–30, 49, 52, 81, 85, 87, 91, 96–7, 99–103, 107, 177, 184–5, 188, 192–3, 195, 204

uncertainty, *see* voter uncertainty
United Kingdom, *see* Britain

van der Eijk, Cees 29–30, 141, 145, 158
veto 141–2, 236, 242–8
voter
competence 6, 32–3, 40, 135–59, 235–42, 249
ideal point 30, 34, 42–50, 58, 67, 68, 91–2, 114–5, 129, 144, 170, 180, 197
ignorance 23, 32–3, 53, 136–8, 142, 240
preferences, *see* ideology
switching 30, 177–81, 194, 197
uncertainty 13, 41, 43, 46, 47–50, 52, 58–9, 88, 90–1, 103, 114, 121–2, 169, 171, 186, 188–9, 191, 197, 241

Wallström, Margot 23
Westlye, Mark C. 52, 87, 90

Zaller, John R. 38–40, 54, 70, 80, 87, 88, 144

Lightning Source UK Ltd.
Milton Keynes UK
UKOW031637051212

203215UK00002B/20/P